W9-CUF-793

THE *Sunset* COOK BOOK

ILLUSTRATED BY EARL THOLLANDER

THE *Sunset* COOK BOOK

Food with a Gourmet Touch

BY THE SUNSET EDITORIAL STAFF

ANNABEL POST
Home Economics Editor, Sunset Magazine

Sunset Food Consultants

HELEN EVANS BROWN

KAY HILLYARD

RUTH B. LANE

EMILY CHASE LEISTNER

JANETH NIX

LOU PAPPAS

Editorial Supervision: DOROTHY N. KRELL

LANE BOOK COMPANY   MENLO PARK, CALIFORNIA

Library of Congress Catalog Card 60-14964

First Edition

First printing October 1960

Copyright © 1960
Lane Book Company, Menlo Park, California

Designed by Adrian Wilson

Composition by A. C. Gollan & Son and MacKenzie & Harris, Inc.
Types: Linotype Times Roman and Monotype Cochin, handset

Paper: Garamond Text, laid finish, made by Champion Paper and Fibre Company

Printed in the United States of America
by the Stecher-Traung Lithograph Corporation

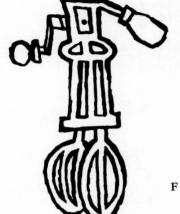

Contents

First Courses & Salads

WE GIVE ATTENTION here to a few recipes for a pleasant opening of a dinner, and to quite a few salad recipes.

The salad, particularly in the West, often is the first course. Sometimes it accompanies the entrée, perhaps taking the place of the vegetable. A few extra trimmings, an accompaniment or two, and the salad becomes the meal itself.

Perhaps the most noteworthy salad contributions of the West Coast are Caesar Salad, Crab Louis, Celery Victor, and Green Goddess Salad. The most popular and most frequently served is the mixed green salad.

Happily, "greens" are becoming available in greater variety, adding color and texture to the mixed green salad. In addition to the common head lettuce, you can now find half a dozen or more other kinds: bronzy Prizehead, butter lettuce, romaine, escarole, frilly chicory, endive, notched-leaf Australian lettuce.

The mixed green salad changes into a hundred salads with flavor additions: snips of anchovies; paper thin cucumber slices; avocado slices or cubes, dipped first in lemon juice; raw cauliflower fans or slices; thin carrot strips; slices of green onions; bits of green pepper; herbs added with discretion; judicious amounts of capers, hot pickled peppers, or artichoke hearts; slices of hard-cooked eggs; pickled or raw mushrooms; and crumbs of Roquefort or any sharp cheese.

Strawberry-Pineapple Cup

You might welcome the first strawberries of the season with this refreshing fruit cup.

1 pint (2 cups) strawberries
1½ to 2 cups fresh pineapple wedges or 1 can (14 oz.) frozen pineapple chunks
2 tablespoons sugar
½ cup white or tawny port

Wash and hull the strawberries; combine with the pineapple, sugar, and wine. Chill for 30 minutes before serving as an opening course or a dessert after a heavy meal. Serves 6.

Spicy Crab Cocktail

½ cup catsup
¼ cup each chili sauce and tangerine or grapefruit juice
2 tablespoons lemon juice
⅓ cup finely sliced celery
1 tablespoon finely sliced green onions, with tops
1 teaspoon prepared horse-radish
Two drops Tabasco
1 cup tangerine or grapefruit segments, chilled
1 cup avocado cubes or balls
2 to 3 cups crab meat
Lemon wedges

Combine catsup, chili sauce, tangerine and lemon juice, celery, onions, horse-radish, and Tabasco. Chill several hours to blend flavors. To serve, add tangerines, avocado, and crab meat to catsup mixture. Spoon into seafood cocktail glasses or into lettuce cups, and serve with lemon wedges. Makes 8 to 10 servings.

Mushroom-Stuffed Artichoke Shells

4 tablespoons (¼ cup) butter
¼ cup dry white table wine
½ teaspoon salt
¼ teaspoon monosodium glutamate
Dash of freshly ground pepper
30 to 40 fresh small mushroom caps (approximately 1 pound)
10 canned or freshly cooked artichoke shells
3 tablespoons water
½ cup commercial sour cream
Watercress sprigs for garnish

In a large frying pan, melt butter and add wine, salt, monosodium glutamate, and pepper. Add mushroom caps and simmer just until tender, stirring constantly. In an electric frying pan (or serving casserole), steam artichoke shells in the water. Stir sour cream into the mushrooms and sauce still in the first pan, and heat just until cream and sauce are blended. Spoon 3 or 4 mushrooms, along with sour cream sauce, into each artichoke shell. Serve hot with a garnish of watercress. Makes 10 servings.

Marinated Artichokes

6 medium sized artichokes
  Boiling salted water
½ cup olive oil or salad oil
5 cloves garlic, minced or mashed
½ cup chopped fresh parsley
¼ cup lemon juice
½ teaspoon salt
  Dash of pepper
  Chicory or other salad greens

Wash artichokes thoroughly under running water. Cut off stems and remove coarse outer leaves. Also cut about 1 inch off the tops, cutting straight across with a sharp knife. Set in a large kettle with stem ends down. Cover with boiling water; cover pan and cook until tender, 30 minutes to 1 hour, depending on the size of the artichokes. Drain well and spread apart the leaves slightly. Combine the oil with garlic, parsley, lemon juice, salt, and pepper. Pour the oil mixture over the artichokes, and continue to pour through the artichokes until the leaves are well coated. Return artichokes to the pan and simmer them for 10 minutes in the oil mixture. Let stand at room temperature at least 1 hour before serving. Arrange on individual salad plates garnished with sprigs of chicory. Serves 6.

Shrimp Cocktail with Caviar Sauce

Arrange cooked, cleaned, and chilled shrimp in cocktail glasses, leaving them whole if small or cutting them into smaller pieces if large. To make the sauce, combine a small jar (2¼ oz.) caviar with 1 cup commercial sour cream and 1 tablespoon lemon juice; chill thoroughly. Pour sauce over shrimp and garnish each serving with a wedge of lemon.

Tuna-Olive Appetizer

The *giardiniera* (Italian pickled vegetables) called for in this recipe are available in markets that carry specialty items.

1 can (7 oz.) solid pack tuna
1 large can (7½ oz.) pitted ripe olives
1 small can (2 or 3 oz.) whole or sliced
  mushrooms
1 can (9 oz.) artichokes
1 jar (3½ oz.) cocktail onions
1 jar (8 oz.) giardiniera
1 can (8 oz.) tomato sauce
3 tablespoons salad oil or olive oil
¼ cup wine vinegar or cider vinegar
1 teaspoon salt

Drain the liquid from the can of tuna, then turn tuna into a bowl, breaking it neatly into fairly large chunks. Add the olives, mushrooms, artichokes, onions, and the giardiniera, all previously drained of their liquids. Then add the tomato sauce, oil, vinegar, and salt. With 2 forks, toss to blend together well, being careful not to mash the chunks of tuna. For best flavor, allow the mixture to stand for several hours or overnight in the refrigerator. Serve as you would a shrimp cocktail, with saltine crackers. Makes 6 to 8 servings.

Italian Appetizer Salad

This salad, in a way, combines *antipasto* with greens. More than an "appetizer" it deserves an important place in the menu.

1 small head cauliflower
1 head each red lettuce, escarole, and curly endive
1 can (1 lb.) each cut green beans, red kidney beans, and garbanzos
2 or 3 green onions, chopped
6 hard cooked eggs, sliced
1 cup olive oil
½ cup vinegar
1½ teaspoons salt
¼ teaspoon pepper
2 tomatoes, sliced
1 can (2¼ oz.) sliced ripe olives
1 or 2 cans (2 oz. each) anchovies (rolled or fillets)

Break apart cauliflower flowerets, and parboil until just slightly tender; drain. Combine in large salad bowl the greens, 3 kinds of beans, green onions, and 4 of the eggs. Toss with dressing made with oil, vinegar, salt, and pepper. Garnish top with tomato slices, remaining egg slices, olives, and anchovies. Serve immediately. Makes 10 to 12 servings.

Cheese-Stuffed Kumquats

4 cups kumquats
Warm water
¾ cup pineapple juice
2 cups sugar
1 large package (8 oz.) cream cheese

Cover kumquats with warm water, bring to a boil; drain. Repeat procedure three times. Cover kumquats with warm water once more, bring to a boil; reduce heat to medium, and cook until the fruit is tender. Drain kumquats and reserve 1 cup of the cooking water. Combine the 1 cup water with pineapple juice and sugar, add kumquats, and cook over low heat for 5 minutes; drain and cool. Split kumquats, remove seed, and fill with softened cream cheese. Chill thoroughly before serving.

Avocados with Pickled Shrimp

1 pound small raw shrimp
⅓ cup white wine vinegar
¼ cup olive oil
½ cup dry white table wine
1 tablespoon each salt, sugar, and pickling spice
1 small onion, chopped
3 medium sized avocados

Peel and devein the raw shrimp. Put them in a saucepan with the vinegar, olive oil, wine, salt, sugar, pickling spice, and onion. Bring to a boil and simmer for 3 minutes, then allow to cool in the liquid. Use as a filling for the avocados which have been halved and peeled. (These shrimp are also very good as appetizers, impaled on toothpicks, served with or without dunking sauce.) Serves 6.

Bean Sprout and Water Chestnut Salad

Use fresh bean sprouts if you can find them — they are much crisper than the canned.

Clean sprouts well or drain the canned ones. To each 2 cups of sprouts, add ¼ cup sliced water chestnuts, ½ cup pineapple chunks, and ¼ cup slivered green pepper. For the dressing, combine 1 cup mayonnaise with 1 teaspoon each soy and curry powder. Mix the dressing through the salad. Arrange salad in lettuce-lined bowl. Sprinkle toasted almonds over the top. Serves 6.

Combination Salad with Browned Butter

For a nutlike flavor, heat 1 to 2 teaspoons of sesame seeds with the butter.

Lettuce
3 large tomatoes
  Salt and pepper
1 large avocado
8 green onions
½ cup (¼ pound) butter

Arrange lettuce leaves on individual plates or large chop plate. Slice tomatoes (which should be cool but not cold), and arrange in lettuce cups; sprinkle with salt and pepper. Halve avocados, peel, and cut each half into 3 lengthwise slices. Arrange over tomato slices. Slice green onions, including part of the green tops, and sprinkle over tomatoes and avocado. Just before serving, pour over hot butter which has been lightly browned over low heat. The butter partially cooks the onion and wilts the lettuce. Serves 6.

Mushroom and Lima Bean Salad

1 package (10 oz.) frozen green lima beans
8 sliced fresh mushrooms or 1 can (4 oz.) sliced mushrooms, drained
1 large onion, chopped
1 tablespoon chopped fresh parsley or 1 teaspoon dry parsley flakes
½ teaspoon oregano
⅓ cup wine vinegar
3 tablespoons olive oil
1 clove garlic, minced or mashed
½ teaspoon salt
¼ teaspoon celery salt
¼ teaspoon pepper
  Onion rings

Cook lima beans according to package directions until tender. Drain, rinse under cold running water, and drain thoroughly again. Toss together with mushrooms, onion, parsley, and oregano.

In a covered jar or container, shake together vinegar, olive oil, garlic, salt, celery salt, and pepper. Pour over bean mixture and toss thoroughly. Chill in refrigerator 1 to 2 hours. To serve, heap into casserole lined with crisp salad greens. Garnish with thinly sliced onion rings. Serves 4.

Raw Cauliflower Salad

1 small head cauliflower, thinly sliced
3 unpeeled red apples, diced
1 cup sliced celery
3 small green onions, sliced
¾ cup chopped parsley or 1 small bunch watercress, chopped
1 clove garlic
½ teaspoon salt
¼ cup red wine vinegar
¼ cup salad or olive oil
Pepper to taste

Chill cauliflower, apples, celery, onions, and parsley or watercress thoroughly so they are very crisp. Rub salad bowl with cut clove of garlic and salt. Shake vinegar, oil, and pepper vigorously in a tightly covered jar. Pour over salad and toss lightly. Taste for seasonings. Serves 6.

Mandarin Oranges in Papaya Halves

Place papaya halves on green leaves. Sprinkle with lemon or lime juice. Fill the centers of the fruit with canned mandarin orange sections and top with a sprig of mint.

Greek Salad

¼ head of iceberg lettuce
¼ head of romaine
18 medium sized radishes
¼ pound crumbled Feta cheese
1 small can (2 oz.) anchovy fillets, minced
2 medium sized tomatoes, cut in small pieces
1 tablespoon chopped fresh parsley
¼ teaspoon dried oregano, crumbled
Freshly ground pepper

Dressing

½ cup olive oil
2 tablespoons tarragon vinegar
½ teaspoon salt
¼ teaspoon freshly ground pepper
2 tablespoons mixed fresh herbs (marjoram, rosemary, tarragon, savory, chives, chervil or parsley)
2 bunches green onions and tops

Two hours before serving, tear the lettuce and romaine into a salad bowl. Add whole radishes, cheese, anchovies, tomatoes, parsley, oregano, and freshly ground pepper. Toss gently, cover with a damp tea towel, and chill.

For the dressing, shake together in a pint bottle oil, vinegar, salt, pepper, and herbs. When ready to serve, pour dressing over salad and toss. Poke green onions straight up in center of salad. Serves 6 to 8.

Hot Potato and Bacon Salad

4 cups cooked potatoes (4 medium sized potatoes), cut in ½-inch cubes
16 slices bacon, cooked and crumbled
1 cup chopped green onions and tops
½ teaspoon salt
Dash of pepper
1½ cups mayonnaise
¼ cup (4 tablespoons) prepared mustard
¼ cup (4 tablespoons) prepared horse-radish
1 cup sliced celery
¼ cup finely chopped carrots
Paprika

Mix together lightly the cubed potatoes, crumbled bacon, green onions, salt, and pepper. Combine the mayonnaise, mustard, and horse-radish in a saucepan; heat, stirring constantly, until sauce bubbles; stir in the celery and carrots. Pour the hot sauce over potato mixture and toss lightly. Sprinkle paprika over top and serve immediately. Serves 8 generously.

Colorful Slaw

2 cups finely shredded cabbage
½ cup sliced small boiling onions
¾ to 1 cup pineapple chunks
½ cup chopped pimiento
½ to ¾ cup sliced stuffed olives
1 cup (¼ lb.) shredded American cheese
¼ cup whipping cream
½ cup mayonnaise
2 tablespoons lemon juice
Salt and pepper to taste

Combine cabbage, onions, pineapple, pimiento, olives, and cheese. Whip the cream and fold into mayonnaise mixed with the lemon juice. Mix into the salad ingredients, season to taste, and refrigerate for 2 hours before serving. Serves 6 generously.

Patio Zucchini Salad

Bright green zucchini, cooked but still crisp.

1 pound zucchini
2 cups water
½ teaspoon salt
1 clove garlic
½ cup chopped onion
½ cup chopped green pepper
½ cup sliced celery
French dressing

Quarter zucchini lengthwise, then cut crosswise into bite-sized pieces. Cook in boiling salted water for 3 minutes, remove from heat, let stand in cooking water for 2 minutes. Drain and chill. Rub garlic clove over inside of salad bowl. Place well chilled zucchini, onion, green pepper, and celery in salad bowl. Pour over French dressing and toss together lightly. Serves 6.

Curried Shrimp

Shuck, clean, and cook shrimp in court bouillon; combine with dressing (1 cup mayonnaise, ½ cup chili sauce, 1 tablespoon curry powder, 1 to 2 tablespoons lemon juice). Serve on endive, chicory, or romaine, and sprinkle with chopped salted almonds.

Ham and Cheese Rice Salad

This salad has some of the heartiness of an oven-baked casserole dish, but you serve it crisp and cold. It can stand alone as a main dish luncheon or supper salad.

1 package (10 oz.) frozen peas
1⅓ cups boiling salted water
1⅓ cups packaged pre-cooked rice
¾ cup mayonnaise
½ cup chopped dill pickle
1 teaspoon grated onion
Lettuce
1 cup slivered Swiss cheese
1 cup slivered cooked ham
Tomato slices

Add peas to the boiling water; cover and cook until water boils again. Stir in rice. Cover, remove from heat, and let stand 10 minutes. With a fork, mix in mayonnaise, dill pickle, and grated onion. Chill thoroughly. At serving time, arrange in 4 to 6 individual casseroles edged with crisp lettuce, or pile into a lettuce-lined bowl. Top salads with slivers of Swiss cheese and ham. Garnish with tomato slices. Offer additional mayonnaise. Serves 4 to 6.

Celery Victor

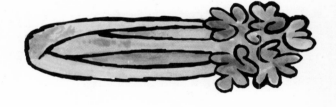

Chef Victor Hirtzler of the St. Francis Hotel in San Francisco first originated this now classic Western salad in the early 1900's.

2 small hearts of celery
1 medium sized onion
2½ cups bouillon (10½ oz. can diluted with 1 can water or 3 beef bouillon cubes dissolved in 2½ cups hot water), or chicken stock
1 cup well-seasoned French dressing
Watercress or shredded lettuce
Coarsely ground black pepper
Anchovy fillets and pimiento strips
Tomatoes and ripe olives (optional)

Wash celery, trim the root end, and cut off all but the smallest leaves. Peel and slice onion. Put whole celery hearts and sliced onion in shallow pan; cover with bouillon. Cover and cook until tender, about 15 minutes. Let cool in stock. Remove hearts, cut in half lengthwise, and place in shallow dish. Pour over French dressing (a garlic-flavored French dressing made with wine vinegar is especially good), and chill several hours.

To serve, drain off most of dressing and place celery on watercress or shredded lettuce. Sprinkle with pepper and garnish with anchovy fillets and pimiento strips. Quartered tomatoes and ripe olives may be used for extra garnish. Serves 4.

Green Goddess Salad

This famous salad was first created in 1915 at the Palace Hotel in honor of George Arliss, who was appearing in San Francisco that year in William Archer's play, "The Green Goddess."

8 to 10 anchovy fillets
1 green onion
¼ cup minced parsley
2 tablespoons minced fresh tarragon or 1 tablespoon dried tarragon soaked in vinegar and then strained
¼ cup finely cut chives
3 cups mayonnaise
¼ cup tarragon vinegar
1 clove garlic
1 large head romaine
1 pound cooked lobster, shrimp, crab meat, or chicken

Chop together the anchovies and green onion until finely minced. Add parsley, tarragon, and chives, and mix lightly. Turn into a bowl and stir in mayonnaise and vinegar, mixing well. Rub a salad bowl with 1 cut clove of garlic and break romaine into bite-sized pieces into the bowl.

Pour over enough dressing to moisten (about 2 cups), toss lightly, spoon on salad plates, and garnish with desired shellfish or chicken. Serves 6. Recipe makes about 1 quart dressing, or enough for 12 servings. (You can store the leftover dressing in a covered container in the refrigerator for at least a week.)

There are many variations to this creamy dressing. Some cooks use sour cream for part of the mayonnaise or anchovy paste instead of the fish fillets. Others use a blender to chop together the parsley, tarragon, chives, and anchovy fillets. Well seasoned French dressing may be used instead of the vinegar.

Curried Rice Salad

An ideal accompaniment for barbecued lamb or barbecued or fried chicken.

2 cups chilled cooked rice
1 green pepper, shredded
2 tablespoons drained pimientos, cut in strips
2 tablespoons raisins
2 tablespoons chopped parsley
2 tablespoons chopped green onion
½ cup olive oil
⅓ cup wine vinegar
1 tablespoon lemon juice
1 clove garlic, minced or mashed
1 tablespoon sugar
½ teaspoon curry powder
Salt and pepper to taste
Salad greens
Green pepper rings
Tomato wedges

Using two forks, toss together the rice, green pepper, pimientos, raisins, parsley, and onion. Chill thoroughly.

Combine oil, vinegar, lemon juice, garlic, sugar, curry powder, salt, and pepper. Just before serving, pour over salad and toss thoroughly.

Arrange salad in a bowl or casserole. Garnish with crisp greens, green pepper rings, and tomato wedges. Serves 4.

Chicken Breast Salad

8 boned chicken breasts
1 small package (3 oz.) cream cheese
¼ cup mayonnaise
2 teaspoons lemon juice
¼ teaspoon grated lemon peel
  Dash of salt
1 finely chopped green onion and top
  Crisp lettuce
2 or 3 large tomatoes, peeled and
  chilled
  Salt and pepper
2 large avocados
½ cup toasted slivered almonds (optional)
  Pitted ripe olives

Cook chicken breasts until tender (you can either pan-fry them in butter, covered to keep them moist, or simmer them in broth). Chill breasts. Remove skin and pat dry. Mix together thoroughly the cream cheese, mayonnaise, lemon juice, lemon peel, salt, and onion.

Coat rounded side of each piece of chicken completely with cheese dressing. Arrange crisp lettuce on 8 dinner-sized plates. Cut tomatoes into 8 thick slices and place on lettuce. Sprinkle with salt and pepper. Arrange a coated chicken breast on each tomato slice. Halve and peel avocados, and cut each half into 4 slices; place 2 avocado slices on each plate. Sprinkle chicken with toasted almonds and garnish with ripe olives. Serves 8.

Chicken-Curry Salad

4 to 5 cups cooked chicken or turkey,
  in large chunks
2 teaspoons grated onion
1 cup celery, cut in diagonal slices
1 cup finely chopped green pepper
¼ cup light cream
⅔ cup mayonnaise or salad dressing
1 teaspoon salt
⅛ teaspoon pepper
1 teaspoon curry powder
2 tablespoons vinegar
  Salad greens

Combine the chicken with onion, celery, and pepper. For the dressing, mix cream with mayonnaise, salt, pepper, curry, and vinegar. Add dressing to the chicken and toss lightly. Refrigerate until time to serve. Arrange the salad in a serving bowl or on individual plates; surround with crisp salad greens. Makes 6 to 8 servings.

Summer Salad

2 cups finely sliced raw spinach
1½ cups sliced peeled cucumbers
⅓ cup sliced green onions, including
  some of the tops
½ cup sliced radishes
1 pint (2 cups) creamed cottage
  cheese
1 cup commercial sour cream
2 teaspoons lemon juice
½ teaspoon salt
  Freshly ground pepper
  Parsley and paprika for garnish

In a bowl combine sliced spinach, sliced cucumbers, onions, and radishes; toss together lightly. Arrange on 4 individual salad plates or in wooden salad bowls. In center of each serving, place a mound of cottage cheese. Blend together sour cream, lemon juice, salt, and pepper, and pour over the salads. Sprinkle top of each salad with a little paprika and chopped parsley, if you wish. Makes 4 servings.

Chef's Wilted Lettuce Salad

4 to 6 slices bacon
4 to 6 cups torn salad greens
3 hard cooked eggs
½ cup slivered cooked ham
3 green onions and tops
¼ cup vinegar
1 teaspoon sugar
  Salt
  Worcestershire
  Pepper
2 tablespoons chopped ripe olives

Cook bacon until crisp; drain. Save 4 tablespoons bacon drippings in pan. Place greens in salad bowl. Chop eggs, arrange on greens with ham. Slice onions and sauté in drippings. Add vinegar and sugar. Add salt, Worcestershire, and pepper to taste. Pour hot dressing over greens, crumble bacon on top, sprinkle with the chopped ripe olives, and toss. Serves 6.

Coconut Crab Salad

1 grapefruit
1 avocado
4 cooked artichoke hearts
½ head iceberg lettuce, shredded
½ cup flaked coconut
1 pound (2 cups) crab meat
½ cup mayonnaise
2 tablespoons dry white table wine
3 tablespoons lemon juice
½ teaspoon salt
  Pepper to taste
  Lettuce

Peel grapefruit and lift segments out of membrane into salad bowl (reserve a few for garnish). Peel avocado, and slice (set aside a few slices and sprinkle with lemon juice). Add to bowl. Slice 2 artichoke hearts into bowl (save 2 for garnish). Add shredded lettuce, coconut, and crab meat.

Mix together dressing of mayonnaise, white wine, lemon juice, salt, and pepper. Pour about half over ingredients in salad bowl. Toss lightly. Heap salad into 6 lettuce-lined bowls; garnish with remaining grapefruit sections, avocado slices, and artichoke slices. Pass salad dressing.

Crab Louis

Which Louis originated this hearty, full-meal salad, we do not know, but Solari's Grill in San Francisco was among the first restaurants to serve it, around 1911.

1 cup mayonnaise
¼ cup whipping cream
¼ cup chili sauce
¼ cup chopped green pepper
¼ cup chopped green onion
  Salt to taste
  Lemon juice to taste
2 heads iceberg lettuce
2 large Dungeness crabs, cracked
  and shelled, or 1½ to 2 pounds
  crab meat
4 large tomatoes
4 hard cooked eggs

Mix together the mayonnaise, whipped cream, chili sauce, green pepper, and green onion. Season with salt and lemon juice to taste. Arrange outer leaves of lettuce on 4 large plates; shred the heart of the lettuce and arrange a bed of shredded lettuce in the center of the leaves. Place the body meat of the crab on the shredded lettuce. Cut tomatoes and eggs in sixths and arrange symmetrically around the crab. Pour over the Louis dressing, and garnish with crab legs. Serves 4.

Exotic Luncheon Salad

2 quarts coarsely cut cooked turkey
1 large can (20 oz.) water chestnuts
2 pounds seedless grapes
2 cups sliced celery
2 to 3 cups toasted slivered almonds
3 cups mayonnaise
1 tablespoon curry powder
2 tablespoons soy
  Boston or bibb lettuce
1 large can (20 oz.) litchi nuts or
  1 large can (1 lb. 13 oz.) pineapple
  chunks

Use turkey breast meat. You will need 2½ to 3 pounds. Coarsely cut the turkey meat from bone into bite sized pieces.

Slice or dice the water chestnuts, and mix them with the turkey meat. Wash the grapes, pick them from their stems, and add, along with the celery and 1½ to 2 cups of the toasted almonds. Mix the mayonnaise with the curry powder and soy. (You may like a couple of tablespoons of lemon juice with it, too.) Combine with the turkey mixture, chill for several hours, then spoon into nests of Boston or bibb lettuce. Sprinkle with the remaining toasted almonds and garnish with the litchi nuts or pineapple chunks arranged on top of each serving. This recipe serves 12 generously or it can be easily multiplied to serve a larger group.

Caesar Salad

Several chefs and restaurateurs claim to have originated this well known green salad. *Sunset* first discovered the salad in a small Coronado restaurant and first published the recipe in March 1945. No one seems to know whether it was created by, or for, a "Caesar." This version was published in *Sunset* in 1957.

Caesar Salad is invariably tossed at the table, where everyone can watch the host or hostess season and mix the greens and drop in each additional ingredient.

1 clove garlic
¾ cup olive oil or other salad oil
2 cups croutons
2 large heads romaine
½ teaspoon salt
  Freshly ground pepper
2 eggs, cooked 1 minute
  Juice of 1 large lemon
6 to 8 anchovy fillets, chopped
½ cup grated Parmesan cheese

Crush garlic in a small bowl, pour over the oil, and let stand several hours. Brown the croutons (preferably made from stale sourdough French bread) in ¼ cup of the garlic oil, stirring often. (If you prefer, you can toast the bread cubes in a slow oven.) Tear romaine into a large salad bowl, sprinkle with salt, and grind over a generous amount of pepper. Pour over remaining garlic oil and toss until every leaf is glossy.

Break the 1-minute eggs into salad; squeeze over the lemon juice, and toss thoroughly. Add chopped anchovies and grated cheese, and toss again. Lastly, add the croutons, toss gently, and serve immediately. Serves about 12.

Hearts of Palm

Cut canned palm pieces in half lengthwise. Pour over them wine vinegar or red table wine and olive oil. Sprinkle with plenty of freshly ground pepper and garnish with pimiento slivers. Chill for a few hours before serving.

Mustard Ring

Try this with ham; it is sweet, tart, and spicy. For contrast to the smooth texture of the mustard-flavored ring mold, fill the center with a crisp cabbage slaw.

4 eggs
¾ cup sugar
1 envelope (1 tablespoon) unflavored gelatin
1½ tablespoons dry mustard
½ teaspoon turmeric
¼ teaspoon salt
1 cup water
½ cup cider vinegar
½ pint (1 cup) whipping cream

Beat eggs in top of double boiler. Mix together thoroughly the sugar and unflavored gelatin; stir in mustard, turmeric, and salt. Add the water and vinegar to the eggs, stir in the sugar mixture, and cook over boiling water until slightly thickened, stirring continuously. Cool until it is thick. Whip cream and stir in. Turn into a 1½-quart ring mold. When firm, unmold and, if desired, fill center with cole slaw to which you might add frozen or canned pineapple chunks or diced winter pears. Garnish with chicory, cress, or other feathery greens. Serves 8.

Jellied Beet and Cabbage Salad

1 can (10½ oz.) consommé
Water
1 package (3 oz.) lemon flavored gelatin
1½ tablespoons vinegar
⅔ cup drained julienne style beets
1 cup finely shredded cabbage
1 tablespoon grated onion
1 teaspoon salt
Dash of pepper
Lettuce
Sour cream dressing

Heat consommé and enough water to make 2 cups liquid. Pour liquid over gelatin and stir until dissolved. Add vinegar. Chill until syrupy. Stir beets, cabbage, onion, salt, and pepper into chilled gelatin. Turn mixture into an 8-inch-square pan. Chill until firm. Unmold salad on shredded lettuce; top with dressing. Serves 6 to 8.

Molded Gazpacho Salad

The ingredients usually used in the Spanish cold soup, *gazpacho,* are used here in a molded salad. It makes a very nice summer meal with cold cuts and hot rolls.

1 envelope unflavored gelatin
About 1½ cups tomato juice
1 large ripe tomato
2 tablespoons vinegar or pickle juice
⅛ teaspoon crushed garlic
1 medium sized cucumber, chopped
1 peeled and seeded green chili, chopped
¼ cup chopped onion
¾ teaspoon salt
⅛ teaspoon freshly ground pepper

Soften the gelatin in ¼ cup of the tomato juice for about 5 minutes. Meanwhile heat 1 cup of the tomato juice; add the gelatin and stir until thoroughly dissolved. Chop the fresh tomato, saving the juice; add vinegar and remaining tomato juice to make ½ cup liquid. Add to the hot mixture with the garlic, cucumber, green chili, onion, salt and pepper. Pour into a 1-quart mold. Chill until firm. Unmold on a bed of crisp greens. Makes 4 to 6 servings.

Ham and Tongue Aspic

Aspic
   3 cans (10½ oz. each) consommé
   1 cup water
   1 medium sized onion, sliced
   2 stalks celery, sliced
   2 envelopes (2 tablespoons) unfla-
      vored gelatin
   ½ cup water

Filling
   Hard cooked egg slices
   Cooked beef tongue slices
1½ cups diced cooked ham
   2 hard cooked eggs, diced
   ⅔ cup chopped celery
   1 green onion, minced
   2 tablespoons finely chopped
      pimiento

Bring to a boil the consommé and the 1 cup water. Add onion, and celery. Cover and simmer 15 minutes. Strain and save liquid. To hot consommé add gelatin that has been softened in the ½ cup water; stir until dissolved. Pour into a 1½ or 2-quart mold, and set mold in ice water that is just a little deeper then the top level of gelatin mixture. Let stand until a layer of aspic about ¼ inch thick has coated sides of mold. Pour out liquid center and save.

Decorate aspic shell with slices of hard cooked egg, dipped first in aspic, then attached to sides and bottom; let chill until eggs hold securely. Pour a little of the aspic (if it gets thick, set in hot water and stir) into mold, and line with thin slices cooked beef tongue. Let chill while you combine with remaining aspic the ham, diced hard cooked eggs, celery, onion, and pimiento. Fill mold and chill at least 4 hours or overnight. Unmold on butter lettuce. Cut and serve with a dressing of mayonnaise flavored to taste with prepared mustard. Serves 8 to 10.

Avocado and Tomato Salad Mold

Avocado Aspic
   1 envelope (1 tablespoon) unflavored
      gelatin
   ¼ cup cold water
   1 cup boiling water
   1 teaspoon sugar
   2 tablespoons lemon juice
   1 cup mashed avocado (1 large)
   ½ cup each commercial sour cream
      and mayonnaise
   1 teaspoon salt
   Pepper and dash of cayenne

Soften gelatin in cold water, pour in boiling water, and stir until dissolved. Add sugar and 1 tablespoon of the lemon juice. Chill until slightly thickened. Immediately after mashing avocado, add the other tablespoon lemon juice, sour cream, mayonnaise, salt, pepper, and cayenne. Mix thoroughly with chilled gelatin. Pour into 2-quart mold. Chill until set.

Tomato Aspic
   1 envelope (1 tablespoon) unflavored
      gelatin
   ¼ cup cold water
   1 cup boiling water
   2 tablespoons sugar
   1 can (10 oz.) tomato soup
   1 tablespoon lemon juice
   ¼ teaspoon salt

Soften gelatin in cold water; dissolve in boiling water. Add sugar, soup, lemon juice, and salt. Pour over firm avocado aspic. Chill until set. Unmold on greens. Serves 8 to 10.

Minced Vegetable Dressing

Use this colorful dressing on wedges of lettuce or over a salad of mixed raw and cooked vegetables.

1 medium sized onion
1 can (4 oz.) pimientos
1 large green pepper
1 cup salad oil
¾ cup sugar
1 tablespoon salt
¾ cup vinegar

Run the onion, pimientos, and seeded green pepper through the medium blade of the food chopper. Put ground vegetables in a quart jar. Add oil, sugar, salt, and vinegar. Shake well. Store in the refrigerator. Shake again each time you use it. Makes 1 quart of salad dressing.

Watercress Dressing

½ bunch watercress
1 clove garlic, minced or mashed
1 cup mayonnaise
  Salt to taste
2 teaspoons lemon juice

Chop watercress and garlic very fine. Stir into mayonnaise; add salt to taste and lemon juice. Chill. Serve over wedges of head lettuce or over a salad of orange and grapefruit segments. Makes 1½ cups of dressing.

Honey Dressing

1 cup salad oil
½ cup catsup
⅓ cup vinegar
⅓ cup honey
1 teaspoon salt
1 teaspoon paprika
1 teaspoon grated onion
1 whole clove garlic

In a mixing bowl or the small bowl of your electric mixer, place the salad oil, catsup, vinegar, honey, salt, paprika, and grated onion. Beat thoroughly with a rotary beater, or beat at medium speed on your electric mixer until very well blended. Add the whole clove of garlic, and let stand about 10 minutes, or until you are ready to use it. Remove the garlic when it has flavored the dressing to your taste. Beat again just before serving. Store in your refrigerator, beating every time you use it. Makes about 2½ cups.

Three-Cheese Dressing

For devotees of blue cheese dressings, this one has an intriguing extra flavor contributed by Sap Sago cheese. Cream cheese blends the other ingredients into a smooth dressing that is delicious on tossed green salads and other vegetable salads.

¼ pound blue cheese
1 large package (8 oz.) cream cheese
4 tablespoons grated Sap Sago cheese
½ teaspoon dry tarragon
1 teaspoon salt
¼ teaspoon pepper
½ clove garlic, mashed
  About ½ cup milk

Using the small bowl of your electric mixer, mix together the blue cheese, cream cheese, and Sap Sago cheese until well blended. Add the tarragon, salt, pepper, and garlic purée. Gradually beat in milk until the dressing is the consistency of medium thick cream. Use immediately, or cover and refrigerate to use later. Makes about 3 cups of salad dressing.

Soups & Chowders

IN THESE DAYS, few soups have much to do with "soup kettle" in the traditional sense—the day-in, day-out, back-of-the-range simmering of ingredients that happen to come its way. Today's soup is much more of a controlled production. Whether the cook sets out to make a seafood chowder, or to capture the essence of an abundance of garden-ripe vegetables, or to satisfy a hunger for old-fashioned split pea soup, the soup remains what it starts out to be: a special blend of special ingredients to suit a particular occasion.

This does not mean that soup-making has become a matter of rigidly following recipes. In fact, to the imaginative cook, there are few categories that allow as much opportunity for ingenuity.

It is interesting, we think, to read this chapter as an over-all picture of what soup has come to mean, considering each recipe as the result of one cook's expedient adventures. You'll find it rich in foreign and regional influences, and rich in well-considered departures from traditional recipes.

Most of all, you will find that today's shortcuts to the traditional soup kettle are not a matter of hit-and-miss can-opener assembly. Canned and packaged ingredients are used freely and wholeheartedly, but not in any way as end products. They are enhanced; they are gratefully blessed for the challenge and the surprises they offer.

Chicken-Mushroom Soup

Chicken broth and sherry give this very creamy mushroom soup an especially rich flavor. If you wish, garnish each serving with shaved almonds instead of mushrooms.

½ pound fresh mushrooms, sliced
¼ cup (4 tablespoons) butter
2 cups chicken stock
3 egg yolks
1 cup light cream
¼ teaspoon salt
   Dash of pepper
2 to 4 tablespoons sherry

Sauté mushrooms in butter for 5 minutes. Set aside 6 slices for garnish. Put chicken stock in the blender, add sautéed mushrooms, and blend until mushrooms are coarsely chopped, less than 1 minute. Add egg yolks and blend 1 or 2 seconds. Turn into a saucepan, add cream and heat slowly, stirring constantly, until slightly thickened. Season with salt, pepper, and sherry. Garnish with the mushrooms. Serves 4 to 6.

Winter Tomato Soup

½ cup chopped celery
2 tablespoons butter or fresh bacon
   drippings
1 can (1 lb.) stewed tomatoes
1 can (10½ oz.) consommé or
   chicken broth
½ cup dry white table wine or ½ cup
   additional chicken broth
1 tablespoon instant minced onion or
   3 tablespoons chopped green onion
1 tablespoon lemon juice
1 tablespoon cornstarch, blended with
   ½ cup water
   Dash of curry powder
   Cheese croutons (optional)

Sauté the celery in butter or bacon drippings until tender, about 5 minutes. Add all remaining ingredients (except croutons); blend well. Simmer 15 to 20 minutes, stirring occasionally. Garnish with cheese croutons. Makes 6 servings.

Bellingham Split Pea Soup

2 cups dried split green peas
2 quarts liquor from boiling smoked
   tongue, or consommé
1 stalk celery, sliced
1 large onion, chopped
1 large carrot, sliced
2 pounds fresh peas, shelled, or 1½
   packages (10 oz. each) frozen peas
1 bay leaf
¼ teaspoon thyme
   Salt and pepper to taste
1 pint light cream

Wash split peas and put in a large kettle with the tongue liquor, celery, onion, and carrot; cover and simmer until tender, about 1½ to 2 hours. (Or cook in a pressure cooker.)

Meanwhile, steam fresh peas until just tender. Press both the soup and the cooked fresh peas through a strainer, or purée the peas in a blender and combine with the strained soup. Add the bay leaf, thyme, salt, and pepper, and simmer for 10 minutes longer, just to blend flavors. When ready to serve, add the cream; heat. Serves 8 to 10.

Pumpkin Soup

2 tablespoons butter
½ green pepper, chopped
1 large tomato, chopped
1 green onion, chopped (include part of the green top)
1 large sprig parsley
1 large sprig thyme, or ¼ teaspoon of the dried herb
1 bay leaf
1 can (1 lb.) pumpkin or 2 cups cooked pumpkin
2 cups chicken stock
1 tablespoon flour
½ cup milk
½ teaspoon each nutmeg and sugar
   Salt to taste

Melt butter in a large pan, add green pepper, tomato, onion, parsley, thyme, and bay leaf; simmer 5 minutes. Add pumpkin and chicken stock and simmer 30 minutes. Press mixture through a food mill or wire strainer. Blend the flour with the milk and stir into the strained soup. Season with nutmeg, sugar, and salt. Heat, stirring often, while you bring soup to a boil; cook about 3 minutes. Serve hot. Makes 4 to 6 servings.

Mushroom Soup Paprika

½ pound fresh mushrooms
1 tablespoon butter
1 teaspoon paprika
1 tablespoon flour
2 tablespoons finely chopped parsley
4 cups beef stock (or beef concentrate dissolved in 4 cups hot water)
1 egg yolk
½ pint (1 cup) commercial sour cream

Wash and slice mushrooms thinly into a saucepan. Sauté in butter along with paprika for 5 minutes, or until golden brown. Sprinkle mushrooms with flour and parsley. Gradually stir in beef stock and simmer slowly 30 minutes. Beat egg yolk slightly; blend with sour cream, and turn into a soup tureen. Gradually pour hot soup over it, stirring well. Makes 6 servings.

Cream Consommé

1 large onion, parboiled
1 tart apple
3 cans (10½ oz. each) consommé
1½ cups whipping cream
   Salt to taste
   Dash each of paprika and curry powder
1 red-skinned apple
   Juice of ½ lemon

Grate the parboiled onion and the unpeeled apple; add to the consommé and cook until tender, about 10 minutes. Purée in a blender or put through a strainer. Stir in cream, and season with salt, paprika, and curry powder. Reheat slowly, just until hot throughout. Serve in small cups, garnished with chopped apple that you have sprinkled with lemon juice. Serves 10.

Strained Onion Soup

2 large onions, sliced
2 tablespoons butter
1 quart beef stock or 3 cans (10½ oz. each) bouillon

Sauté onions very slowly in butter. When they are completely wilted but not brown, add beef stock or bouillon and simmer for 20 minutes, replacing with water any liquid that evaporates. Strain, pressing all the juices from onions. Correct seasoning; serve in bouillon cups. Serves 6.

Cheese Soup with Condiments

Let each person select his own toppings for this soup — serve chopped green pepper, thin pimiento strips, toasted almond slivers, crumbled crisp bacon, and popcorn.

2 tablespoons each chopped onion, butter, flour
2 chicken bouillon cubes
6 cups milk
1¼ cups shredded sharp Cheddar cheese
Pinch of dry mustard
Salt, pepper, paprika

In the top of a double boiler over direct heat, sauté onion in melted butter until golden. Stir in flour and bouillon cubes; blend in milk. Place over hot water and cook until slightly thickened. Add cheese and mustard and continue cooking until cheese melts, stirring occasionally. Season to taste with salt, pepper, and paprika. Serve immediately. Serves 4 to 6.

Cream of Avocado Soup

You can serve this delicate soup hot or cold. Sprinkle it with crumbled bacon or crisp garlic croutons.

1 large ripe avocado
2 cans (14½ oz. each) evaporated milk
1 pint (2 cups) fresh milk
½ teaspoon celery salt
½ teaspoon garlic salt
¼ teaspoon monosodium glutamate
Salt and pepper to taste

Peel avocado, remove seed, and run it through a blender or press through a sieve. Beat the evaporated milk into the avocado pulp; then stir in the fresh milk. Add seasonings and heat enough to blend all ingredients. Serves 6 to 8.

Ham and Celery Soup

1 ham bone with meat on it
2 chicken backs
1 quart water
¼ small cabbage, finely shredded
2 stalks celery with tops, sliced
6 green onions, chopped
1 can (10½ oz.) cream of celery soup
½ soup can water
Salt and pepper to taste
½ cup coarsely grated raw carrots

Simmer ham bone and chicken backs in the water until meat falls from bones. Remove bones and put all meat pieces into the broth; add cabbage, celery, and onions, and cook 15 minutes. Add celery soup and water; season with salt and pepper. Simmer until well blended, but do not boil. Serve in large soup bowls, and top with coarsely grated raw carrots. Serves 8.

Boula

1 can (10 oz.) clear turtle soup
1 can (10½ oz.) cream of pea soup
1 soup can water
2 tablespoons sherry
½ teaspoon lemon juice
¼ cup whipping cream

Combine turtle and pea soups with the can of water. Bring to the boiling point, stir in sherry and lemon juice, and ladle into 6 heat-proof soup bowls or large ramekins. Whip cream and drop a tablespoonful on top of each bowlful of soup. Place under the broiler until cream forms a thick, brown layer. Serve immediately to 6 persons.

Spinach Herb Soup

Whirl the vegetables in your blender if you prefer a smooth-textured soup.

2 tablespoons butter
⅓ cup chopped green onions and tops
2 tablespoons finely chopped parsley
2 tablespoons finely chopped chives
1 cup chopped watercress
1 cup chopped lettuce
½ cup finely chopped fresh spinach
½ teaspoon salt
⅛ teaspoon pepper
½ teaspoon dried tarragon, crushed
4 cans (10½ oz. each) consommé
½ cup light cream

Melt butter in a large saucepan; add green onions and tops, parsley, chives, watercress, lettuce, spinach, salt, pepper, and tarragon; cook over low heat for 15 minutes. Pour in consommé and continue cooking 15 minutes. Before serving, stir in cream and bring just to a boil. Serves 8.

Beef Vegetable Soup

Beef shank bone with meat (about 1¼ lbs.)
1½ quarts water
2 bay leaves
⅓ cup chopped celery leaves
3 sprigs parsley
1 tablespoon salt
1 package (1¼ oz.) dehydrated onion soup
1 can (1 lb.) seasoned stewed tomatoes
1 cup diced carrots
1 cup diced potatoes
1 cup sliced celery
3 tablespoons uncooked rice
1 quart water
1 teaspoon salt
½ teaspoon pepper

In a large kettle, put the soup bone, 1½ quarts water, bay leaves, celery leaves, parsley, and the 1 tablespoon salt. Cover and simmer until the meat is tender, about 2½ hours; remove the bone and meat. (Cool broth if you wish to skim off all fat.)

Cut meat from bone and return to the broth. Mix in the onion soup. Add the stewed tomatoes, carrots, potatoes, celery, rice, the 1 quart water, 1 teaspoon salt, and pepper. Cover and simmer until the vegetables are tender, about 25 minutes. Makes 8 to 10 generous servings.

Cream of Cucumber Soup

3 medium sized cucumbers
¼ cup (4 tablespoons) butter
1 teaspoon finely chopped chives
3 tablespoons flour
1½ teaspoons salt
    Freshly ground black pepper to taste
1 quart milk
    Chopped parsley or paprika

Cut cucumbers in half lengthwise and scoop out the large seeds. Coarsely shred the unpeeled cucumbers. Melt butter in the top part of a large double boiler or saucepan; add cucumbers and chives and sauté until lightly browned. Blend in flour, salt, and pepper. Scald milk and gradually stir in. Place over hot water and cook, stirring occasionally, until thickened. Serve hot or cold, garnished with parsley or with paprika. Serves 6.

Country Supper Soup

This soup is even better made a day ahead so that flavors will have a chance to blend and mellow.

½ pound lean sliced bacon, cut in small pieces
2 cans (10¾ oz. each) condensed onion soup
1 can (1 lb. 13 oz.) solid pack tomatoes
1 cup diced carrots
1 cup sliced celery
1 cup diced potato
½ pound zucchini, diced
1 clove garlic, minced or mashed
1 small bunch parsley, chopped
9 cups water
1 bay leaf, crumbled
    Generous pinch each thyme, marjoram, and basil
    Salt and pepper to taste
2 cups broken uncooked spaghetti
2 cans (1 lb. each) cooked dried lima beans
¼ cup grated Parmesan cheese

In a large kettle, combine the bacon, soup, tomatoes, carrots, celery, potato, zucchini, garlic, parsley, water, and the seasonings. Bring to a boil, then cover and simmer gently for 1 hour, stirring occasionally. Add spaghetti and continue cooking for 30 minutes longer, stirring frequently. Just before serving add lima beans (including liquid) and cheese. Taste and season with more salt and pepper if necessary. Serve in heated bowls and pass additional grated Parmesan cheese. Makes about 4 quarts soup. Serves 8 to 10 generously.

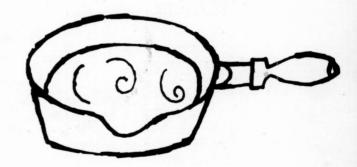

Barley Bean Soup

2 slices beef shank, sawed into pieces 1½ inches thick
2 small ham knuckles
½ cup dried navy beans
¼ cup pearl barley
2 sliced celery tops
1 onion, chopped
8 cups cold water

Place beef shank, ham knuckles, navy beans, barley, celery tops, and onion in a large kettle. Pour over cold water; cover and simmer 3 hours. Remove meat, and when cool enough to handle, slice from the bone and cut in small pieces. Return meat to soup, season with salt and pepper, and heat. Serve with a sprinkling of chopped parsley. Serves 8.

Crab Bisque

1 cup crab meat
½ cup sherry
1 can (11 oz.) tomato soup
1 can (10½ oz.) green pea soup
1 soup can light cream
¼ teaspoon curry powder
½ teaspoon paprika

Put crab meat in a bowl, pour over sherry, and let stand 1 hour. Blend together the tomato and green pea soups, cream, curry, and paprika. Heat slowly, but do not boil. Add the crab meat. Reheat to boiling point and serve immediately. Serves 6.

Hearty Clam Chowder

Serve this with a dark bread, a tray of cheese, and a bowl of chilled fruit.

4 slices bacon, cut in small cubes
3 green onions and tops, chopped
5 medium sized potatoes, peeled and
  cut in ½-inch cubes
2 tablespoons chopped green pepper
1 stalk celery, sliced
1 carrot, finely sliced
1 clove garlic, mashed or minced
2 cups water
1 teaspoon salt
½ teaspoon pepper
1 teaspoon Worcestershire
4 drops Tabasco
2 cups chopped raw clams (with juice)
1 pint (2 cups) light cream

In a large heavy kettle, sauté bacon until crisp; add green onions and tops, potatoes, green pepper, celery, carrot, and garlic. Pour in water and season with salt, pepper, Worcestershire, and Tabasco. Cover pan and simmer 15 minutes, or until potatoes are tender. Mash mixture slightly with a potato masher. (If you prefer a thicker soup, mash potatoes well.)

In a separate pan, heat clams in their juice for 3 minutes, or until tender. Add clams to vegetable mixture; pour in cream. Stir well, then heat just until piping hot, but do not boil. Serves 4 as a main course.

Geragure

Because rockfish has solid, firm meat, it is an excellent choice for chowders. In this Armenian dish called *Geragure* (it means "meal"), both rockfish and crab retain their identity as they bubble in the tomato broth.

1 medium sized onion, sliced
½ clove garlic, mashed or minced
1½ tablespoons olive oil
1 cup water
1 can (1 lb. 4 oz.) solid pack
  tomatoes
1 teaspoon salt
½ teaspoon pepper
1 cup crab meat, fresh or canned
1½ pounds rockfish fillets

In a heavy kettle, sauté onion and garlic in olive oil until golden brown, then add water, tomatoes, salt, and pepper, and simmer for 20 minutes. Drop in crab meat and continue cooking for 10 minutes. Cut fillets in thin strips, then drop into tomato mixture and simmer very slowly for 20 minutes. To avoid breaking up fish, do not stir the mixture, but shake pan occasionally. Serve immediately. Makes 6 servings.

Cioppino

Serve this famous fish stew as a main course, accompanied by crusty French bread and a salad of mixed greens. It's a bit messy to eat, so have a large supply of paper napkins on hand.

¼ cup (4 tablespoons) chopped fresh marjoram
2 tablespoons chopped fresh rosemary
2 tablespoons chopped fresh sage
2 tablespoons chopped fresh thyme
4 tablespoons chopped fresh sweet basil
½ cup chopped fresh parsley
4 cloves garlic, mashed or minced
4 small red peppers, finely chopped
1 quart (4 cups) coarsely chopped Swiss chard (approximately 1 large bunch)
40 raw cockle clams
2 large cooked crabs, cleaned and cracked
36 raw prawns, 12 to 20 count
2 pounds sea bass, rockfish, or other firm fleshed white fish
2 large cans (1 lb. 13 oz. each) solid pack tomatoes
1 small can (6 oz.) tomato paste
¾ cup olive oil
2 tablespoons salt
2 teaspoons freshly ground pepper
1 cup dry white table wine

Combine the marjoram, rosemary, sage, thyme, and sweet basil; add parsley, garlic, and chopped red peppers; toss all together with the Swiss chard. Arrange clams in the bottom of a large, heavy 8-quart kettle with a tight fitting cover. Sprinkle part of the herb and Swiss chard mixture over the clams; put the cracked crab in next, and sprinkle with another layer of herbs and chard. Add the prawns, another layer of the herb mixture, and arrange the sea bass on top. (If fresh herbs are not available, substitute one-fourth as much fresh dried herbs.)

Mix together tomatoes, tomato paste, olive oil, salt, and freshly ground pepper and pour over all. Cover and simmer for 30 minutes; pour in wine, and simmer 10 minutes longer, or until the seasonings are well blended. Serve in big soup bowls with plenty of the sauce. Be sure to dip down to the bottom of the kettle for the clams. Serves 12.

Fisherman's Stew

2½ pounds filleted salmon
2 tablespoons salad oil or olive oil
1 clove garlic, mashed or minced
¼ teaspoon each thyme, basil, and rosemary
¼ teaspoon each whole allspice and whole black peppers, crushed
½ teaspoon salt
1 onion, thinly sliced
½ cup sliced celery
1 tablespoon chopped parsley
Dash of cayenne
1 cup each clam broth and dry white table wine
1 can (1 lb.) solid pack tomatoes
1 tablespoon sugar
1 lemon, thinly sliced
1 cup cooked small shrimp
6 slices French bread, toasted and buttered

Cut fillets so you will have 6 pieces. Heat oil and garlic in a large, deep frying pan; fry salmon 3 minutes on each side. Sprinkle over the thyme, basil, rosemary, allspice, pepper, salt, onion, celery, parsley, and cayenne. Pour in clam broth and wine and simmer for 20 minutes, or until fish flakes with a fork. Carefully remove fish. Add the tomatoes, sugar, and sliced lemon to the clam broth mixture. Boil rapidly until mixture is reduced one-third and sauce is quite thick. Return salmon to sauce, along with shrimp, and heat slowly for 10 minutes. To serve, place a slice of buttered and toasted French bread in each flat soup dish; arrange a salmon fillet on each piece of toast, and surround with the sauce. Serves 6.

Seafood Gumbo

Ham and bacon give a smoky flavor and extra richness to this outstanding soup.

2 tablespoons butter
½ cup diced bacon (approximately 6 slices)
½ cup chopped green onion
1 clove garlic, mashed or minced
2 tablespoons flour
1 can (1 lb.) okra
1 can (1 lb.) solid pack tomatoes
1 cup diced ham, cut in ¼-inch cubes
2 teaspoons finely chopped fresh thyme or ½ teaspoon powdered thyme
2 bay leaves
7 cups boiling water
1 pound shucked small, raw shrimp
¾ pound flaked crab meat
½ cup uncooked rice

Melt butter in a large, heavy kettle. Add bacon, green onion, and garlic, and sauté until onion is limp and clear. Sprinkle in flour and stir until blended. Add okra, tomatoes, ham, thyme, and bay leaves; pour in boiling water. Stirring often, simmer for 45 minutes. Add shrimp and crab to broth and continue cooking 15 minutes. Cook rice by your preferred method. To serve, spoon 3 tablespoons of cooked rice into 8 heated bowls, then ladle over piping hot gumbo mixture. Serves 8.

Fish Soup

2 pounds fresh or frozen cod or halibut
½ cup olive oil
2 cloves garlic, mashed or minced
½ cup finely chopped parsley
½ cup sliced green olives (2 oz. jar)
1 cup canned or fresh tomatoes
2 cups water
¼ cup dry white table wine

Cut fish into 2-inch-square pieces. In a covered saucepan, combine the oil, garlic, parsley, sliced olives, and tomatoes. Cook over medium heat 5 minutes. Add the fish and continue cooking 5 minutes, stirring frequently to prevent sticking. Add water, cover saucepan, and simmer until the fish can be flaked with a fork, about 10 minutes. Add wine before serving. Serves 6.

Curried Cream of Chicken Soup

¼ cup minced onion
2 tablespoons butter
1 tablespoon curry powder
2 cups rich chicken stock
2 cups (1 pint) whipping cream
3 egg yolks
Salt and pepper to taste
1 large apple, finely diced
Juice of ½ lemon (1½ tablespoons juice)

Cook onion in butter until wilted; stir in curry powder and then chicken stock. Simmer for 5 minutes, add cream, and bring to a boil. Beat the egg yolks slightly and beat ½ cup of the hot stock into them slowly. Combine mixtures and cook gently until thickened, but do not boil. Season with salt and pepper and chill. Serve garnished with the diced apple that has been soaked in lemon juice. Serves 6.

Gazpacho

The original Spanish recipe for this icy cold soup called for layers of bread. This West Coast version has been described as "almost a liquid salad."

4 large very ripe tomatoes, peeled and chopped
1 large cucumber, peeled and diced
1 medium sized onion, finely minced
1 green pepper, seeded and finely minced
1 cup tomato juice
1 tablespoon wine vinegar
3 tablespoons olive oil
1 small clove garlic, mashed or minced
Salt and pepper to taste

Mix the tomatoes, cucumbers, onion, green pepper, tomato juice, vinegar, oil, and garlic; add salt and pepper to taste. Chill soup until icy. Serve in small glasses, with an ice cube in each, or spoon into bowls lined with lettuce leaves. Serves 6 to 8.

Chilled Vegetable Soup

As creamy and delicate as vichyssoise, but with mysterious garden fresh flavor.

1 cup coarsely diced raw potatoes
1 cup fresh or frozen green peas
¼ cup sliced green onions
1½ cups chicken bouillon
⅛ teaspoon celery salt
⅛ teaspoon curry powder
1 cup (½ pint) whipping cream

Add the potatoes, peas, and green onions to the chicken bouillon in a saucepan. Bring to a boil; reduce heat, cover, and simmer until the vegetables are just tender, about 10 minutes. Turn this vegetable mixture into your electric blender and blend until smooth, about 30 seconds, or put through a fine strainer. Mix in the celery salt, curry powder, and cream. Chill very thoroughly before serving. Makes about 4 servings.

Jellied Borsch

This is not a true borsch, but rather a very pleasant semi-jellied beet soup. The sauerkraut juice and sour cream contribute a refreshing tang.

2 cans (1 lb. 4 oz. each) diced beets
1 can (10½ oz.) consommé
1 cup sauerkraut juice
2 whole cloves
1 onion, chopped
  Water
  Salt to taste
1 envelope (1 tablespoon) unflavored gelatin
¼ cup cold water
  Sour cream
  Chopped dill leaves or chives

Combine beets, consommé, and sauerkraut juice; simmer with the cloves and onion for 10 minutes; strain (the beets may be used in salad). Measure liquid and add enough water to make 5 cups. Boil 1 cup of the liquid, add salt to taste; add gelatin which has been softened in the ¼ cup cold water, and stir until it is dissolved. Stir in remaining 4 cups of liquid. Chill. Serve in bowls or cups surrounded with ice; top each serving with a spoonful of sour cream and a sprinkling of dill or chives. Serves 6.

Vichyssoise

4 leeks or 1 large bunch green onions, finely chopped (use white part only)
1 large onion, finely sliced
¼ cup (4 tablespoons) butter
1 quart chicken broth or strong chicken bouillon (6 bouillon cubes to 4 cups boiling water)
3 large potatoes, peeled and thinly sliced
½ pint (1 cup) whipping cream
1 cup milk
  Salt and pepper
  Chopped chives

Over low heat cook chopped leeks or green onions and sliced onion in butter until soft, but not browned. Add chicken broth and potatoes, and cook, covered, until potatoes are tender, about 20 minutes. Press through a fine sieve, or blend in an electric blender. Pour in cream and milk and season to taste with salt and pepper. If too thick, thin with additional milk. Chill thoroughly. Serve cold with finely chopped chives or chopped green onion tops sprinkled over the top. Serves 8.

Meats

THE WESTERN COOKS who contributed these recipes are well aware of the place of fruits and nuts in meat cookery, and as you glance through these pages, you will find these foods used freely and imaginatively. Ham is prepared with walnuts, pork chops are stuffed with prunes and apricots, corned beef is basted with an orange and lemon mixture, Swiss steak receives a garnish of tomatoes, olives, and artichoke hearts.

You will also find an international background here as you read such recipe titles as: Sauerbraten, Quick Sukiyaki, Tournedos Nicoise, Greek Meat Balls, Indonesian Pork Broil, Schweinspfeffer, Cantonese Ham, Veal Mozzarella.

But as you read — and as you try some of the recipes — you will realize that this is not at all a collection of recipes for foreign dishes. If you are looking for *the* authentic Veal Scallopini, or a Sauerbraten exactly like one you remember from long ago, you are not likely to find them. These recipes are international in background, but in background only. They have been built by individual cooks, partially from rules, partially from memory, partially from pure inspiration.

There is no worship here of "foreign" in the sense of strange or exotic. Rather, "foreign" is allied in meaning to "tradition"— the best of the traditions of another culture, applied to the ingredients at hand.

Triple Roll Roast

As colorful as it is flavorful. When the meat is sliced, each piece displays concentric rings of beef, pork, and veal.

1 pound each top round beef steak, veal steak, and pork steak, cut ¼ inch thick
Salt and pepper
2 tablespoons chopped parsley
1 cup consommé
1 tablespoon chopped parsley
½ cup sliced celery
1 sliced onion
4 whole cloves

Trim meat and bone; cut enough fat in small pieces to measure ½ cup. Season meat with salt and pepper. Stack meat in layers, starting with the top round, then the pork, and ending with the veal. Sprinkle the 2 tablespoons chopped parsley over the meat as you make the layers. Roll up meat; tie. Heat the ½ cup fat in a heavy kettle; brown meat roll on all sides. Pour in consommé; add the 1 tablespoon chopped parsley, celery, onion, and cloves. Cover and bake in a 325° oven for 2½ hours. Strain sauce; thicken for gravy. Serves 8 to 10.

Braised Rump Roast

4-pound rump roast
1 teaspoon celery salt
¼ teaspoon pepper
1 clove garlic, peeled and partially crushed
2 tablespoons salad oil, shortening or bacon drippings
¾ cup water
1 tablespoon each honey and vinegar
2 tablespoons soy
½ teaspoon ground ginger
1 to 2 tablespoons soy, depending on saltiness desired
2 tablespoons cornstarch

Rub cut sides of meat with celery salt and pepper. In a heavy kettle, brown garlic in the oil; remove garlic. Brown meat on all sides in the oil. Combine water, honey, vinegar, 2 tablespoons soy, and ginger; pour over meat. Cover and simmer for 2 hours, or until meat is tender.

Transfer meat to a hot platter. Mix the 1 to 2 tablespoons soy and cornstarch, stir into drippings. Bring to a boil and cook, stirring, about 5 minutes until gravy is thickened. Serves 8 to 10.

Beef Round in Sour Cream Gravy

4 thin slices salt pork
1 large onion, sliced
1 green onion, chopped
1 large carrot, peeled and sliced
1 clove garlic, minced or mashed
4 pounds beef bottom round or rump
1 teaspoon pepper
½ teaspoon salt
¾ cup dry red table wine
¾ cup commercial sour cream
3 tablespoons each flour and water
1 tablespoon lemon juice

Lay 2 slices salt pork in the bottom of a heavy kettle. Add onions, carrot, and garlic, and sauté lightly. Remove vegetables from pan and set aside. Rub meat well with pepper and salt, and brown on all sides. Reduce heat; stir in wine and sour cream, blending until smooth. Add sautéed vegetables and cover with remaining salt pork. Cover kettle and cook slowly 2½ hours.

Transfer meat and vegetables to a hot platter and discard salt pork. Blend flour paste into the juices and cook until smooth. Stir in lemon juice. Slice meat and pour over gravy. Serves 8.

Sauerbraten

4-pound top round roast
Salt and pepper
2 cups cider vinegar
2 cups port wine
1 large onion, sliced
1 large green pepper, sliced
1 large carrot, thinly sliced
Tops of 1 bunch celery (leaves only)
8 sprigs parsley, chopped
1 teaspoon whole black peppers
2 to 4 bay leaves, crumbled
1 teaspoon salt
2 teaspoons marjoram
4 cloves garlic, minced or mashed
2 teaspoons rosemary
2 teaspoons thyme
1 teaspoon sweet basil
¼ teaspoon ginger
3 tablespoons butter
5 or 6 gingersnaps
½ pint (1 cup) commercial sour cream

Salt and pepper meat, then place in a marinade of the vinegar, port, sliced vegetables, and seasonings. Let stand in refrigerator 4 or 5 days, turning twice a day. Remove roast from marinade, drain well, then brown on both sides in butter; add marinade, and simmer for 3 to 4 hours, or until tender. Remove roast to hot platter. Stir crumbled gingersnaps and sour cream into gravy and stir until thick and smooth. Do not boil. Serve with sliced roast. Serves 10 to 12.

Tournedos Nicoise

Authentic *tournedos* are slices of beef tenderloin or fillet, but you can substitute another cut of steak. Cook the beans and potatoes in advance and keep warm in casseroles in the oven. Have the prepared tomato sauce in a saucepan, ready for reheating. The meat must be sautéed at the last moment.

4 medium sized tomatoes
3 tablespoons butter
1 clove garlic, minced or mashed
1½ teaspoons crumbled or dried tarragon
8 slices beef tenderloin or fillet, cut at least ¾ inch thick
Butter
Salt and freshly ground pepper to taste
3 packages (10 oz. each) French-cut string beans, cooked and well buttered
3 dozen small potatoes, cooked and turned in butter
Parsley
Spiced crab apples for garnish

Peel, chop, and strain tomatoes; then simmer slowly in the 3 tablespoons butter, along with the garlic and tarragon, until flavors are just blended, about 10 minutes. Using 2 large frying pans, brown steaks in butter to desired doneness, and season to taste with salt and freshly ground black pepper. To serve, overlap steaks on a large, round platter, forming a crown. Place a spoonful of the fresh tomato sauce on each. Surround with alternate mounds of hot green beans and lightly browned potatoes. Garnish with parsley and preserved crab apples. Serves 8.

Beef Teriyaki

2 pounds boneless beef steak
1¾ cups soy
½ cup sugar
½ teaspoon crushed garlic
1 tablespoon grated fresh ginger or
  2 tablespoons minced preserved
  or candied ginger
½ teaspoon monosodium glutamate
  (optional)

Cut meat into 4 pieces and place in a bowl. In a pan combine the soy, sugar, garlic, ginger, and monosodium glutamate, if used. Heat just until sugar is dissolved; cool. Pour mixture over meat and marinate for 1 hour or longer. Remove meat from marinade and grill over glowing coals, or broil in your oven until done to your liking. (Leftover marinade keeps well in the refrigerator for several weeks.) Slice each steak into finger-sized pieces and serve one steak to a person. Makes 4 servings.

Steak Diane

Some *maitres d'hotel* add chopped onion, wine, and other extras, but this is one of the simplest and best ways to prepare this dish.

Slice tenderloin beef very thin, and give it a few whacks with a meat mallet to flatten it even more; sprinkle with salt and pepper to taste. Have your pan very hot, and use just enough butter to keep meat from sticking. Brown steaks quickly, a minute or so on each side.

For every 4 to 6 steaks, add to pan ¼ cup (4 tablespoons) butter; also add ½ teaspoon Worcestershire sauce for each steak. Heat until butter melts, then pour over steaks and serve. These cook so quickly that they can be done to order in an electric frying pan at the table.

Curried Beef with Vegetables

2 slices bacon, cut in small pieces
2 tablespoons butter
1 medium sized onion, sliced
2 pounds round steak, cut in 1-inch
  cubes
½ cup flour mixed with 1 teaspoon salt,
  ¼ teaspoon pepper, and 1½ tablespoons curry powder
  Water
2 bay leaves
1 cup each diced celery and diced
  carrots
2 cups cubed potatoes
1 cup fresh or frozen green peas
1 tablespoon lemon juice

In a heavy kettle or Dutch oven, cook bacon, butter, and onion until the onion is golden brown. Remove onion and bacon with a slotted spoon; set aside. Dredge the meat in the seasoned flour and brown well in the fat remaining in the pan. Sprinkle meat with any of the flour mixture left over, add water to cover, bay leaf, and the onion and bacon. Simmer for 1 hour, or until meat is nearly tender, adding more water if needed. Add celery, carrots, and potatoes, and cook until vegetables are done and meat is tender. Add the peas during the last 10 minutes. Remove the bay leaf, add lemon juice, and thicken the gravy, if desired. Serves 6.

Swiss Steak, California Style

1 cup dry white table wine
3 tablespoons wine vinegar
1 canned green chili, finely chopped
1 tablespoon brown sugar
1 teaspoon salt
¼ teaspoon garlic powder
2 pounds beef round steak, cut 1½ to 2 inches thick
2 tablespoons shortening

Sauce

1 cup drained marinade
½ cup bouillon
¼ cup chili sauce
2 tablespoons chopped onion
2 teaspoons each cornstarch and water

Garnish

3 medium sized tomatoes, quartered
½ cup pitted ripe olives
1 small can (4 oz.) artichoke hearts, drained

Mix first 6 ingredients for marinade. Trim any excess fat from meat. Place meat in pan or bowl, and marinate in refrigerator overnight. The next day, drain meat well, saving marinade. In a large pan with cover, brown meat on both sides in heated shortening. Add marinade, bouillon, chili sauce, and chopped onion. Cover pan and simmer meat until tender, about 1¼ hours. Skim any fat from liquid. Blend cornstarch with water and stir into liquid. Cook until thickened. Add tomatoes, olives, artichoke hearts. Heat.

Place meat on heated serving platter. Arrange garnish around and on top of meat. Spoon on a little of the sauce. Serve the remainder separately. Makes 6 servings.

Fruited Corned Beef

9 pounds corned beef round (2 pieces, 4 to 5 pounds each)
Water
Whole cloves
1 cup brown sugar, firmly packed
½ cup fine dry bread crumbs
1 teaspoon dry mustard
Grated peel and juice of 2 medium sized oranges
Grated peel and juice of 2 lemons
2 cups cider

Cover meat with cold water, bring to a boil, and remove scum. (If beef seems very salty, pour off water and add fresh.) Simmer slowly 3 hours, or until just barely tender. Cool in the cooking liquid. Place drained corned beef in baking pan; score fat and stud with cloves. Combine brown sugar, crumbs, mustard, and grated orange and lemon peels. Pat meat with crumb mixture. Place in a moderate oven (350°) to brown slightly. Baste frequently with a mixture of the orange and lemon juices and cider. Continue baking 30 minutes or until heated through. Slice to serve. Serves 18.

Quick Sukiyaki

The traditional sukiyaki dinner is a ceremony. This is a simplified version — every ingredient is available from your grocer — but we recommend that you cook it at the table as the Japanese do. (Use an electric frying pan, or a *wak* on a *hibachi*.) Prepare the vegetables ahead of time and arrange them in colorful bowls.

1½ pounds round steak, 1 to 2 inches
    thick
4 small white boiling onions
2 bunches green onions
2 green peppers
1 small head celery
1 small box fresh mushrooms or
    1 can (6 oz.) sliced mushrooms
1 pound spinach
½ cup soy
1 bouillon cube
½ cup water
½ teaspoon monosodium glutamate
2 tablespoons sugar
    Salt to taste

Trim fat from meat; save big pieces to render out for drippings. Using a very sharp knife, cut meat across grain in slices ⅛ to 1/16 inch thick. (If slices are large, halve or quarter them to make bite-size pieces.) Cut white onions into eighths; slice green onions lengthwise, then cut crosswise in 1½-inch strips; seed green peppers and cut in small strips with slanted sides; slice celery diagonally in ½-inch-wide strips; slice the mushrooms lengthwise (stems, too) in pieces ⅛ inch thick; wash spinach, remove stems, and cut large leaves in half.

Mix together in a pitcher soy, bouillon cube which has been dissolved in the ½ cup water, monosodium glutamate, sugar, and salt.

To start the first batch of sukiyaki, render out meat fat in a heavy pan under high heat; remove cracklings. Add one-half of the meat; cook and stir until meat is brown. Add half the white onions, green pepper, and celery, and stir lightly; add half the soy mixture, and stirring often, cook rapidly for 5 minutes. Stir in half the green onions and mushrooms, and cook for 1 minute. Mix in half the spinach and cook 1 minute. Serve at once with rice.

Because sukiyaki cooks quickly, wait until your guests are halfway through the first batch before starting the second.

This recipe will serve 4 persons with plenty for second helpings. Sukiyaki has such flexible proportions that it is easy to double or triple the ingredients for a crowd.

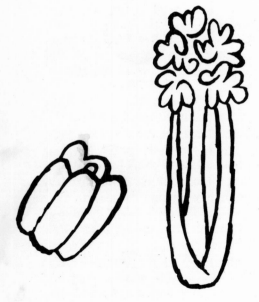

Meat Ball Curry

1 cup dry bread crumbs
3 cups milk
½ cup finely chopped onions
2 tablespoons butter
2 pounds ground beef
2 eggs
2 teaspoons salt
Pepper to taste
Butter for frying

Sauce

1 medium sized onion, chopped
1 cup sliced celery
2 tablespoons butter
1 can (10½ oz.) bouillon
1 soup can water
2 teaspoons curry powder
3 tablespoons flour mixed with 3 table-
    spoons water
Salt and pepper to taste

Soak crumbs in milk; sauté the ½ cup chopped onions in butter until tender. Combine soaked crumbs, onion, ground beef, eggs, salt, and pepper, and beat with an electric mixer until blended, smooth, and rather shiny. Chill for 1 hour.

Form chilled meat mixture into balls; if you wet your hands in cold water, you'll find it easier to shape the meat into balls. Fry balls in a small amount of melted butter over moderate heat, adding more butter when necessary. Shake the pan occasionally; this helps to keep the meat balls round.

As you remove each batch of meat balls from pan, add 2 to 3 tablespoons water to drippings, stir around, and save to use in sauce.

To make sauce, sauté chopped onion and celery in butter until just barely tender. Add drippings from frying meat balls, bouillon, water, and curry. Simmer several minutes. Thicken with flour and water paste and season to taste with salt and pepper. Add meat balls; cook until heated through. Serve with rice to 6 to 8 persons.

Greek Meat Balls

4 slices French bread
1 cup water
2 pounds ground beef
1 small onion, grated or finely
    chopped
¼ cup cracker meal
1 cup finely chopped parsley
1 tablespoon salt
¼ teaspoon celery seeds
½ teaspoon pepper
½ teaspoon monosodium glutamate
¼ cup grated Parmesan cheese
3 eggs
    Flour (approximately 2 cups)
    Olive oil or salad oil

Sauce

½ of the olive oil left in the frying pan
½ bottle of catsup
2 cups water

Remove crusts from French bread; pour water over bread and let stand until it absorbs moisture. Add ground beef, chopped onion, cracker meal, parsley, salt, celery seeds, pepper, monosodium glutamate, cheese, and eggs to the bread, and work ingredients with your hands until soft and well blended.

Drop meat mixture, a tablespoon at a time, into flour; roll each tablespoonful of meat into a ball, and roll balls in flour until all the moist spots disappear. Into a heavy frying pan, pour olive oil to a depth of ½ inch; heat oil until you can brown a bread cube in 1 minute. Drop a few of the meat balls in the pan at one time. Brown well, turning only once. Remove and keep warm while you finish browning all the meat.

Bring oil, catsup, and water to a boil; add meat balls. Cover and simmer gently for 30 minutes, turning meat balls only once. Serves 10 with 4 to 5 meat balls for each person.

Leg of Lamb Mexican

This cooking method plus the wine and orange marinade-baste combine to give lamb a crisp crust and an intriguing flavor.

5 or 6 pound leg of lamb
1 cup dry red table wine
½ cup orange juice
¼ cup chili sauce
¼ cup water
1 tablespoon chili powder
2 tablespoons olive oil
1 medium onion, finely chopped
2 cloves garlic, minced
1 tablespoon chopped fresh oregano or ¾ teaspoon dry oregano
1 teaspoon cumin seed, crushed
1 tablespoon brown sugar
Salt and pepper to taste

Place meat in a deep glass or enamel pan. Combine remaining ingredients and pour over meat; let stand in the refrigerator 24 hours, turning occasionally. Lift meat from marinade, let drain, and place on a rack in a baking pan. Roast in a very hot oven (450°) for 15 minutes. Reduce oven temperature to moderate (350°), pour marinade over meat, and continue cooking for about 2½ hours or until meat is tender, basting frequently. Add a few tablespoons of boiling water to pan juices if they tend to cook down quickly; skim off fat, and serve juices with meat. Makes 8 to 10 servings.

Roast Lamb with Worcestershire

Square lamb shoulder or boned and rolled shoulder (2½ to 4 pounds)
½ cup (¼ pound) butter
1 bottle (10 oz.) Worcestershire
2 cups water

Remove all excess fat from meat. Place meat in a roasting pan with a cover. Melt butter and mix with Worcestershire and water. Pour over meat, cover pan, and bake in a moderate oven (350°), 30 minutes to the pound. Baste occasionally. Remove cover for the last 30 minutes of roasting to brown meat. Thicken drippings for gravy. Serves 2 to 4, depending on size of shoulder and appetites.

Lamb Shanks with Red Wine

6 lamb shanks
Water
Celery tops
3 sprigs parsley
¼ teaspoon thyme
1 bay leaf
1 clove garlic, peeled and halved
1½ teaspoons salt
¼ teaspoon pepper
¾ cup flour seasoned with salt and pepper
1½ cups dry red table wine
½ cup salad oil

Put lamb shanks in a large pan; add enough water to barely cover shanks. Season with celery tops, parsley, thyme, bay leaf, garlic, salt, and pepper. Cover and simmer 1 hour. Remove shanks from broth; strain broth and reserve. Roll lamb in seasoned flour, and place in a greased baking pan. Mix wine and oil together; pour over meat. Bake in a moderately hot oven (375°) for 1 hour, or until crisply browned. Turn occasionally and baste frequently. Make gravy from the drippings and the reserved broth. Serves 6.

Fruited Lamb Shanks

Salt and pepper
4 lamb shanks
Flour
½ cup currants or raisins
1 cup cooked prunes
1 cup cooked dried apricots
2 tablespoons each cider vinegar, lemon juice, and honey or light corn syrup
½ cup sugar
½ teaspoon each cinnamon, allspice
¼ teaspoon ground cloves
1 cup water

Salt and pepper meat and roll in flour; place in a greased casserole or baking pan and cover. Bake in a moderate oven (350°) for 1½ to 2 hours, or until meat is tender. Meanwhile combine currants, prunes, apricots, vinegar, lemon juice, honey or syrup, sugar, spices, and water in a saucepan. Bring to a boil and cook slowly for about 5 minutes. Drain fat from the meat, pour the fruit sauce over the meat, cover again and bake in a hot oven (400°) for an additional 30 minutes. Spoon fruit and pan juice over meat to serve. Makes 4 servings.

Lamb Chops with Sour Cream-Olive Sauce

6 large loin or shoulder lamb chops, cut 1 inch thick
Salt and pepper
½ teaspoon crumbled dried tarragon
1 teaspoon dry mustard
2 tablespoons sherry
⅓ cup commercial sour cream
2 tablespoons sliced stuffed green olives

Place meat on a broiling rack and broil. For well done chops, allow about 8 minutes broiling time for each side. Sprinkle chops with salt and pepper to taste, then remove to a platter and keep hot. Scrape pan drippings into a small saucepan and add the tarragon, mustard, and sherry; simmer for 1 minute. Stir in sour cream and sliced olives. Stirring, heat but do not boil. Pour over chops and serve at once. Serves 6.

Lamb Chops, Italian Style

This mint-flavored marinade doubles as a basting sauce.

½ cup red wine vinegar
3 sprigs fresh mint, chopped
1 clove garlic, minced or mashed
6 shoulder lamb chops, cut 1 inch thick
Salt to taste

Combine wine vinegar, chopped mint, and garlic. Marinate chops in this mixture for 1 hour or longer, turning once. Remove chops from marinade and broil or barbecue, basting once or twice with the remaining marinade. For well done chops, allow about 8 minutes' broiling time for each side of the meat. Sprinkle with salt to taste. Serves 6.

Schweinspfeffer

Like sauerbraten, this "matures" for a couple of days in a marinade.

2 cups dry red table wine
1 cup vinegar
1 cup water
1 medium sized onion, chopped
1 clove garlic, mashed or minced
1 carrot, coarsely chopped
⅛ teaspoon crumbled sage
¼ teaspoon powdered thyme
1 teaspoon salt
½ teaspoon whole black peppers
2 pounds pork butt, cut in 1½-inch squares
1½ teaspoons bacon fat or meat drippings
2 teaspoons sugar
2 tablespoons flour
1 cup bouillon

Combine wine, vinegar, water, onion, garlic, carrot, sage, thyme, salt, and peppers in a saucepan; bring to a boil; then pour over meat squares. Let stand for 2 days, turning pork occasionally. Remove meat from marinade and pat dry on paper toweling. Brown quickly in fat or drippings. Remove meat from pan and place in a large heavy kettle with a tight fitting lid. Stir sugar and flour into meat drippings and cook until lightly browned, then stir in bouillon and 1 cup of the marinade. When liquid is boiling, pour over meat. Cover pan, and stirring occasionally, simmer slowly for 2 hours. Serves 8.

Roast Pork Tenderloin, Chinese Style

Garnish platter with watercress sprigs, spiced purple plums, preserved kumquats.

3 pork tenderloins (about ¾ lb. each)
1 cup chicken stock
¼ cup each soy and honey
2 tablespoons sherry
1 tablespoon lemon juice
½ clove garlic
1 teaspoon each cinnamon and salt
¼ teaspoon powdered ginger
2 tablespoons cornstarch

Combine chicken stock, soy, honey, sherry, lemon juice, garlic, cinnamon, salt, and ginger. Marinate the meat for 2 hours in this mixture. Drain meat, reserving marinade. Coat meat with cornstarch. Place in a shallow roasting pan. Bake in a moderately slow oven (325°) about 1 hour, 30 minutes. Baste frequently with marinade. To serve, slice on the diagonal. Serves 6.

Stuffed Spareribs

2 sides (about 4 lbs.) spareribs
2 teaspoons salt
6 apples, peeled and sliced thin
1 cup seeded (or seedless) raisins

Place one side of spareribs on rack in oven roasting pan. Sprinkle with 1 teaspoon salt. Arrange apples and raisins over meat, but keep about 1 inch inside the edge of the meat. Place second side of spareribs on top and secure with toothpicks to keep fruits well sealed in. Sprinkle with remaining salt. Bake in moderate oven (350°) for 2 hours. Serves 4 to 6.

Sherried Glazed Spareribs

After the preliminary baking, you might glaze the spareribs over very low coals instead of in the oven. Brush them frequently with the marinade.

1 side (about 2 lbs.) spareribs
Salt and pepper to taste
1 can (8 oz.) tomato sauce
½ cup sherry
½ cup honey
2 tablespoons wine vinegar
2 tablespoons minced onion
1 clove garlic, minced or mashed
¼ teaspoon Worcestershire

Sprinkle the whole side of spareribs with salt and pepper. Place in a shallow pan and bake in a hot oven (400°) for 40 minutes. Drain off all the fat that has collected in the pan.

Combine tomato sauce, sherry, honey, vinegar, onion, garlic, and Worcestershire; pour over spareribs. Lower oven temperature to moderate (350°) and bake ribs 1 hour longer or until tender. Serves 2 to 3.

Fruit-Stuffed Pork Chops

Dried fruit and pork chops alternate in this attractive entrée, which resembles a stuffed pork loin. Baste frequently with ginger ale to keep the meat moist and give it a brown glaze.

6 loin pork chops
Salt to taste
15 dried prunes, soaked
15 dried apricots, soaked
2 cups ginger ale
Orange slices
Maraschino cherries

Brown chops on both sides in rendered fat. Season with salt. Place 3 soaked prunes and 3 soaked apricots on a chop, place a second pork chop on top, and repeat layers of fruit and chops, ending with a chop. Tie with string. Place in a shallow baking pan, with the fat side up; pour over 1 cup ginger ale. Cover and bake in a moderate oven (350°) for 45 minutes; remove cover and continue baking 45 minutes longer, basting with remaining ginger ale. Garnish with orange slices and maraschino cherries. Serves 6.

Cheese-Puffed Pork Chops

The toppings for these chops are very much like cream puffs, but flavored with Parmesan cheese and onion. The puffs are also excellent baked on veal steaks.

4 pork chops, cut 1 inch thick
Salt and pepper to taste
2 tablespoons butter
⅓ cup flour
⅔ cup milk
1 egg, slightly beaten
1 small onion, grated
½ cup grated Parmesan cheese
1 teaspoon salt
¼ teaspoon pepper

Brown chops on one side in a heavy frying pan; sprinkle with salt and pepper to taste. Melt butter in a saucepan; blend in flour; slowly stir in milk. Cook, stirring constantly, until mixture makes a very thick paste; add egg and beat well, cooking until mixture is shiny. Stir in the onion, cheese, salt, and pepper, and mix well. Turn over chops and place a spoonful of batter on top of each. Brown bottom of chops for 5 minutes; then place in a moderate oven (350°) for 30 minutes. Serves 4.

Oven-Barbecued Pork

1½ teaspoons salt
1½ tablespoons sugar
 2 cloves garlic, minced or mashed
 5 tablespoons soy
 3 tablespoons applesauce
 2 tablespoons sherry
 2 pounds boned loin of pork, but-
   terflied and laid flat

Combine salt, sugar, garlic, soy, applesauce, and sherry. Marinate meat in mixture for 2 to 3 hours. Place meat in roasting pan; pour in half the marinade. Roast in a moderately hot oven (375°) for 1 hour, or until tender. Baste occasionally with remaining marinade. Serves 6 to 8.

Indonesian Pork Broil

Serve skewers on a bed of hot, steamed, lightly salted rice.

3 tablespoons peanut butter
2 tablespoons soy
2 tablespoons ground coriander
1 tablespoon ground cumin
1 small clove garlic, minced or mashed
½ teaspoon chili powder
2 pounds lean pork

Make a paste by blending peanut butter, soy, coriander, cumin, garlic, and chili powder. Cut meat into 1-inch cubes. Rub paste well into meat cubes. Let stand 30 minutes. Thread onto about 12 thin skewers, with about 4 meat cubes on each. Broil slowly (about 15 minutes on each of two opposite sides) about 6 inches from the heat. Turn only once. Serve on rice with small bowls of dipping sauce. Makes 6 servings.

Spicy Dipping Sauce

½ cup soy
1 tablespoon molasses
1 tablespoon crushed red pepper
1 clove garlic, minced

Combine all ingredients. Allow to stand 1 hour. Strain into small bowls.

Glazed Ham Loaf with Horse-Radish Sauce

A spiced peach syrup glaze, a horse-radish sauce — and highly gratifying results.

2 pounds uncooked smoked ham,
   ground
1½ pounds fresh pork, ground
 1 cup cracker crumbs
 2 eggs
 1 cup hot milk
 1 cup spiced peach syrup

Mix together thoroughly the ground meats, cracker crumbs, eggs, and hot milk. Shape into a loaf and place in a 9-inch-square pan. Pour over as much peach syrup as will soak into the loaf. Bake in a moderate oven (350°) for 45 minutes, basting several times with the remaining spiced syrup. Accompany with horse-radish sauce. Serves 8 generously.

Horse-radish Sauce

½ cup whipping cream
1 tablespoon prepared horse-radish
1 teaspoon sugar
½ teaspoon lemon juice

Whip cream until stiff and fold in horse-radish, sugar, and lemon juice. Spoon into a sauce bowl. Chill for several hours. Makes about 1 cup.

Mustard Cream Ham

You can serve canned ham or any cold, cooked, boned ham with this cream mask.

1 pint (2 cups) whipping cream
1 tablespoon dry mustard
½ teaspoon seasoned salt
Watercress or parsley

Whip cream to soft peaks; beat in mustard and salt. Swirl over the entire surface of the ham. Sprinkle with finely chopped watercress or parsley. Topping is enough for a 5-pound ham.

Cantonese Ham

1 center slice ham, cut ¾ inch thick
¼ cup soy
¼ cup sherry
½ cup sliced green onions and tops
¼ teaspoon powdered ginger
¼ cup water
1 tablespoon salad oil

Place ham in baking dish and cover with a mixture of the soy, sherry, green onions, ginger, and water; let stand in marinade for 1 hour. Remove ham from marinade, dry with paper towel. Brown ham on both sides in the oil in a heavy frying pan. Pour over the marinade, cover, and simmer for 20 minutes. Serves 4 to 6, depending on size of ham slice.

Caramelized Ham with Walnuts

2 ham slices, about 1 pound each
2 teaspoons vinegar
2 tablespoons dark brown sugar
½ cup chopped walnuts
2 tablespoons cooking oil
2 cups boiling water
½ cup sherry

Rub ham slice surfaces with vinegar and sugar. Let stand 15 minutes. Lightly toast walnuts in oil. Drain oil into large frying pan. Over high heat, quickly brown ham on both sides in the hot oil. (The caramelizing of the sugar is important to the color and flavor.) Add toasted walnuts, boiling water, and sherry. Cook slowly, uncovered, until liquid disappears and ham is tender. Serve with nuts atop ham slices. Serves 6.

Cashew Veal

1½ cups cashews
¼ cup (4 tablespoons) butter
3 pounds veal steak, sliced ½ inch thick
Salt and pepper
Flour
2 medium onions, finely chopped
2 cloves garlic, minced or mashed
½ teaspoon dry mustard
2 cups boiling water
1 teaspoon Worcestershire

In a large frying pan, sauté cashews in melted butter for about 3 minutes; remove cashews. Cut veal into 1½-inch squares. Season with salt and pepper; dust lightly with flour. Brown in butter that remains in frying pan. When meat is almost brown, add onions, garlic, and mustard. When meat browns and onions are soft, add boiling water and Worcestershire. Cover and cook over low heat about 1½ hours or until veal is tender. About 5 minutes before removing from heat, add nut meats. Serves 8.

Veal Steak à la Norge

Norwegian cooks serve this meat sauce over game birds and venison steaks as well as over veal.

6 veal steaks
2 tablespoons oil or shortening
Salt and pepper to taste
½ cup slivered gjetost (Norwegian goat cheese)
½ pint (1 cup) commercial sour cream

Pan-fry the steaks in hot oil on both sides, cooking until tender. Season with salt and pepper to taste, and remove to a warm platter. Stir slivered cheese into the sour cream and heat slowly until cheese melts. Return meat to the pan of sauce and simmer 3 minutes. Serves 6.

Veal Balls in Pastry Shells

1 slice bread
¼ cup light cream
1 pound ground veal
1 egg
1 teaspoon salt
¼ teaspoon each nutmeg and mace
½ teaspoon onion juice
Flour
½ cup (¼ pound) butter
2 tablespoons each butter and flour
1 cup each light cream and water
½ cup dry white table wine
¼ teaspoon mace
1 teaspoon grated onion
9 to 12 baked pastry tart shells

Soak bread in cream for 5 minutes; add the ground meat, egg, salt, nutmeg, mace, and onion juice. Mix lightly; roll mixture into marble-sized balls. Roll balls in flour; brown in the ½ cup butter; transfer to top of double boiler.

To make sauce, blend together the 2 tablespoons butter and flour; add to the pan drippings and cook until browned. Add cream, water, ¼ cup of the wine, mace, and onion. Stirring, cook until smooth and thickened. Pour sauce over meat balls; cover and cook over hot water 30 minutes. Stir in the remaining ¼ cup wine. To serve, spoon about 10 small meat balls and some of the sauce into each pastry shell. Serves 9 to 12 depending on size of pastry shells.

Veal Scallopini

2 pounds veal round, sliced ¼ inch thick
Salt and pepper to taste
Flour
½ cup (¼ pound) butter
½ pound fresh mushrooms, sliced
1 large onion
1 sprig each fresh rosemary, parsley, and oregano or marjoram, or ¼ teaspoon each of the dried herbs
½ teaspoon salt
¼ teaspoon pepper
1 cup dry white table wine
1 tablespoon sugar

Sprinkle meat with salt and pepper, and dredge in flour. Melt 4 tablespoons (¼ cup) of the butter in a frying pan, and brown meat slowly on both sides; remove to a platter and keep warm. Sauté mushrooms in 2 tablespoons of the butter until golden; remove from the pan and set aside. Finely chop together the onion, rosemary, parsley, and oregano, and sauté in the remaining 2 tablespoons butter until onion is golden brown.

Add mushrooms, salt, pepper, wine, and sugar; cook until hot, but no longer. Spoon over meat; serve at once to 6 to 8 persons.

Veal Mozzarella

Serve this with a platter salad of carrot sticks, sliced tomatoes, and olives.

1 large onion, chopped
3 tablespoons finely chopped green pepper
2 cloves of garlic
1 small can (2 oz.) sliced mushrooms, drained
6 tablespoons olive oil
2 cans (6 oz. each) tomato paste
2 cans (8 oz. each) tomato sauce
Pinch of oregano
1 bay leaf
½ teaspoon salt
¼ teaspoon pepper
1 pound veal cutlets, sliced ¼ inch thick
1 egg, beaten
½ cup milk
1 teaspoon salt
Pepper
½ cup fine dry bread crumbs
¼ pound Mozzarella cheese, sliced

Sauté onion, green pepper, 1 clove minced garlic, and mushrooms in 2 tablespoons of the olive oil until golden brown. Stir in tomato paste, tomato sauce, oregano, bay leaf, salt, pepper. Simmer 20 minutes. Rub meat with the other clove of peeled garlic. Mix together egg, milk, salt, and pepper. Dip meat in egg-milk mixture, then in crumbs, coating both sides. Brown meat in the remaining 4 tablespoons olive oil; place in an 8 by 12-inch baking dish; pour over sauce. Bake in moderate oven (350°) 30 minutes. Place sliced cheese over meat and bake 5 minutes longer. Serves 6.

Veal Sauté

This is a party dish, and in party proportions.

8-pounds veal stew, cut in 1 to 1½-inch cubes
4 teaspoons salt
½ teaspoon pepper
½ cup salad oil
2 cans (4 oz. each) sliced mushrooms, drained, or ½ pound fresh mushrooms, sliced
2 cloves garlic, minced or mashed
1½ cups coarsely chopped onion
1 cup diagonally sliced celery
2 medium sized green peppers, seeded and cut in strips
2 large cans (1 lb. 13 oz. each) solid pack tomatoes
1 cup dry red table wine
4 tablespoons cornstarch or 8 tablespoons flour

Season meat with salt and pepper, and brown in oil; remove. Sauté mushrooms and garlic in drippings for 5 minutes; add onion and celery and sauté until onion is clear. Stir in green pepper, tomatoes, wine, and browned meat. Cover and simmer until meat is tender, about 1½ hours. Mix cornstarch with enough cold water to make a paste, and stir in. Bring to a boil and cook, stirring, about 5 minutes until thickened. Serves 18.

Lemon Veal Steak

1 pound veal round steak
1 clove garlic, halved
3 tablespoons butter
1 lemon, sliced
  Salt
  Paprika
1 large onion, sliced
1 large tomato, sliced
½ cup consommé, or beef or veal stock
  Chopped parsley

Rub meat with garlic. Cut meat into ⅜-inch slices. In a large frying pan, melt butter, then brown meat quickly. Remove from heat, and squeeze juice of one lemon slice over all the meat. Season with salt and paprika. Arrange onion and tomato slices over the meat. Pour consommé over all. Cover and cook slowly 15 minutes. Add remaining lemon slices, cover, and cook 15 minutes more, or until meat is tender. Remove meat to serving plate, and sprinkle with chopped parsley to garnish. Makes 4 servings.

Liver in Mushroom Wine Sauce

The tart wine sauce is a delicious complement to liver. An electric frying pan works especially well for cooking this dish.

3 tablespoons butter
1 pound young beef liver, sliced thin
3 sprigs parsley, chopped
1 small can (2 to 4 oz.) sliced mushrooms (or ¼ lb. sliced fresh mushrooms, sautéed in butter)
  Juice of 1 lemon
¼ cup dry red or white table wine
  Salt and freshly ground pepper

Melt the butter in a frying pan over medium heat and brown liver well on both sides. Lower temperature. Sprinkle parsley over top of meat and add mushrooms, including mushroom liquid, lemon juice, and wine. Cover and cook slowly, turning the liver occasionally, until tender, 10 to 15 minutes. Add more wine during the cooking, if necessary, to keep it moist. Add salt and pepper to taste. Serve immediately with the pan juices spooned over it. Makes 3 to 4 servings.

Liver Pot Roast

Here, a chunk of liver gains the stature of a roast. There's gravy enough for rice.

¼ cup (4 tablespoons) flour
2 teaspoons salt
½ teaspoon pepper
  3-pound piece baby beef liver
4 tablespoons bacon drippings
1 onion, sliced
1 cup dry white table wine
½ cup consommé or bouillon
2 tablespoons vinegar
¼ teaspoon whole black peppers
2 small bay leaves
½ lemon, thinly sliced
1 tablespoon bacon drippings

Combine flour, salt, and pepper; sprinkle over liver and roll meat in it until well coated. Heat the 4 tablespoons bacon drippings in a heavy kettle with a tight fitting cover; brown meat well on all sides in drippings. Add onion, then pour in wine and consommé. Season with vinegar, whole peppers, bay leaves, sliced lemon, and the 1 tablespoon bacon drippings. Cover pan and simmer slowly for 1 hour, or until meat is tender. Remove liver to a serving platter and keep hot.

Thicken sauce for gravy, if desired. Slice liver before serving with gravy. Serves 8 to 10.

Fish & Shellfish

SOMETIMES IN READING recipes for the preparation of fish, you may wonder whether the intent is to arrive at the taste of the fish, or to arrive at the sauce.

The recipes here were selected not to mask, but to enhance. For the person who creates the perfect companion sauce must first have a profound admiration for the fish itself. Behind each recipe is the fine art of fish cookery—the gentle poach, the simple broil, the low-heat sauté, the pre-bath of lemon juice.

In this chapter, you can see that the wide world has innumerable ways with fish. Note the use of wines, sour cream, curries, even chili.

There is another phase in the art of fish cookery that endears it to the cook. This is the irresistible influence of fish on the total menu. One cook we know says it this way: the minute she decides on fish for dinner, she plans the meal with one eye on luxuries—chilled white wine, marinated artichoke hearts, garden fresh butter lettuce, strawberries and cream—and the other eye on color—red tomatoes or purple-red beets or bright orange carrots, bright green peas or dark green broccoli or yellow green baby limas.

It is certainly true that the delicacies of the sea are worthy of and have a very special affinity for the delicacies of the garden and the vineyard.

Clam-Cheese Pie

Crisp bacon points up this fluffy, soufflé-type pie. Cross strips of cooked bacon on top or sprinkle with bacon crumbs just before serving.

1 large package (8 oz.) cream cheese
4 eggs, separated
2 cans (7 oz. each) minced clams
1 teaspoon minced onion
¼ teaspoon Tabasco
Pinch of salt (about ⅛ teaspoon)
Pastry-lined 9-inch pie pan

Soften cheese and break up with a fork; add the egg yolks and beat well. Drain clams thoroughly; add clams and seasonings to the cream cheese mixture. Beat egg whites until stiff and fold in; pour mixture into unbaked pastry-lined pan. Bake in a moderate oven (350°) for 45 minutes, or until crust is brown and filling is firm. Remove from the oven and let set for 5 minutes before cutting in wedges. Serves 6.

Imperial Crab

This recipe can be used either for an entrée or for tiny appetizers, depending on how you shape the crab mixture before deep-fat frying.

1 egg
1 pound (2 cups) crab meat
1 cup mayonnaise
½ teaspoon dry mustard
½ green pepper, chopped
1 cup unsalted cracker crumbs
Fat for deep fat frying

Beat the egg well. Add crab meat, mayonnaise, mustard, and green pepper. Shape into small balls or form into patties. Roll in cracker crumbs. Fry in deep fat at 350° for about 6 minutes, or until golden brown. Makes about 5 servings as an entrée, or about 20 appetizers.

Crab Puff Soufflé

Pink with crab meat and flecked with the green of parsley, this soufflé is a delight to the eye as well as to the palate.

¼ cup (4 tablespoons) butter
¼ cup flour
½ teaspoon salt
1 cup milk
3 eggs, separated
½ cup mayonnaise
½ teaspoon salt
Dash pepper
1 teaspoon each paprika and chopped fresh parsley
½ pound (1 cup) or 1 can (6½ oz.) crab meat

In a saucepan melt butter over low heat. Stir flour and salt into the butter to make a smooth paste. Add milk slowly, stirring constantly, until thickened. Remove sauce from heat; cool. Beat the egg whites until stiff but not dry; set aside. Beat egg yolks into white sauce; fold in mayonnaise. Stir in salt, pepper, paprika, parsley, and crab meat. Gently fold in beaten egg whites. Pour into a 1½-quart soufflé dish. Bake in a hot oven (400°) 25 minutes, or until brown and puffed. Serve immediately. Makes 4 servings.

Crab Curry

You may wish to serve additional condiments in separate dishes. Good here would be: chutney, chopped green onions, chopped hard cooked egg.

¼ cup chopped onion
½ clove of garlic, minced or mashed
¼ cup (4 tablespoons) butter
2 teaspoons curry powder
2 tablespoons flour
1 pint (2 cups) light cream
1½ pounds (3 cups) fresh crab meat or 3 cans (6½ oz. each) crab meat, flaked
½ teaspoon salt
Dash of cayenne
Pinch of thyme
2 egg yolks
4 cups hot steamed rice (1⅓ cups uncooked rice)
Condiments: crisp bacon, chopped salted peanuts, chopped sweet pickle

Sauté onion and garlic in butter until limp but not browned; add curry powder and cook over very low heat for 10 minutes. Blend in flour and gradually add the cream. Cook, stirring constantly, until thickened. Remove from heat and strain into the top of double boiler. Place sauce over boiling water and add crab, salt, cayenne, and thyme; cook until heated through.

Stir slightly beaten egg yolks into the sauce. Cook just until heated through. Spoon over hot rice turned out on a hot chop plate, and sprinkle with bacon, peanuts, and sweet pickle. Serves 6 to 8.

Seafood with Olive Rice

1 large can (1 lb., 13 oz.) tomatoes
¼ cup catsup
1 medium sized onion, sliced
1 clove garlic, mashed or minced
2 teaspoons sugar
½ teaspoon Tabasco
¼ cup (4 tablespoons) butter
¼ cup flour
1 tablespoon chili powder
½ cup clam juice
½ pound (1 cup) crab meat
½ pound fresh shrimp
1 jar (12 oz.) fresh Pacific oysters, drained
Salt and pepper to taste
3 cups hot cooked rice
Garlic-flavored ripe olives, heated

Simmer together for 15 minutes the tomatoes, catsup, onion, garlic, sugar, and Tabasco; strain. Melt the butter, stir in flour and chili powder to make a smooth paste. Gradually add clam juice and tomato sauce, stirring. Boil 5 minutes. Add crab meat, shrimp, and oysters. Heat thoroughly, but do not boil. Add salt and pepper to taste. Arrange rice in a ring on a heated platter; fill center with hot seafood chili. Garnish with olives heated in olive liquid. Serves 6.

Lobster Tails Thermidor

A distinguished supper entrée . . .

5 pounds frozen lobster tails (1 or 2 per person, depending on their size)
3 tablespoons butter
1¼ cups sherry
2½ teaspoons dry mustard
1½ tablespoons minced chives
1½ tablespoons each chopped fresh tarragon and parsley (or about ½ teaspoon each of the dried herbs)
Salt and pepper
1¼ cups whipping cream
Grated Parmesan cheese

Thaw lobster tails and boil in salted water 20 minutes, or until tender. Remove meat from shells, and dice. In a saucepan, melt butter; add lobster meat and sherry, and simmer 10 minutes. Add mustard, chives, tarragon, parsley, and salt and pepper to taste. Stir in cream; then heat, but do not allow to boil.

Fill lobster tail shells with creamed mixture, place in a shallow baking pan, and sprinkle generously with cheese. Bake in hot oven (400°) for 15 minutes, or until cheese is melted. (You can prepare the lobster tails, up to the point of baking, ahead of time; then pop into the oven after your guests arrive.) Serves 8.

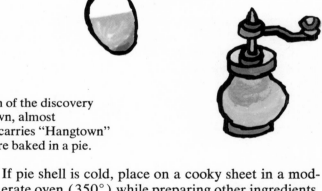

Hangtown Pie

Since the first anniversary celebration of the discovery of gold in California, held in Hangtown, almost any combination of eggs and oysters carries "Hangtown" in its name. In this version, the two are baked in a pie.

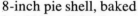

8-inch pie shell, baked
1 jar (12 oz.) fresh oysters
Flour
1 egg, slightly beaten with 1 tablespoon water
Fine dry bread crumbs or cracker meal
2 tablespoons each butter and lard (or bacon fat)
4 eggs, slightly beaten
2 tablespoons cream
Salt
Pepper
2 tablespoons minced chives
2 tablespoons butter

If pie shell is cold, place on a cooky sheet in a moderate oven (350°) while preparing other ingredients. Roll oysters in flour, dip them in egg and water mixture, and then roll in crumbs. Fry in a mixture of the butter and lard until golden brown on both sides. Blend slightly beaten eggs, cream, salt, pepper, and chives. Melt the 2 tablespoons butter in a small frying pan, add egg mixture, and scramble until eggs are set. Spread scrambled eggs in bottom of pie shell. Arrange oysters on top. Cut in wedges, serve on hot plates, and garnish with lemon wedges and pickles, if you wish. Serves 5.

Oysters Kirkpatrick

This famous oyster recipe originated in San Francisco's Palace (now the Sheraton-Palace) Hotel and was named in honor of its manager, John C. Kirkpatrick.

For each serving, push 6 cleaned and shucked oysters, each on a half shell, down into ½ inch of rock salt spread in a pie tin. Sprinkle each oyster with 2 drops lemon juice, salt, and pepper.

Cover each oyster with a tablespoon of tomato purée; strip with partially cooked bacon; cover with shredded Swiss cheese.

Sprinkle with paprika and more lemon; then bake in very hot oven (450°) for 10 minutes or until oysters curl and cheese bubbles.

Scallops Supreme

2 pounds scallops, fresh or frozen
½ cup light cream
¼ cup dry white table wine
2 teaspoons lemon juice
1 teaspoon crushed instant minced onion or ½ teaspoon scraped fresh onion
¼ cup finely chopped green pepper
½ teaspoon finely chopped fresh rosemary or ⅛ teaspoon crushed dried rosemary
½ teaspoon salt
¼ teaspoon freshly ground pepper
¾ cup soft bread crumbs
  Butter

Arrange scallops in 6 individual baking dishes, 6 large scallop shells, or a 1½-quart shallow baking dish.

Mix together cream, wine, lemon juice, onion, pepper, rosemary, salt, and pepper. Pour in equal portions over each dish of scallops (at this point, you can refrigerate scallops to cook later in the day). Just before baking, top each dish with about 2 tablespoons soft bread crumbs. Dot with butter and bake in a very hot oven (450°) for 15 minutes. Slide scallops under the broiler for a few seconds for additional browning, if desired. Makes 6 servings.

Shrimp Custard Tarts

  Pastry based on 3 cups flour
1 pound cleaned, cooked shrimp
4 slices bacon
¼ cup grated Parmesan cheese
4 eggs
2 cups milk
2½ teaspoons minced fresh thyme or chervil (or use ½ teaspoon of the dried herbs)
¾ teaspoon Tabasco
  Salt and pepper

Line 8 individual foil pie or tart pans with pastry. Arrange shrimp on bottom of each pan. Cook bacon until crisp; crumble and sprinkle over the shrimp. Sprinkle a layer of cheese over the bacon. Beat eggs slightly; add milk, thyme, Tabasco, salt, and pepper. Pour into pastry-lined pans. Bake in a very hot oven (450°) for 10 minutes; reduce heat to 350°, and bake 20 minutes, or until filling is set. Serves 8.

Deep Fat-Fried Prawns

The batter and sauce used here are also good for deep fat-frying chunks of lobster or halibut and chunks of eggplant, sweet potatoes, and carrots.

1½ pounds raw prawns (15 to 20 count)
1 egg
1 cup water
1 cup flour
  Sesame oil or salad oil
½ cup fish stock
2 tablespoons soy
2 tablespoons sherry
  Grated fresh ginger

Shuck, clean, and butterfly prawns. (Cut almost through rounded side of prawns; lift out sand vein.) Mix egg and water slightly; add flour and stir just until flour is moistened. Heat 2 inches of sesame or salad oil (or combination) in a pan; dip shrimp in batter, then cook in hot deep fat until golden brown; drain. Combine the fish stock, soy, and sherry. Serve the sauce cold with the hot shrimp. Pass a separate dish of the grated fresh ginger. Serves 4 to 6.

Cheese-Coated Halibut Sticks

2 pounds halibut fillets, 1 inch thick
½ cup salad oil
1 teaspoon salt
1 clove garlic, minced or mashed
1 cup commercially grated American cheese
½ cup fine dry bread crumbs

Cut the halibut into pieces approximately 1 inch wide by 2 inches long. Combine the oil, salt, and garlic. Marinate the halibut steaks in the oil for 1 to 2 minutes, then drain. Roll in the grated cheese and then in the dry crumbs. Place on an oiled baking sheet so that pieces do not touch. Bake in a very hot oven (450°) for 12 minutes. Serve immediately, with or without fish sauce. Serves 6.

Halibut with Dill Pickle Sauce

2 pounds halibut fillets, 1 inch thick
2 cups (1 pint) commercial sour cream
5 tablespoons chopped green onion
5 tablespoons finely chopped green pepper
4 tablespoons (¼ cup) chopped dill pickle
2 tablespoons finely chopped parsley
2 tablespoons lemon juice
½ teaspoon dry mustard
½ teaspoon basil
½ teaspoon salt
¼ teaspoon pepper

Arrange the halibut fillets in an 8 by 12-inch baking pan. Mix together sour cream, green onion, green pepper, dill pickle, parsley, lemon juice, mustard, basil, salt, and pepper; pour sauce over fish. Bake in a moderate oven (350°) for 30 minutes, or until fish flakes with a fork. Serves 6 to 8.

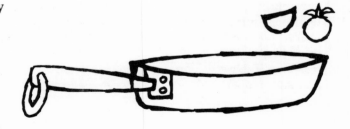

Russian Salmon Pie

Pastry for 9-inch 2-crust pie
2 pounds cooked or canned salmon
3 hard cooked eggs, sliced
2 teaspoons dill weed
Salt and pepper to taste
2 tablespoons butter
1 cup medium cream sauce
1 egg, beaten

Line a 9-inch pie pan with half of the pastry. Flake salmon; put half of the fish in the pastry shell. Cover the layer of salmon with half of the egg slices. Sprinkle with dill weed, salt, and pepper; dot with butter. Repeat layers. Pour over cream sauce, top with pastry, seal edges, prick top, and glaze with beaten egg. Bake in a hot oven (425°) for 30 to 35 minutes or until well browned. Makes 5 or 6 servings.

Salmon and Oysters en Casserole

2 tall cans (1 lb. each) red salmon
2 jars (12 oz. each) oysters
½ cup (¼ pound) butter
¾ cup flour
4 cups milk (or substitute 1 cup sherry for 1 cup of the milk)
1 teaspoon dried sweet basil
2 teaspoons salt
1 teaspoon pepper
2 teaspoons monosodium glutamate
2 tablespoons lemon juice
2 cups shredded Cheddar cheese (about ½ lb.)
Thin tomato slices
Small Cheddar cheese slices

Cut salmon into chunks, and arrange in bottom of a buttered 3-quart casserole. Poach oysters in their liquor until edges curl; add butter if the liquid evaporates. Drain; reserve liquid. Place oysters over salmon.

Melt ½ cup butter; stir in flour to make a smooth paste. Gradually add milk, then reserved oyster liquid, sweet basil, salt, pepper, monosodium glutamate, and lemon juice. Add the shredded cheese, and heat until sauce is thick and smooth and cheese is melted. Pour sauce over salmon and oysters. Bake in a moderate oven (350°) about 30 minutes. Just before serving arrange tomato slices, topped with small cheese slices, over top of casserole; broil until cheese melts. Serves 8.

Salmon Fillets with a Mayonnaise Mask

½ cup mayonnaise
2 tablespoons lemon juice
1 egg, separated
2-pound salmon fillet
Paprika

Mix together mayonnaise, lemon juice, and egg yolk. Beat egg white until stiff, and fold in.

Place salmon fillet on piece of heavy paper or foil. Cut out paper around fish. (Paper keeps the salmon skin from sticking to the broiler pan.)

Grill salmon until fish flakes easily. Swirl top with the mayonnaise mask, and then sprinkle with paprika. Broil for 2 minutes under high heat. Serve at once. Serves 4 to 6.

Sole in White Wine Sauce

8 pieces fillet of sole (about ⅓ pound each
2 cups water
Juice of 1 lemon
Salt and pepper
Butter
2 medium sized white onions, thinly sliced
1 clove garlic, thinly sliced
10 whole peppercorns
1 bay leaf
¾ cup dry white table wine
¼ cup water
3 tablespoons butter
3 tablespoons flour
¼ teaspoon salt
Dash of cayenne
½ cup plus 2 tablespoons light cream
2 packages (4 servings each) instant mashed potatoes
About 8 mushroom crowns
Butter
2 teaspoons crushed dried chervil

Rinse sole in water mixed with the lemon juice. Pat dry with a cloth. Sprinkle each piece on one side with salt and pepper, and dot each with about ¾ teaspoon butter. Fold each piece over in half lengthwise and place in a shallow baking dish.

Scatter onion and garlic slices over sole. Sprinkle with peppercorns; tuck in bay leaf. Add wine and water. Cover and poach in a moderate oven (350°) for 15 minutes. Drain and save fish stock; discard onions, garlic, peppercorns, and bay leaf. (If you plan to serve the fish right away, keep fish warm, otherwise refrigerate.) Handle folded pieces carefully, for they fall apart easily.

Melt the 3 tablespoons butter in a saucepan; blend in flour, salt, and cayenne. Slowly add fish stock and cream; stirring constantly, cook until thickened. (You can use sauce immediately or reheat.) Arrange fish on a board or ovenproof platter. Prepare instant mashed potatoes according to package directions; put through a pastry bag, using rosette tip, to decorate board edge. Spoon hot sauce over fish, and garnish with large mushroom crowns sautéed in butter; sprinkle with crushed chervil. Place in a very hot oven (450°) for about 5 to 7 minutes, lightly browning potato border. Makes 4 to 6 servings.

Fillet of Sole with Shrimp

4 large fillets of sole, or 6 smaller fillets (fresh or frozen, thawed)
Salt and pepper to taste
¼ cup dry white table wine
2¼ cups hot water
2 tablespoons lemon juice
3 tablespoons each butter and flour
½ teaspoon Tabasco
1 tablespoon each minced green pepper and green onion
2 tablespoons minced fresh or dried chervil
1 cup shrimp, fresh or canned
Salt to taste
1 cup buttered soft bread crumbs

Sprinkle the fillets with salt and pepper and marinate several hours in white wine. Transfer to a frying pan, cover with the hot water and lemon juice, and simmer 10 minutes. Lift fish to a buttered baking dish. Cream the butter and flour together and add to the liquid remaining in pan. Add all the remaining seasonings, shrimp, and salt to taste. Cook, stirring, until thickened. Strew half the crumbs over the fish, cover with the sauce, and sprinkle with the rest of crumbs. Bake in a moderate oven (350°) about 15 minutes; then set under broiler, if needed, to brown top. Garnish with lemon wedges and chervil or parsley. Serves 4 to 6.

Fish Soufflé Martinique

4 sole fillets (approximately 1 pound)
1 teaspoon salt
1 tablespoon chopped parsley
6 whole black peppers
½ cup dry white table wine
¼ cup (4 tablespoons) butter
2 tablespoons flour
½ cup milk
   Salt and pepper to taste
3 eggs, separated
2 egg whites
2 tablespoons grated Parmesan cheese
2 egg yolks, slightly beaten
   Chopped parsley

Place fillets in a greased baking dish; season with salt and sprinkle with parsley and whole black peppers. Pour in wine and dot with 2 tablespoons of the butter. Cover with foil and bake in a hot oven (400°) for 15 minutes. Pour fish stock out of dish and set aside. Melt another 2 tablespoons butter, and blend in flour. Add milk gradually and, stirring, cook until thick. Add salt and pepper. Beat 3 egg yolks with 2 tablespoons fish stock; stir in a little hot white sauce and return to pan; stirring, cook 1 minute. Beat the 5 egg whites until stiff and fold in sauce. Sprinkle fish fillets with cheese. Spoon over soufflé mixture, and bake in a hot oven (400°) for 20 minutes. Serve with a sauce made by thickening ½ cup fish stock with the remaining 2 egg yolks. Sprinkle with parsley. Serves 2 to 4.

Crumb-Topped Swordfish

2 tablespoons salad oil
2 pounds swordfish steaks
   Juice of 1 lemon (3 tablespoons)
1 teaspoon salt
¼ teaspoon pepper
1 cup finely chopped onion
½ cup chopped parsley
1 cup (½ pint) commercial sour cream
¼ cup dry bread crumbs
2 tablespoons butter

Coat baking dish with salad oil. Arrange swordfish in the dish in a single layer. Sprinkle fish with lemon juice, salt, and pepper. Cover with the chopped onion, then add a layer of the parsley. Spoon sour cream over the top. Sprinkle with bread crumbs; dot with butter. Bake in a moderately hot oven (375°) for 25 minutes. Serves 6.

Curried Swordfish

2 slices swordfish, approximately 4 by 8 inches, each cut 1½ inches thick
3 cups boiling water
1 teaspoon salt
½ teaspoon whole black peppers
1 bay leaf
1 tablespoon lemon juice
3 tablespoons butter
1 tablespoon chopped onion
2 tablespoons flour
1 teaspoon curry powder
¼ cup light cream
   Paprika

Place swordfish slices in a large frying pan and cover with boiling water. Add salt, peppers, bay leaf, and lemon juice. Simmer, uncovered, over low heat for 15 minutes, or until fish is just tender. With a wide spatula, lift fish out of stock and place on ovenproof platter or drip pan. Strain the stock and measure out 1½ cups.

Melt butter, sauté the onion in it until limp, then blend in the flour. Gradually pour in the strained fish stock and cook until thickened. Blend in curry and cream. Pour sauce over fish slices and slip under the broiler for 5 minutes, or until lightly browned. Sprinkle lightly with paprika. Cut into pie-shaped wedges. Serves 6 to 8.

Poached Trout with Broccoli

In this elegant but easy recipe, the trout is poached, then baked with broccoli and a mushroom-cheese sauce.

1½ pounds fresh broccoli
  5 or 6 medium sized trout, cleaned
    Juice of 1 lemon
  1 cup dry white table wine or chicken stock
  1 cup fresh mushrooms
  2 tablespoons butter
  2 tablespoons flour
½ cup whipping cream
½ teaspoon salt
⅔ cup shredded American cheese

Cook broccoli until just tender-crisp. Remove heads and tails from trout, if you wish. Sprinkle trout with lemon juice and let stand 15 minutes. Simmer in heated wine or chicken stock until almost tender, about 5 minutes. Remove trout; arrange with broccoli in a shallow baking dish.

If mushrooms are small, leave whole; cut larger ones in halves or quarters. Sauté in butter until lightly browned. Add flour and mix until well blended. Gradually stir in cream and ½ cup of the poaching liquid. Cook, stirring constantly, until mixture boils and thickens. Reduce heat and stir in salt and cheese until blended. Spoon over fish in baking dish. Bake, uncovered, in a moderately hot oven (375°) for 20 to 25 minutes. Serves 5 or 6.

Trout in Parchment

All the delicate flavor of fresh trout is retained by this method of parchment cookery.

6 medium sized trout, cleaned
  Salt and pepper to taste
2 tablespoons butter
2 tablespoons finely chopped onion
2 tablespoons finely chopped parsley
¼ teaspoon dried dill weed
⅓ cup grated raw carrot
2 small tomatoes, cut in 6 slices
  Lemon juice
  Boiling water

Use whole trout with their heads and tails removed. Or cut larger trout into serving size pieces (bone them, if you wish). For each trout or serving, cut a piece of parchment paper about 18 to 20 inches square. Oil or wet both sides of the parchment. Place each serving of fish on a square of paper. Sprinkle fish with salt and pepper. Divide butter, onion, parsley, dill weed, carrot, and tomato slices among the packages. Add a squeeze of lemon juice to each. Bring corners of paper together and tie firmly like little bags.

Drop in boiling water in a large kettle. Cover and boil until tender, 15 to 25 minutes, depending on size of fish. Or cook in a covered steamer, allowing 5 to 10 minutes extra cooking time. Serve fish in thin parchment containers with the juices that form inside the bag. Makes 6 servings.

Trout in Butter Sauce

4 medium sized trout, cleaned
Salt to taste
Flour
½ cup (¼ pound) butter
½ teaspoon mace
Dash of freshly ground black pepper
4 fresh sage leaves,
or ¼ teaspoon dried sage
Grated peel and juice of 1 lemon
Parsley
Lemon slices

Sprinkle fish inside and out with salt. Roll in flour; shake off excess. Heat ¼ cup of the butter in a frying pan (use one that is large enough so that trout lie flat) and brown fish on both sides, taking care not to burn. Transfer cooked fish to a warm platter and keep hot. Place in the frying pan the other ¼ cup butter, mace, pepper, sage leaves (cut in fine strips), lemon peel, and lemon juice. Heat until butter melts and bubbles; pour over trout. Garnish with parsley and lemon slices. Serve immediately. Makes 4 servings.

Sweet-Sour Tuna

1 can (1 lb. 4 oz.) pineapple chunks
2 tablespoons butter
2 cups green pepper strips
1 chicken bouillon cube
1 cup boiling water
2 tablespoons cornstarch
1 tablespoon soy
2 tablespoons vinegar
⅓ cup sugar
2 cans (7 oz. each) solid pack tuna
Dash of pepper
2 cans (4 oz. each) chow mein noodles

Drain syrup from pineapple and set aside (you should have about 1 cup). Cook the pineapple chunks in the butter for 3 minutes. Measure out ⅔ cup of the pineapple syrup and pour half of it into the pineapple. Add green pepper strips; cover and simmer 10 minutes. Dissolve bouillon cube in boiling water and stir into pineapple mixture. Mix cornstarch with remaining ⅓ cup pineapple syrup and stir in. Add soy, vinegar, and sugar.

Cook, stirring constantly, until thick and clear. Break tuna into chunks and fold gently into mixture. Add pepper and heat until tuna is hot. Serve over crisp noodles which have been heated in a moderately slow oven (325°) until hot. Serves 6 to 8.

Tuna Pancakes

2 tablespoons chopped pimiento
4 tablespoons chopped green pepper
1 tablespoon butter
2 cans (7 oz. each) tuna
½ cup mayonnaise
2 eggs
¼ teaspoon salt
1 cup milk
⅔ cup sifted flour
1 cup commercial sour cream
¼ cup light cream
½ cup shredded Cheddar cheese

Sauté pimiento and green pepper in butter. Add tuna and mayonnaise and mix thoroughly. Make 16 pancakes (6 inches in diameter) with batter made by beating together the eggs, salt, milk, and flour. Spread tuna mixture on pancakes, and roll. Place filled pancakes in baking pan, seam side down. Combine sour cream with light cream and spoon over pancakes. Sprinkle with Cheddar cheese, and bake in a moderate oven (350°) for 15 minutes. Serves 8.

Poultry

IT IS NOT DIFFICULT to account for the affectionate regard which thousands of cooks — and diners — have for poultry dishes. These dishes carry with them the quality of specialness; they seem to say "occasion."

From the hostess' viewpoint, the tender, juicy chicken, like her sister bird, the turkey, is dependably fine eating, catering to varied tastes by offering a choice in parts. Like the perfect guest, it has a personality range that admits it to any party: marinated and barbecued, it satisfies hearty appetites; stuffed and baked, it lives up to holiday traditions; boned and basted in sherry-butter, it pleases the most discriminating palate.

To the cook, poultry is an open invitation to embellishment and variation. Broiling, baking, pan frying, or oven frying — herbs, spices, wines — marinades, sauces, dressings, stuffings — sour cream, mushrooms, nuts, fruits — curry, tettrazini, teriyaki. The variations, and the variations within variations, are infinite. And each combination seems to establish itself as a unique taste experience — its own particular dish.

From the viewpoint of hostess-cook, concerned with serving at the peak of perfection, there is yet another virtue: most poultry dishes not only will wait, but like to wait. In many of the recipes included here, the principle is the casserole one of combining compatible ingredients — and a blending time improves them.

Braised Chicken with Cashew-Rice Stuffing

These braised chicken fryers have a delicately spiced brown rice stuffing.

2 cups steamed browned rice
1 cup coarsely chopped cashew nut meats
3 tablespoons each melted butter and sherry or apple juice
½ cup each chopped onion and diced celery
1 clove garlic, minced or mashed
½ teaspoon freshly ground pepper
¼ teaspoon each ground ginger and mace
⅛ teaspoon each crumbled dried savory and thyme
2 tablespoons minced parsley
2 frying chickens, about 2 pounds each
  Flour seasoned with salt and pepper
4 tablespoons each butter and bacon drippings
1½ cups dry white table wine or chicken broth

For the stuffing toss together rice, nut meats, melted butter, sherry, onion, celery, garlic, pepper, ginger, mace, savory, thyme, and parsley. Stuff the chickens lightly; skewer the openings closed, and truss the legs together with twine. Dust with seasoned flour and, using a large Dutch oven, brown on all sides in a mixture of the butter and drippings. Pour in ½ cup of the wine or broth; cover and simmer until tender, about 1 hour. Baste occasionally and add more wine when needed.

Remove chickens to a hot platter, and thicken liquid, if desired. Serves 4 to 6.

Fruited Chicken

6 to 8 pieces chicken (breast, legs, thighs)
⅓ cup flour
1½ teaspoons salt
½ teaspoon paprika
1 teaspoon curry powder
4 tablespoons salad oil or shortening
1 cup dry white table wine or chicken broth
6 to 8 orange segments
1 cup pitted Bing or Royal Anne cherries
6 to 8 pineapple spears
1 avocado, cut in crescents
  Sprigs of mint

Shake chicken pieces in paper bag with flour, salt, paprika, and curry. Brown gently on all sides in oil. Remove to large baking pan or oblong casserole. Add the wine, cover, and bake in a moderately hot oven (375°) for 20 minutes. Remove from oven and arrange orange segments, cherries, and pineapple spears over the chicken. (If liquid has cooked away, add ½ cup more wine or water.) Return to oven and continue baking, uncovered, until chicken is tender, about 20 to 25 minutes longer.

Remove chicken to chop plate or platter; arrange fruit over and around chicken. Garnish platter with crescents of avocado and sprigs of fresh mint. Serves 6 to 8.

Breast of Chicken Gourmet

¼ cup (4 tablespoons) butter
4 chicken breasts
½ cup dry white table wine
2 tablespoons butter
½ medium sized onion, finely chopped
¼ cup dry white table wine
½ pint (1 cup) commercial sour cream
   Salt and white pepper to taste

Melt the ¼ cup butter in frying pan; add the chicken breasts, from which you have removed skin, and cook until just delicately brown; turn occasionally. Sprinkle the ½ cup wine over the chicken, cover, and steam until tender, 20 to 25 minutes.

Melt the 2 tablespoons butter in another pan; cook onion in it, but do not allow it to brown. Stir in the ¼ cup wine and the sour cream; remove from heat. When chicken is tender, pour sour cream sauce over it; add salt and white pepper to taste, and heat together only long enough to warm the cream again. Serves 4.

Breast of Chicken with Almonds

2 chicken breasts
   Salt to taste
   Flour
1 egg
¼ cup almonds, very finely chopped
3 tablespoons butter
2 tablespoons sherry
   Paprika
1 cup (½ pint) whipping cream

Sprinkle the chicken breasts with salt, then roll in flour. Dip in slightly beaten egg and then roll in the finely chopped almonds. Sauté in butter until golden brown on both sides and tender, about 25 minutes, handling carefully to avoid knocking off the almonds. Remove the chicken and place in a very low oven to keep hot. If you have a chafing dish, turn the chicken drippings into the pan. If not, continue in the frying pan. Add the sherry, a generous dash of paprika, and the whipping cream to the drippings; blend well, then simmer slowly for 5 to 10 minutes. Add the chicken breasts, sprinkle with additional toasted almonds; serve from chafing dish or frying pan. Serves 2 generously.

Chicken Jubilee

6 to 8 chicken breasts
½ cup flour
¼ teaspoon garlic salt
½ teaspoon paprika
1½ teaspoons salt
4 tablespoons salad oil or shortening
1 cup chicken broth or dry white
   table wine
2 cups pitted Bing cherries
½ cup (or more) brandy

Shake chicken breasts in paper bag with flour, garlic salt, paprika, and salt. Fry slowly to a rich golden brown in salad oil. Arrange in baking pan and add broth. Cover and bake in a moderately hot oven (375°) for 20 minutes. Remove cover and add cherries.

Return to oven and bake, uncovered, 15 to 20 minutes longer, or until chicken is tender. Place on top of range, pour over brandy, heat long enough to warm brandy (do not allow to boil), then set aflame. When brandy stops burning, serve chicken with the cherries and the sauce. Serves 6 to 8.

Skillet Barbecued Chicken

For the cook who considers "barbecue" a flavor, not a cooking method.

1 frying chicken cut in serving size pieces
¼ cup salad oil
2 tablespoons vinegar
2 tablespoons brown sugar
⅓ cup catsup
1 teaspoon Worcestershire
¼ teaspoon garlic salt
1 teaspoon salt
½ teaspoon pepper
½ teaspoon each celery seed and parsley flakes
¼ cup water

Wash the chicken pieces and drain well. Put chicken giblets on to simmer in water to cover, if you care to add them to the sauce later. In electric frying pan or other large heavy frying pan, combine salad oil with vinegar, brown sugar, catsup, Worcestershire, garlic salt, salt, pepper, celery seed, parsley flakes, and water. Set in the chicken pieces and cook uncovered over medium heat, turning to brown evenly. Cook until tender, about 35 minutes. Remove pieces to a warm platter. Skim oil from sauce left in pan. Add 1 cup stock from cooking giblets (or water); stir to loosen all the browned particles in pan. Add chopped giblets, if desired. Serve sauce over chicken. Serves 4.

Herb-Buttered Chicken

Cracked wheat pilaff and a salad-garnish of chilled orange and grapefruit sections are satisfying accompaniments.

1 frying chicken (approximately 3 lbs.) cut in serving size pieces, or 4 large chicken breasts
Salt and pepper
½ cup (¼ pound) softened butter
½ teaspoon finely chopped fresh tarragon
1 tablespoon finely chopped green onion
1 cup fine soft bread crumbs

Wipe chicken with a damp cloth; season with salt and pepper. Cream half the butter with tarragon and onion, and spread over chicken. Roll in crumbs. Brown slowly in the remaining butter in a fryer or in a heavy skillet that has a tight fitting lid. Cover and cook until tender, about 1 hour. Add a little water if necessary. Serve chicken with Herb Sauce.

Herb Sauce

1 tablespoon each finely chopped tarragon and parsley or ½ teaspoon each of the dried herbs
1 tablespoon finely chopped green onion
2 teaspoons dry mustard
1 teaspoon salt
¼ teaspoon freshly ground black pepper
½ cup olive or salad oil
¼ cup tarragon wine vinegar

Combine tarragon, parsley, green onion, mustard, salt, pepper, olive oil, and vinegar. Let stand at least 15 minutes to give flavors a chance to blend. Heat, and whip or beat just before serving. Serves 4.

Lemon Chicken

Lemon and mint are the refreshing overtones. If you have kumquats or limequats, try them in place of the lemons.

6 to 8 pieces of frying chicken
(breasts, legs, thighs)
1 whole lemon
⅓ cup flour
1½ teaspoons salt
½ teaspoon paprika
4 tablespoons salad oil or shortening
2 tablespoons brown sugar
1 lemon, thinly sliced
1 cup chicken broth
2 sprigs fresh mint

Wash chicken and drain on paper towels. Grate the peel from the lemon and set aside; cut lemon in half and squeeze the juice over the pieces of chicken, rubbing each piece with the juice. Shake in a paper bag with the flour, salt, and paprika. Brown chicken slowly in the salad oil. Arrange in casserole or baking pan.

Sprinkle grated lemon peel over the chicken, add the brown sugar, and then cover with the thinly sliced lemon. Pour in the broth and place the mint over the top. Cover and bake in a moderately hot oven (375°) until chicken is tender (40 to 45 minutes). Remove mint before serving. Serves 6 to 8 if chicken pieces are large.

Orange-Almond Chicken

1 frying chicken (about 3½ pounds),
cut up
1 teaspoon salt
¼ teaspoon pepper
1 teaspoon paprika
⅓ cup butter
1 cup orange juice
⅔ cup slivered almonds or chopped
filberts, toasted

Wash the chicken and pat it dry. Combine the salt, pepper, and paprika; rub into the chicken until thoroughly coated. Melt butter in a large frying pan with a cover. Sauté the chicken pieces until golden brown on both sides. Cover the frying pan, reduce heat, and cook for 25 to 30 minutes, or until chicken is tender. Remove chicken to a warm platter and keep hot in a warm oven. Pour the orange juice into frying pan, stir to loosen all the browned particles, then cook over high heat until it is reduced by half. (If you prefer a thicker gravy, blend 1 teaspoon cornstarch with an equal amount of water; stir into the reduced orange juice; cook until thickened.) Pour over the chicken. Sprinkle with toasted almond slivers and serve at once. Serves 3 to 4.

Chicken in Wine

1 frying chicken (2½ to 3 pounds),
    cut in serving size pieces
1 clove garlic, halved
1 teaspoon salt
1 tablespoon lemon juice
¼ cup dry white table wine
1 bay leaf
3 tablespoons olive oil
1 tablespoon flour
¼ cup each chopped onion and green
    pepper
1 cup diced carrot
½ cup sherry

Rub chicken with the cut clove of garlic and the salt. Mix together a marinade of the lemon juice, white wine, and bay leaf; add chicken pieces and let stand at least 2 hours. Remove chicken and pat dry; reserve the marinade. Brown chicken on all sides in hot oil. Transfer browned chicken to a 2-quart casserole. Blend flour into the drippings, stirring until smooth. Add onion, green pepper, carrot, and the marinade, and heat thoroughly; pour mixture over chicken. Add sherry. Bake in a moderate oven (350°) for 40 minutes, or until chicken is tender. Remove bay leaf before serving. Serves 4.

Chicken with Pimientos and Tomatoes

1 medium sized onion, chopped
1 clove garlic, minced or mashed
4 medium sized tomatoes, chopped
¾ teaspoon salt
¼ cup chicken broth, water, or
    dry white table wine
½ cup olive oil or salad oil
1 clove garlic, whole
6 large pieces frying chicken
    Salt and pepper to taste
½ cup thinly sliced ham, cut in strips
1 can or jar (4 oz.) pimientos, cut
    in thin slices
¼ cup finely chopped parsley

Cook the onion, minced garlic, tomatoes, salt, broth, and ¼ cup of the oil in a covered pan over low heat until the tomatoes are completely done, 30 to 40 minutes. Press through a wire strainer.

Heat remaining ¼ cup oil with garlic; remove garlic. Season the chicken with salt and pepper. Sauté the chicken in heated oil until it's a light golden brown on all sides. Add the ham, and cook about 5 minutes. Add the pimientos and parsley. Pour over the puréed tomato sauce; cover and simmer until the chicken is tender. Makes 6 servings.

Patio Chicken

2 pounds chicken breasts and legs
    or 1 frying chicken
1 cup bread crumbs
1 teaspoon onion salt
¼ teaspoon garlic salt
½ teaspoon each pepper, monosodium
    glutamate, crushed savory, and
    curry powder
1 cup mayonnaise

Roll chicken in a mixture of the bread crumbs, onion salt, garlic salt, pepper, monosodium glutamate, savory, and curry powder.

Arrange crumb-coated chicken on a greased cooky sheet, skin side up and with no overlapping. Place in a hot oven (400°) for 15 minutes to set the crumbs so they will stick to chicken. Remove from oven; with a brush, coat chicken generously with mayonnaise. Reduce heat to slow (300°) and bake for 1 hour, or until chicken is done but not dry. Serve hot or cold. Serves about 4.

Chicken Hawaiian

Colorful and flavorful with pimiento, dates, almonds, and rings of pineapple.

1 package frozen chicken breasts
1 package frozen chicken legs or thighs
¼ cup soy
¼ cup dry white table wine
Juice of 1 lime
1 clove garlic, mashed or minced
1 teaspoon curry powder
1 teaspoon minced ginger root
¼ teaspoon dried thyme
¼ teaspoon dried oregano
¼ teaspoon freshly ground pepper
2 medium sized onions, thinly sliced
¼ cup (4 tablespoons) butter
2 cups uncooked rice
8 slices of pineapple
1 tablespoon butter
½ cup toasted slivered almonds
16 dates (approximately ½ package), sliced
1 pimiento, cut in small pieces
¼ cup dry white table wine

Thaw chicken breasts and legs; cut each chicken breast into 2 pieces. Mix together soy, wine, lime juice, garlic, curry, ginger root, thyme, oregano, and pepper (no salt). Pour over chicken and marinate for several hours, turning chicken occasionally. Fry the onions in 2 tablespoons of the butter until light yellow and remove from pan.

Add the other 2 tablespoons butter to pan and then fry the chicken pieces (which have been drained and dusted with flour) until brown on all sides. Pour in the marinade, cover, and steam until tender, about 45 minutes, uncovering pan for the last 15 minutes. While chicken is steaming, cook rice by your preferred method. Sauté the pineapple slices in the tablespoon of butter until lightly browned. To serve, mix the almonds, dates, and pimiento with the rice and heap on a large chop plate. Arrange chicken and fried pineapple slices around the rice. Add the other ¼ cup wine to the drippings in the pan and swish around. Serve gravy separately. Serves 8.

Chicken Breasts Sauterne with Avocado

Avocado slices provide a flavorful garnish for savory chicken.

8 large chicken breasts
1½ teaspoons salt
1 teaspoon paprika
¼ cup flour
¼ cup (4 tablespoons) butter
¼ cup finely chopped onion
⅓ cup tomato catsup
3 tablespoons wine vinegar
1 teaspoon Worcestershire
¾ cup dry white table wine or ½ cup chicken broth and ¼ cup white wine
4 cups hot steamed cracked wheat pilaff
1 large avocado

Remove skin from chicken breasts and dust with a mixture of the salt, paprika, and flour. Brown in melted butter until the chicken is a rich golden color on all sides. Combine onion, catsup, vinegar, Worcestershire, and wine. Pour over chicken, cover, and simmer until chicken is tender, about 45 minutes.

Mound hot cracked wheat in the center of a hot chop plate and surround with the chicken breasts. Spoon sauce over the breasts, then peel and slice the avocado and arrange the slices between the chicken breasts, pinwheel fashion. Serves 8.

Turkey Sauté aux Fines Herbes

4 pounds turkey parts (2 legs and 2 thighs, or 1 leg, 1 thigh, and 1 breast), or a turkey quarter
½ cup flour
2 teaspoons salt
  Freshly ground pepper to taste
3 tablespoons each butter and salad oil
1 cup dry white table wine
½ cup sliced mushrooms
1 teaspoon each crumbled dried tarragon and thyme
1 teaspoon each chopped parsley, chives, and green onions
  Chicken or turkey stock
2 tablespoons flour
2 tablespoons butter

Have your meat man saw turkey parts crosswise into 1½-inch-thick steaks. Rub meat with a mixture of flour, salt, and pepper. Brown steaks in butter and salad oil, turning to brown both sides. Add wine, mushrooms, tarragon, thyme, parsley, chives, and green onions.

Cover and simmer turkey until tender, about 50 minutes. Remove meat to a hot platter, add enough chicken or turkey stock to the pan to make 2 cups, and thicken with a roux made with the flour and butter. Simmer 3 minutes, pour over turkey, and serve. Serves 4 to 6.

Turkey and Oyster Fricassee

4 to 5 pound baby turkey
½ cup flour, seasoned with salt and pepper
  About ½ cup butter
3 cups water
¼ teaspoon each mace, nutmeg, and pepper
1 small onion, sliced
1 teaspoon salt
3 anchovy fillets
½ cup sherry
4 tablespoons each butter and flour
1 cup light cream
1 egg yolk
  Juice of 1 lemon
1 cup button mushrooms
1 teaspoon capers
1 dozen oysters

Cut up turkey, roll in seasoned flour, and fry in butter until browned. Place in deep casserole or heavy kettle with a tight fitting cover and add water, spices, onion, salt, anchovies, and sherry. Simmer gently until turkey is tender. Melt butter, and blend in cream and flour. Stir into turkey carefully; let it come to the simmering point, then turn heat very low and slowly stir in slightly beaten egg yolk and lemon juice. Add mushrooms, capers, and oysters and heat just long enough to curl the edges of the oysters. Serves 8.

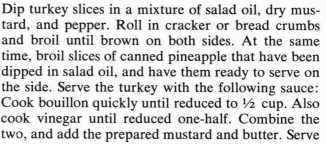

Turkey Diablo

6 thick, cooked turkey slices cut from breast
½ cup salad oil
1 teaspoon dry mustard
  Few grindings of black pepper
  Fine cracker or dry bread crumbs
6 slices canned pineapple, dipped in salad oil
1 can (10½ oz.) bouillon
½ cup tarragon vinegar
1 tablespoon prepared mustard
2 tablespoons butter

Dip turkey slices in a mixture of salad oil, dry mustard, and pepper. Roll in cracker or bread crumbs and broil until brown on both sides. At the same time, broil slices of canned pineapple that have been dipped in salad oil, and have them ready to serve on the side. Serve the turkey with the following sauce: Cook bouillon quickly until reduced to ½ cup. Also cook vinegar until reduced one-half. Combine the two, and add the prepared mustard and butter. Serve as soon as the butter is melted. Serves 6.

Curried Turkey with Almonds

¼ cup (4 tablespoons) butter
6 tablespoons flour
2 cups milk
½ teaspoon salt
½ teaspoon paprika
¼ teaspoon pepper
¼ teaspoon curry powder
2 teaspoons water
1 bay leaf
2 cups diced cooked turkey
1 cup blanched almonds, slivered and toasted
1 cup cooked peas

Melt butter in a 2-quart saucepan and blend in flour. Scald milk; gradually pour into saucepan while stirring. Add salt, paprika, pepper, curry powder moistened in water, and bay leaf. Stirring constantly, simmer until thick. Remove bay leaf. Mix in turkey, almonds and peas. Heat thoroughly. Serve on buttered toast or rice or in the center of a noodle ring. Garnish with parsley. Serves 6.

Turkey Puff

½ cup finely chopped onion
½ cup diced celery
2 tablespoons butter
2 cups cooked turkey or chicken
1 can (10½ oz.) chicken noodle soup
½ cup light cream
1 can (2 or 3 oz.) mushroom slices or pieces, drained
2 tablespoons diced pimiento
½ cup slivered toasted almonds
½ teaspoon salt
½ teaspoon freshly ground pepper
4 eggs, separated
½ cup shredded Cheddar cheese

In a large pan, sauté the onion and celery in butter. Add the turkey, soup, cream, mushrooms, pimiento, almonds, salt, and pepper; blend well. Cook over low heat just until hot. Pour into a buttered 2-quart casserole. Beat the egg yolks, add cheese; fold in egg whites, beaten until stiff, but not dry. Pour egg-cheese mixture over top of casserole. Bake in a moderate oven (350°) for 30 minutes. Serves 6.

Citrus-Stuffed Duck

Tart, sharp, or spicy stuffings and accompaniments are best for contrast with the flavor of duck. To garnish this duck, surround it with broiled apricot halves.

½ cup coarsely chopped walnut meats
3 cups 1-inch bread cubes
½ cup hot water
1 tablespoon grated orange peel
Pulp of 1 orange, chopped
2 cups sliced celery
1 egg
½ teaspoon salt
Dash of pepper
¼ teaspoon poultry seasoning
¼ cup melted butter
4 to 5-pound duck, ready to cook weight
1 teaspoon salt

Arrange nut meats in a single layer in a shallow pan; turning occasionally, toast in a slow oven (300°) for 5 to 7 minutes; remove from oven. Increase heat to 350°, and toast bread cubes until golden brown. Heat water, pour over bread cubes, and let stand 10 minutes. Combine nut meats, bread cubes, orange peel, orange pulp, and celery. Beat egg with the ½ teaspoon salt, pepper, and poultry seasoning; combine with bread cube mixture. Pour melted butter into stuffing and toss well.

Rub inside of duck with the 1 teaspoon salt. Spoon stuffing into duck; sew openings. Place the bird, breast side up, in a roasting pan. Bake, uncovered, in a moderately slow oven (325°) for 2 to 2½ hours or until tender. For a crisper skin, increase heat to a hot oven (400°) the last 30 minutes of baking. Serves 3 to 4.

Duck Mandarin Style

A typical Oriental marinade and a sauce containing tangerine sections and a generous amount of orange juice result in surprisingly good flavor.

1 duck, 5 to 6 pounds, cut for fricassee
¼ cup soy
1 tablespoon sugar
½ teaspoon salt
1 teaspoon ground ginger
¼ cup salad oil
1 clove garlic
2 cups water
1 cup orange juice
2 tablespoons cornstarch
¼ cup water
2 cups tangerine or orange sections

Marinate the pieces of duck in a mixture of the soy, sugar, salt, and ginger for about two hours, turning occasionally. Heat oil with garlic. Remove garlic, and sauté duck in oil until browned. Pour in 2 cups of water and the orange juice. Cover and simmer gently until tender, 1½ to 2 hours depending on tenderness of duck. Remove duck, arrange on platter and keep warm in oven. Thicken sauce with cornstarch mixed with ¼ cup water. Add tangerine or orange sections (or slices) and cook 5 minutes. Pour orange sauce over the duck. Serve with steamed rice to 6 persons.

Roast Squab Stuffed with Wild Rice

1½ cups uncooked wild rice
2 tablespoons finely chopped parsley
½ cup finely sliced celery
¼ cup (4 tablespoons) chopped onion
1 medium sized apple, cored, peeled, and chopped
3 cups water
1 teaspoon salt
8 squabs
½ cup (¼ pound) butter, melted
1 teaspoon salt
½ teaspoon pepper
¼ teaspoon monosodium glutamate
½ cup sauterne

Wash rice thoroughly, then place in a large pan with parsley, celery, onion, apple, water, and 1 teaspoon of the salt. Cover and boil for 20 minutes. Drain. When rice is cool enough to handle, stuff squabs with mixture; truss. Season melted butter with 1 teaspoon salt, pepper, and monosodium glutamate; then roll squab in the mixture. Place squabs, breast up, on a rack in a roaster. Pour wine over. Cover pan; then bake in a moderate oven (350°) for 30 minutes. Increase heat to a hot oven (400°), and continue cooking for 30 minutes. Remove cover and, basting occasionally, bake for 15 minutes longer to brown. Use drippings for gravy. Serves 8.

French Roast Squab

4 slices onion, cut ¼ inch thick
4 squabs
2 cups canned (drained) or fresh seedless grapes
½ cup (¼ pound) butter, melted
½ teaspoon salt
¼ teaspoon pepper
⅛ teaspoon monosodium glutamate
¼ cup (4 tablespoons) sauterne
½ cup hot water
1 bouillon cube

Place 1 slice onion in the neck opening of each squab; then stuff each bird with ½ cup grapes. Truss. Season ¼ cup of the melted butter with salt, pepper, and monosodium glutamate; then roll whole birds in mixture. Place squabs on rack in an uncovered roaster. Pour over it the wine, remaining ¼ cup melted butter, and the water in which you have first dissolved the bouillon cube. Basting frequently, roast uncovered in a slow oven (300°) for about 2 hours, or until the leg moves easily. Serves 4.

Chicken Livers with Water Chestnuts

1 pound fresh chicken livers, or thawed frozen chicken livers
4 slices bacon, cut in ½-inch pieces
2 tablespoons chopped green onions
¼ cup flour
¼ teaspoon monosodium glutamate
½ teaspoon salt
⅓ cup sliced canned water chestnuts
½ cup light cream
2 tablespoons chopped green onion tops

Cut the chicken livers in half, removing any connecting tissue. Place the bacon pieces in a frying pan and sauté until lightly browned. Add the chopped green onions and cook about 1 minute. Combine the flour, monosodium glutamate, and salt, and toss the livers in flour until well coated. Add to the frying pan, and sauté about 5 minutes, turning so they brown evenly. Add the sliced water chestnuts and cream. Bring the mixture just to the boiling point. Serve immediately, plain or on crisp toast. Top each serving with chopped green onion tops. Makes 4 servings.

Chicken Livers and Avocado in Sour Cream

¼ cup chopped onion
¼ cup chopped green pepper
1 clove garlic, whole (optional)
½ pound fresh chicken livers or thawed
   frozen chicken livers
2 tablespoons butter
1 small ripe avocado, diced
¾ cup commercial sour cream
½ teaspoon Worcestershire
½ teaspoon paprika
   Salt and pepper to taste

Sauté onion, pepper, garlic, and livers in butter until livers are just cooked, about 10 minutes. Remove clove of garlic. Add diced avocado (if desired save a few cubes to use as a garnish) and cook gently until heated through (about 1 minute). Stir in sour cream just to heat. Add Worcestershire, paprika, salt, and pepper. Serve on hot buttered toast rounds. Makes 2 servings.

Walnut and Mushroom Stuffing

¾ cup chopped onion
½ pound fresh mushrooms, sliced,
   or 2 cans (4 oz. each) sliced
   mushrooms, drained
¾ cup butter
3 quarts (1½ loaves) soft bread cubes
¾ cup chopped walnut meats
¾ teaspoon salt
½ teaspoon pepper
2 teaspoons rubbed sage
½ teaspoon marjoram
½ to 1 cup chicken stock

Slowly cook onion and mushrooms in butter until lightly browned, pour over bread cubes and toss to blend. Add nut meats, salt, pepper, sage, marjoram, and enough broth to moisten; mix lightly. This amount of stuffing is ample for an 18 to 20 pound turkey. If you use a smaller turkey, the extra dressing can bake in a moderate oven (350°) for 35 minutes.

Water Chestnut Stuffing

1 cup chopped onion
½ cup chopped green pepper
½ cup sliced celery
1 cup (½ pound) butter
8 cups bread cubes, toasted
2 cups sliced water chestnuts
1 tablespoon soy
1 tablespoon grated fresh ginger or
   candied ginger (rinsed first of the
   sugar)

Sauté onion, green pepper, and celery in butter until limp. Combine with the bread cubes, water chestnuts, soy, and ginger; toss lightly. If the mixture is very dry, add a little hot water to moisten slightly. Makes 10 cups stuffing.

Game

TRADITIONALLY, the dinner featuring game is an occasion—a special event celebrating the return of the hunter. It is invariably approached with enthusiasm. Interest in game cookery is out of all proportion to the frequency of the preparation of game. Perhaps the fascination with the subject is due to scarcity and the threat of the disappearance of this very special food from the table.

However, as hunter-hosts know, enthusiasm for the eating of game is not shared equally by everyone. In planning a game dinner, select your guests carefully. Don't waste time and great food on the unappreciative.

Most of the recipes that grace this chapter are written for those epicures who appreciate the unique flavor of game. A few simple rules are evident: While to dilute the true flavor of game is no crime, to distort it or confuse it is mockery. Avoid overcooking. Game birds, with the exception of geese, are naturally dry, and you must add fats. When gamey flavors are to be minimized, marinate. But don't go so far that a new flavor is substituted.

Not the least of the pleasures of game cookery is the business of saucing. For ideas on this, see the chapter on sauces. And for evidence that the hunter-chef is in his environment at the barbecue, see the chapter on barbecuing.

Roast Wild Duck

There is no doubt that a duck on the rare side is more tender and juicy than one that is on the well done side. However, there's no need to apologize for your taste if you don't like rare duck.

No one agrees on roasting time. A very hot oven (475°) will produce a rare, but not raw, bird in the following times: Small duck (teal) 10 to 12 minutes; medium size (sprig), 12 to 15 minutes; large size (Mallard), 15 to 20 minutes.

The duck may be stuffed, if desired, but generally it is not. Often a slice of onion, a rib of celery, and a piece of apple are put into the cavity — or use a sprig of parsley and 2 or 3 juniper berries instead.

Put ducks in a pan, breast side up; rub with olive oil or bacon grease. Roast in a very hot oven (475°) for the preferred length of time, basting a few times with the cooking fat.

Duck à l'Alsacienne

This method is good for a duck whose age leaves something to be desired. Cut the birds in pieces and rub with flour. Cook in butter or shortening until lightly browned. Add 1 cup white table wine, 1 bay leaf, 2 juniper berries, 1 small onion, 1 teaspoon salt, 1 sprig parsley, and 3 peppercorns for every 2 ducks. Cover and cook slowly until tender.

Remove duck pieces to platter. Strain sauce, correct seasoning, and pour over the duck. Surround with sauerkraut that has been simmered for 2 hours in white table wine (1 cup wine to each pint of sauerkraut); season with salt and pepper.

Duck à l'Orange

Braise duck as for Duck à l'Alsacienne (above), but omit juniper berries. Strain sauce, and to it add the juice and the shredded zest (outer peel) of 2 oranges. Pour back on the duck, heat, and serve garnished with sliced peeled oranges.

Grilled Breast of Wild Duck with Gravy

Remove breasts from the number of ducks to be served. Sauté quickly in half salad oil and half butter just until tender; do not overcook. Place on a hot platter and serve at once with Duck Gravy.

Duck Gravy

1 small onion, minced
 Hearts, livers, and gizzards from the ducks, chopped fine
3 tablespoons butter or drippings
2 cups hot stock or water

Sauté onion, hearts, livers, and gizzards in butter or drippings until lightly browned. Add stock, cover, and simmer 45 to 50 minutes, or until tender. (If liquid evaporates too rapidly, add additional stock in small amounts.) Season to taste and thicken slightly with a little flour-water paste before serving. The addition of drippings from previously roasted duck will give a richer color to this gravy.

(To make stock for gravy, cook remaining portions of the birds in water to cover, with a few pieces of celery and some onion, salt, and pepper. When meat is tender, remove from the bones and use to make a savory hash.)

Crumb-Coated Roast Dove

A crusty coat of seasoned bread crumbs coats the outside of the bird.

¾ cup fine dry bread crumbs
½ teaspoon crumbled oregano
⅛ teaspoon pepper
 1 clove garlic, minced or mashed
 4 sprigs parsley, finely chopped
 6 doves
 3 teaspoons salt
⅓ cup olive oil
 3 tablespoons catsup
 3 tablespoons water

Combine bread crumbs, oregano, pepper, garlic, and parsley. Set aside. Thoroughly clean doves and pat dry. Sprinkle them with salt; brush with olive oil. Completely coat the outside of each dove with the crumb mixture; arrange in a large greased utility pan. Combine catsup, water, and any remaining olive oil and crumbs; pour over birds. Cover with foil. Roast in a moderate oven (350°) for 2 hours, or until doves are tender. Add a small amount of water to the pan if needed. Serves 6.

Roast Wild Goose

1 wild goose, cleaned and dressed
⅓ cup vinegar
1½ cups dry white table wine
   Juice of 2 lemons
   Juice of 1 orange
1 small onion, sliced
⅛ teaspoon nutmeg
1 small bay leaf
   Few celery leaves
   Few sprigs of parsley
   Salt and pepper
3 apples, peeled
3 celery stalks

Place goose in marinade made by combining vinegar, wine, lemon juice, orange juice, onion, nutmeg, bay leaf, celery leaves, and parsley. Let stand 3 to 4 hours, turning and basting frequently. Remove goose from marinade and rub cavity with salt and pepper.

Place peeled apples and celery stalks inside. Truss goose and place breast side up in a roasting pan. Sear for 20 minutes in a very hot oven (450°), then turn goose breast side down, cover pan, lower heat to moderate (350°), and continue roasting for 1 to 1½ hours, or until tender. Baste occasionally with the marinade and pan drippings.

Batter-Fried Wild Goose

1 wild goose, cleaned and skinned
½ cup dry red table wine
¼ teaspoon dried basil
   Flour
2 eggs
   Flour seasoned with salt and pepper to taste
   Bacon drippings or salad oil for frying

With a sharp knife, cut the meat from the breast in ¼-inch-thick slices; cut the meat in as large pieces as possible. Cut the meat from the thighs in lengthwise strips, removing as much of the tough tendon as possible. Marinate slices of goose meat in wine seasoned with basil for at least 2 hours. Dip drained and dried goose slices in flour first, then in slightly beaten egg, and finally in seasoned flour. Fry quickly in hot bacon drippings, about 5 minutes on each side. The meat should still have a tinge of pink. Serves 4.

Pheasant Salmi

6 green onions and tops, chopped
3 tablespoons butter
5 tablespoons browned flour
1 cup stock (made from cooking pheasant bones in water seasoned with 2 stalks celery)
¼ cup (4 tablespoons) sherry
2 tablespoons orange juice
¼ teaspoon grated orange peel
   Salt
1 cup pecan stuffing or other leftover stuffing
2 to 3 cups cooked pheasant meat, cut in bite-size pieces

Sauté onions in butter until lightly browned; add browned flour, and stirring, cook 2 minutes. (To brown flour, sprinkle into a heavy frying pan, and stirring, cook over medium heat until it is a light beige.) Add the stock, sherry, orange juice, and grated peel; stirring, cook until smooth and thickened; taste and add salt if desired. Add stuffing to the gravy mixture, along with the meat, and cook just long enough to heat through. Serve over mashed potatoes or split buttered biscuits. Serves 4 to 6.

Pecan-Stuffed Pheasant

The pecans add a crunchy texture to a fluffy bread stuffing, and they supply additional fat to keep the bird moist.

¼ cup (4 tablespoons) butter
1⅓ cups dry bread crumbs
⅔ cup coarsely broken pecan meats
2 pheasants
2 tablespoons flour
¾ teaspoon salt
¼ teaspoon pepper
¼ cup (4 tablespoons) butter
1½ cups hot water
⅓ cup sherry

Melt the 4 tablespoons butter and pour over bread crumbs; add pecan meats and toss lightly. Stuff mixture into pheasants, then truss birds. Combine the flour, salt, and pepper, and lightly sprinkle over pheasants. Melt the other 4 tablespoons butter in a heavy frying pan; brown each pheasant on all sides, then transfer to a roasting pan. Add hot water and sherry to the browned butter, then pour mixture over the birds. Cover and bake in a moderate oven (350°) for 1 hour.

Baste pheasants with liquid in the pan every 15 minutes. Remove cover and continue baking for 20 minutes, or until the birds are crisp and brown. Remove birds to a platter and keep hot while you thicken drippings for gravy. Serves 6.

Hassenpfeffer

1 large or 2 small rabbits
2 cups red wine vinegar
2 cups dry red table wine
2 cups sliced onions
4 teaspoons salt
1 teaspoon coarsely ground black pepper
½ teaspoon crushed juniper berries (optional)
½ teaspoon whole cloves
¼ teaspoon thyme
3 bay leaves
½ cup flour
½ teaspoon salt
½ cup shortening
1 cup water or stock
Salt to taste
2 teaspoons sugar

Cut up rabbits as you would chickens. Combine vinegar, wine, onions, the 4 teaspoons of salt, pepper, juniper berries, cloves, thyme, and bay leaves. Marinate rabbits in this mixture in the refrigerator for 2 days, turning occasionally.

Drain, saving marinade; dry meat, then rub with flour which has been seasoned with the ½ teaspoon of salt. Sauté in shortening until brown. Drain fat. Strain marinade, add water or stock, and add to the meat. Simmer, covered, for 45 minutes, or until tender. Correct seasoning, adding salt to taste. Add sugar. Arrange on a platter and thicken the sauce with *beurre manie* (butter and flour kneaded together) if necessary. You might serve it with potato pancakes or potato dumplings. Serves 6.

Sweet and Sour Moose

Long simmering in a sweet-sour sauce tames the wild flavor of moose.

2 pounds moose, cut in 2-inch cubes
2 cups water
2 teaspoons salt
8 whole cloves
8 whole allspice
1 cinnamon stick, broken in small
   pieces
1 tablespoon sugar
4 tablespoons (¼ cup) flour
1 tablespoon shortening
½ cup vinegar
1 medium sized onion, chopped

Simmer meat cubes in water seasoned with salt, cloves, allspice, cinnamon stick, and sugar until tender, about 1½ hours. While meat is cooking, spread flour in a shallow baking pan and brown in a moderate oven (350°) for 10 minutes. Melt shortening, blend in flour until smooth. Drain stock from meat and stir it into flour mixture along with vinegar. Stirring, cook until smooth and thick. Pour gravy over meat, add onion, and continue simmering for 30 minutes. Serves 6.

Venison Pot Roast

If you prefer venison with a mild flavor, you'll like this approach.

6-pound venison pot roast
3 cloves garlic, slivered
½ pound salt pork or 1 cup bacon
   drippings
4 tablespoons (¼ cup) flour
½ teaspoon each salt and sage
¼ teaspoon pepper
3 tablespoons salt pork or bacon
   drippings
4 cups tomato juice
¼ cup wine vinegar
2 bay leaves
2 whole cloves
5 whole black peppers
½ teaspoon each onion salt, garlic salt,
   and celery salt
¼ teaspoon thyme
2 teaspoons Worcestershire
1 can (10½ oz.) mushroom soup
6 each onions, carrots, and potatoes

Cut all fat off the meat (in venison the flavor is concentrated in the fat, and if left on, it gives a gamey taste to the meat). Wipe meat with a damp cloth wrung out in mild vinegar. Cut slits in meat on all sides and insert small slivers of garlic in each slit. Lard with strips of salt pork. Or using a pastry brush, coat well with bacon drippings. Mix together flour, salt, sage, and pepper; rub into meat.

Heat 3 tablespoons salt pork or bacon drippings in a heavy kettle with tight fitting cover. Brown meat slowly on all sides. Lift meat out and slip a low rack in the bottom of the kettle. Replace meat, then add tomato juice, wine vinegar, bay leaves, cloves, peppers, onion salt, garlic salt, celery salt, thyme, and Worcestershire. Cover and simmer over low heat for 2 hours. Baste with the liquids 3 or 4 times during cooking.

After meat has cooked 2 hours, add mushroom soup and stir until it is well blended with tomato juice. Peel onions, carrots, and potatoes; surround meat with the vegetables. Cover and continue cooking for an additional hour, or until vegetables are done to your liking.

If you wish a slightly heavier gravy, pour off sauce and strain; thicken slightly with a flour and water mixture. Pass gravy to pour over the sliced meat. Serves 10.

Roast Leg of Venison with Chestnut Sauce

When you take venison out of your freezer for this meal, leave the meat wrapped while it thaws, then place it in the marinade.

1 leg of venison (shank removed)
4 slices bacon
3 cups dry red table wine
1 onion, sliced
1 clove garlic, mashed or minced
1 bay leaf
4 juniper berries (optional)

Sauce

1½ pounds shelled and peeled
    chestnuts
1½ cups bouillon
¼ cup (4 tablespoons) butter
4 tablespoons (¼ cup) flour
1 cup of reserved marinade
    Salt and pepper
1½ cups commercial sour cream

Lard venison with the bacon slices. Put meat in a deep kettle and marinate for 24 hours in the mixture of the red table wine, onion, garlic, bay, and juniper berries. Turn several times during marinating. Pour off marinade and reserve for basting and for the sauce. Place meat in a roasting pan; insert a meat thermometer in the fleshiest part of the leg, making sure that it does not touch the bone. Roast in a very hot oven (450°) for 20 minutes to brown; reduce heat and continue cooking at 350° until thermometer reads 140° for rare or 160° for medium, about 20 minutes to the pound. Baste with 1 cup of the marinade occasionally during cooking.

To make sauce, cook the shelled chestnuts in bouillon just until tender, but not broken; drain, reserving stock. Melt butter, sprinkle over flour, and stir and cook 3 minutes. Pour in 1 cup reserved stock from cooking chestnuts, and the 1 cup reserved marinade; stirring, cook until smooth and thickened. Add chestnuts and heat through. Season with salt and pepper to taste, then carefully stir in sour cream and heat gently so cream will not curdle. Serve sauce with the sliced meat in place of gravy.

Braised Venison à la Forestiere

This is good treatment for tougher cuts of venison.

3 pounds venison
    Marinade (see page 82)
¼ cup shortening
2 tablespoons flour
½ cup tomato purée
3 crushed juniper berries (optional)
    Herb bouquet of parsley, bay, and
    thyme
1 cup stock (venison or bouillon)
½ pound mushrooms, sliced
3 shallots or green onions, chopped
2 tablespoons butter
4 tablespoons flour

Cut meat in chunks and marinate in either of the marinades on page 82 for about 24 hours if you use the raw marinade or 4 hours if you use the cooked marinade. Drain; sauté in shortening to seal, then sprinkle with 2 tablespoons flour, and continue to cook until brown. Add 1 cup of the marinade, tomato purée, juniper berries, and herb bouquet. Cover and simmer until almost tender (about 1½ hours), adding water or stock to replace evaporation. Cool, and skim off fat.

Sauté mushrooms and shallots in butter for 5 minutes. Blend in the 4 tablespoons flour, cook a minute, and combine with meat and liquid. Simmer until thickened, and serve with toast. Serves 6 to 8.

Venison Scallopini

1½ pound piece venison steak
    Salt, pepper, and flour
 1 egg
 ⅓ cup light cream
 1 cup fine cracker crumbs
 1 cup grated Parmesan cheese
 ¼ cup minced parsley
 ¼ cup butter
 1 clove garlic, minced
 ½ cup sherry or Marsala wine
 ½ cup venison broth or water

Slice venison into serving size pieces, about ⅜ inch thick, and pound well. Sprinkle meat with salt and pepper, then dredge in flour. Beat egg slightly and stir in cream. Mix together cracker crumbs, Parmesan cheese, and parsley. Dip each meat slice into egg and cream mixture and then into Parmesan crumbs until well coated. Heat butter and garlic together in heavy frying pan with a cover. Add crumbed meat slices and brown on both sides. Pour in wine and broth, cover, and bake in a moderately hot oven (375°) for 45 minutes to 1 hour, or until tender. Serves 4 or 5.

Raw Marinade for Game

 1 bottle (⅘ quart) dry red table wine
 ¼ cup red wine vinegar
 2 large carrots, sliced
 2 large onions, sliced
 6 shallots or green onions, chopped
 ½ teaspoon each whole peppercorns, whole cloves, juniper berries (optional), and thyme
 1 tablespoon salt
 3 or 4 sprigs parsley
 1 bay leaf

Combine all ingredients. Pour over the meat, cover with foil, and keep cool. Turn meat several times. Small pieces of meat are usually marinated for 24 hours, larger pieces for 2 or 3 days. If the marinade completely covers the meat, turning is not necessary. Some cooks pour a little oil on top of the marinade to seal out the air. Makes about 1 quart marinade.

Cooked Marinade for Game

This is used when there is not time for long marinating. When it is poured hot over the meat, it hastens the flavoring and tenderizing process.

 4 bay leaves
 ½ teaspoon thyme (or 4 sprigs fresh thyme)
 4 whole cloves
 6 whole allspice
 1 clove garlic
 6 whole peppercorns
 1 sliced onion
 2 sprigs parsley, chopped
 2 cups dry red table wine
 1 jigger (1½ ounces) brandy

In a mortar, bruise bay leaves, thyme, cloves, allspice, garlic, and peppercorns. Add remaining ingredients. Bring to a boil and pour over the meat. Marinate from 4 to 24 hours, turning occasionally. Makes about 1 pint of marinade.

Barbecue Specialties

THERE ARE MANY good reasons for cooking outdoors, but in this chapter we are concerned with just one: Does the charcoal broil contribute to the goodness of the food?

The method may call for spit, skewers, or grill, but always the heat of the coals is the essential difference between barbecuing and other kinds of cooking. And the coals should make a difference in the food.

Smoke flavors are not overlooked, but they are imparted by the smoke of various woods or herbs rather than by the angry, acrid smoke of burning fat.

Watching the barbecue cook, you will see that he manipulates either the coals or the distance between coals and meat as carefully as he does the oven thermostat. There are "hot coals," "medium coals," and "low to medium coals." Swordfish is grilled 4 inches above hot coals. Turkey steaks are broiled about 8 inches from the fire. Chicken, to be cooked slowly, gets a special arrangement: the coals are pushed to each end of the barbecue, and the chicken is placed in the middle of the grill.

The barbecue is reaching out into all parts of the menu — even into the hors d'oeuvre department. Hot, skewered appetizers of every description are easy to prepare, and allow guest participation. For ideas on this barbecue specialty, refer to the chapter on Party Food.

Barbecued Chuck with Mushroom Stuffing

Here, flavorful beef chuck roast is split into steaks, stuffed with a sautéed mushroom mixture, then tied and barbecued.

3 to 4-pound chuck roast, sliced through the center
⅔ cup dry red table wine
⅓ cup salad oil
3 cloves garlic, minced or mashed
⅛ teaspoon each rosemary, marjoram, and thyme
Freshly ground pepper to taste
½ pound fresh mushrooms, sliced, or 2 cans (4 oz. each) sliced mushrooms
6 tablespoons butter
3 green onions, finely chopped
¼ cup finely chopped parsley

Ask your meat man to saw a 2-inch-thick chuck roast through the center to make 2 chuck steaks, each 1 inch thick. (If possible, have it cut from the chuck steak section — close to the rib end — so the bones will be smaller and the meat more tender.) Or you can start with 2 chuck steaks of the same size. With a sharp knife, cut out the long, slender blade bone in each steak, but leave the other large bone that is on the side of each steak.

For marinade, mix together wine, oil, garlic, rosemary, marjoram, thyme, and pepper. Turn into a large, shallow baking dish, add meat, and let marinate overnight, turning occasionally.

For stuffing, sauté fresh mushrooms in butter until golden brown, or drain canned mushrooms. Mix in chopped green onions and chopped parsley. Spoon mushroom mixture over 1 chuck steak and arrange the second steak on top. Tie securely with string. Barbecue over medium coals about 45 minutes, allowing 20 to 25 minutes on each side for medium rare. To serve, cut away string and slice slightly on the diagonal into strips about ⅛ inch thick. Serve mushroom stuffing on the side. Makes 4 servings.

Oyster-Stuffed Market Steaks

It may be gilding the lily, but for superlative steak for an extraordinary occasion, try stuffing market steaks (also sold as Delmonico, Spencer, or boned-rib steaks).

4 market steaks, cut 1 inch thick
¼ cup finely sliced celery
2 tablespoons chopped onion
¼ cup butter
1 can (8 oz.) small oysters
Water, stock, or dry white table wine
½ package (8 oz. size) herb-seasoned stuffing mix
Salt to taste

Cut lengthwise pockets in steaks. Do not cut back or sides; leave enough rim around edge so filling won't break through. Lightly fill pocket with oyster stuffing (see below). Each steak will take ⅓ to ½ cup stuffing. Skewer edges together with strong toothpicks or little metal skewers. Grill over hot coals (about 5 minutes each side for rare steak).

To make stuffing, sauté celery and onion in butter until soft. Drain and save liquor from oysters. Add water, stock, or white table wine to oyster liquid to make ½ cup liquid. Add to sautéed celery and onions along with oysters, stuffing mix, and salt. Mix lightly.

Barbecued Whole Fillet

Give this tenderest of steaks the regal treatment it deserves.

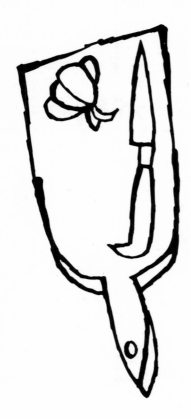

Purchase the whole fillet (about 4 to 6 pounds) or a center fillet roast (about 2½ to 3 pounds).

The fillet can be barbecued right on the grill or on the spit. If you do it on the grill, turn it quite often, exposing all sides to the heat. It's a lean cut, so brush frequently with a mixture of half melted butter, half oil. Or you may choose to have your meat man lard the fillet, wrapping a layer of fat around the meat so it self-bastes as it grills. It will take about 30 minutes to grill a whole fillet if you like it rare. Timing will be about the same when you spit roast.

For the most dramatic serving, place the charcoal-browned whole tenderloin on a handsome platter or board, surround with brimming relish-filled "tomato box" garnishes (see below), sprigs of watercress, and a log of blue-cheese butter (also below). Then carve generous, thick slices and serve as individual steaks. Place a pat of the blue-cheese butter on each steak serving.

To serve this superior meat to a larger number of people, slice thin and offer as sandwiches on crusty buttered hot French bread. For a beautiful serving, cut a long, thin loaf of French bread in half lengthwise. Spread cut surfaces generously with plain or seasoned butter. Heat. Arrange thin slices of the savory grilled steak on one half of the bread, thin slices of onions, tomatoes, and radishes or cucumbers on the other. Arrange the bread halves side by side, and cut diagonally across both to make 12 to 15 servings.

Tomato Box Garnish

Select large, firm tomatoes with stems, if possible. Cut off tops to use for lids. Hollow out inside of tomato, leaving a shell. Heap full of favorite relishes — small radish roses, carrot curls, tiny onions and pickles, ripe and green stuffed olives. Set lids on top of tomatoes so relishes show.

Blue-Cheese Butter Roll

Blend ½ pound (1 cup) soft butter and ¼ pound blue cheese with 1 tablespoon finely chopped green onions, fresh rosemary, or basil. Place on a sheet of waxed paper, shape into a log, and roll in finely chopped parsley. Wrap with waxed paper; refrigerate until firm. Serve on watercress.

Teriyaki Steak Strips

If barbecuing flank steak is new to you, you're in for a delightful surprise when you taste these juicy, tender strips. We like these teriyaki-seasoned steak strips served with brown rice or quick-cooking cracked wheat.

2 pounds flank steak
1 cup undiluted beef consommé (or ½ cup each consommé and red or white wine)
⅓ cup soy
1½ teaspoons seasoned salt
¼ cup chopped green onions with tops
1 clove garlic, minced or mashed
3 tablespoons lime juice
2 tablespoons brown sugar or honey

Have your meat man remove the membrane, but don't have the meat scored in a mechanical tenderizer.

Cut meat into 1-inch-wide strips, diagonally, from top to bottom. Marinate in refrigerator overnight in a marinade made by combining consommé, soy, salt, green onions, garlic, lime juice, and brown sugar or honey.

Drain meat and save marinade. Using a hinged broiler, grill very quickly over hot coals (about 2 minutes on each side) while brushing with marinade. Turn only once. Serves 5 or 6.

Spit-Barbecued Leg of Lamb

A leg of lamb on the spit is practically self-basting and needs little watching.

5 to 6-pound short-cut leg of lamb
4 cloves garlic, split
½ teaspoon crumbled dried oregano
1 teaspoon salt
4 tablespoons (¼ cup) melted butter
Juice of 1 lemon

Make several cuts in lamb, and insert split cloves of garlic and a mixture of oregano and salt. With any remaining oregano and salt, rub the outside of the meat. Insert the spit almost parallel to the bone and place over medium coals. Mix butter and lemon juice, and brush the meat. Basting once or twice, barbecue 1¼ to 1½ hours (140° on a meat thermometer) for medium rare. Serves 6 to 8.

Barbecued Breast of Lamb

2 cups dry red table wine
¼ cup vinegar
1 teaspoon sweet basil or rosemary
2 cloves garlic, crushed
2 teaspoons salt
Pepper to taste
1 onion, sliced
4 pounds breast of lamb (have breast left whole)

Mix together the wine, vinegar, basil or rosemary, garlic, salt, pepper, and onion. Marinate meat overnight in this mixture. Drain; weave meat on spit, and roast over charcoal, basting with the marinade. (Be sure the fat drops in *front* of the fire, so it won't flare.) It will take an hour or so for the lamb to become crisply brown and tender. Serves 4 to 6.

Lamb Shish Kebabs

Use the spicy marinade and basting sauce for barbecued lamb chops, too.

8 or 9-pound leg of lamb
18 small boiling onions
1 pound mushroom caps
6 medium sized tomatoes, quartered
1 can (6 oz.) tomato paste
½ cup dry white table wine
½ cup white wine vinegar
2½ to 3 tablespoons olive oil or
    salad oil
2 tablespoons hot prepared mustard
1½ medium sized white onions, minced
1½ tablespoons Worcestershire
¾ teaspoon each dried rosemary and
    oregano
    Salt to taste

Have your meat man prepare the leg for kebabs, or cut it yourself into 1¼ to 1½-inch cubes, removing gristle. Precook onions, and wash mushroom caps.

Several hours before you plan to start barbecuing, arrange meat and vegetables compactly on large skewers, starting and ending with cubes of meat. Place the filled skewers in a large, shallow baking pan, and marinate in sauce made by combining all of the remaining ingredients. Turn kebabs several times while they marinate. Broil over coals, basting with the marinade and turning occasionally for even browning and cooking. Broiling will take 15 to 20 minutes. Makes 6 kebabs.

Barbecued Split Leg of Lamb

If you wish, marinate the meat ahead of time in your favorite red wine marinade, or brush with garlic butter during barbecuing.

Ask your meat man to bone a 5 to 6-pound leg of lamb, keeping meat in one piece. Insert 2 skewers through the meat at right angles. Place the fat side down on the grill over medium hot coals. Turn once, using the skewers as holders. Meat will be medium rare in about 45 minutes. To carve, start at one end and cut meat across the grain into ¼-inch-thick slices. Serves 6.

Barbecued Lamb Steaks

Ask your meat man for a long-cut leg (it has the large loin in it) weighing between 7 and 8 pounds, and have him cut it crosswise into 12 steaks about ¾ inch thick.

Place on grill over medium hot coals; brush with warm garlic sauce, made by combining 4 cloves crushed garlic with 3 tablespoons each melted butter and salad oil. Grill 15 minutes altogether, or about 8 minutes on each side, for medium rare. Serves 12.

Skewered Veal Barbecue

⅓ cup soy
1 large onion, chopped
2 tablespoons salad oil or olive oil
1 tablespoon dried oregano
2 or 3 veal steaks, ½ to ¾ inch thick
  Burgundy or claret wine
1 can (1 lb. 13 oz.) sliced pineapple

Mix together the soy, onion, oil, and oregano to make the marinade. Cut the veal steaks into 1 to 1½-inch squares. Put the veal squares in a bowl, pour in the marinade, then add enough Burgundy to cover the meat when packed down in the bowl. Let the meat marinate all day and turn it in the marinade from time to time. Cut the pineapple slices into quarters.

About 2 hours before time to barbecue, string meat on the skewers with a piece of pineapple between every two pieces of meat. You'll have to work carefully on the pineapple as it is apt to split if skewers are large. Arrange the skewers on a shallow pan, pour over the sauce and marinate, turning occasionally, until time to barbecue over coals. Barbecuing takes about 20 minutes in all, turning 4 times. Baste with the marinade when you turn them. This fills 6 good-sized skewers.

Spit-Roasted Pork

1 can (1 lb.) apple sauce
¾ cup dry white table wine
½ cup soy
2 tablespoons salad oil
1 cup chopped onion
1 clove garlic, minced or mashed
1 teaspoon ground ginger
  Whole leg of fresh pork, boned and
  rolled (net weight 12 pounds)

Combine half of the apple sauce (1 cup) with the wine, soy, salad oil, onion, garlic, and ginger. Marinate the pork in this mixture for at least 1 hour. Place on spit, and roast over medium coals until well done, 6 to 7 hours for the 12-pound roast (internal temperature on meat thermometer should read 185°). Baste frequently with the marinade as it roasts. When done, remove from spit, slice and serve on a large platter. For a sauce to go with the meat, add the remaining 1 cup apple sauce to the marinade that's left; heat and serve. Serves 12.

Barbecued Spareribs

4 pounds spareribs
1 cup each catsup and water
2 medium sized onions, finely chopped
2 cloves garlic, minced or mashed
2 tablespoons Worcestershire
2 teaspoons prepared mustard
2 teaspoons salt
1 teaspoon pepper

Grill ribs over a medium fire for about 1 hour, turning them frequently, and basting often with a sauce made by combining all of the remaining ingredients. Serves 6.

Spicy Ham Steak

¼ cup melted butter
1 cup sherry
1 cup pineapple juice
2 teaspoons ground cloves
¼ cup dry mustard
¼ cup firmly packed brown sugar
2 teaspoons paprika
1½ cloves garlic, minced
1 center-cut slice ham, 1 inch thick

Combine all ingredients except ham and mix well. Slash edges of ham and marinate in sherry and pine-apple mixture for 3 hours; turn several times. Grill over low to medium coals for 20 minutes, basting frequently with marinade and turning occasionally. Carve ham into individual portions and serve hot. Makes 4 to 6 servings.

Celestial Shrimp

2 pounds uncooked jumbo prawns
½ cup each soy, salad oil, and sherry
1 tablespoon minced green or crystal-lized ginger

Slit backs of prawns with a pair of pointed scissors, then wash out the sand veins. Marinate them for 2 hours in a mixture of the soy, salad oil, sherry, and ginger. Drain, put in a fine-meshed hinged broiler, and cook over coals for 3 minutes; turn and cook 2 or 3 more minutes, or until the shells are pinkly browned. Serve immediately to 6 people.

Grilled Fish with Herbs

This method of cooking fish is popular in Provence.

Use any whole firm-fleshed fish. Clean, remove head if you wish, and make a few diagonal incisions in both sides. Brush with olive oil and sprinkle with salt and pepper. Lay a few branches of fennel across the fish on both sides, and fasten in a greased hinged broiler. (If you don't have fennel, use thyme, or bay leaves, or dill, preferably branches, though the crushed herbs may be sprinkled on.) Grill the fish on both sides, sprinkling a few times with a little more oil. When it's cooked, arrange it on a fireproof platter, and put a few heaps of dried herbs around it, douse with brandy, and light. When the flames die down, serve with lemon wedges and Rémoulade Sauce (page 125).

Western Trout Barbecue

⅔ cup butter
1 cup tomato juice
1 cup dry white table wine
¼ cup (4 tablespoons) cider vinegar
2 tablespoons brown sugar
1½ teaspoons salt
1 teaspoon each Worcestershire, paprika, and chili powder
¼ teaspoon pepper
1 clove garlic, mashed or minced
1 small onion, minced
Small trout or larger trout cut in 3-inch pieces

Combine all the ingredients for the sauce and simmer for 10 minutes. When ready to cook trout, skewer cleaned fish on long-handled forks, dip in sauce, and roast over low coals for 10 to 15 minutes. Dip fish in sauce often to keep it moist.

Swordfish Barbecue

½ cup soy
¼ cup catsup
¼ cup chopped parsley
½ cup orange juice
2 cloves garlic, mashed
2 tablespoons lemon juice
1 teaspoon pepper
1½ to 2 pounds swordfish, 1 inch thick

Combine in a small bowl soy, catsup, parsley, orange juice, garlic, lemon juice, and pepper. Mix well. Marinate swordfish in this mixture for 1 hour. Grill about 4 inches above hot coals for about 8 minutes. Turn fish (use kitchen tongs to prevent breakage) and grill 7 minutes on other side. Brush with marinade frequently during broiling. Serves 4.

Squab or Chicken Barbecue

6 squabs or 3 broilers
1 cup (½ pound) butter
3 cloves garlic, sliced
1 teaspoon monosodium glutamate
2 tablespoons minced parsley
Salt, pepper, paprika
1 tablespoon Worcestershire
4-inch sprig rosemary or 1 teaspoon dried rosemary

Split squab down the back and flatten, or cut broilers in half.

Melt butter, add garlic, heat until browned; remove garlic. Add monosodium glutamate and parsley and simmer a few minutes.

Add salt, pepper, and paprika to taste, Worcestershire, and rosemary. Pour over split squabs or broilers and let stand at least 1 hour before barbecuing, turning once. Do not refrigerate. Broil squab or chicken over coals, using the sauce left in the pan to baste the squab or chicken as it grills. Serves 6.

Barbecued Chicken

3 to 3½ -pound frying or roasting
   chicken (or equivalent quantity
   of chicken parts)
1 medium sized onion, chopped
2 tablespoons oil or shortening
2 tablespoons vinegar
2 tablespoons brown sugar
¼ cup lemon juice
1 can (8 oz.) tomato hot sauce
3 tablespoons Worcestershire
1½ teaspoons prepared mustard
1 cup water
   Celery salt, salt, and pepper to taste

Cut chicken into serving size pieces. Brown onion in oil; then add remaining ingredients and simmer for 30 minutes. After marinade has cooked, pour over chicken and marinate overnight. Build charcoal fire in barbecue, then push coals to each end and put chicken on the middle of the grill — not directly over coals. Cook chicken slowly for 2 to 2½ hours. You don't have to watch it too closely, but you should turn it several times, brushing frequently with the remainder of the marinade. Serves 4 to 6.

Broiled Turkey Steaks

Buy a large, hard-frozen, eviscerated tom turkey — the bigger the better. Have your meat man cut it on his power saw into 1-inch transverse slices, starting at the front of the breastbone, and working back to about where the thighs join the body. If you're serving a large number of people, have him cut more slices — one slice will make two good servings. The two ends that are left can be kept frozen until you need them.

Now lay frozen slices out in a large flat pan (you can stack them) and drizzle on enough cooking oil to coat each one. As the slices thaw, the oil and juices will make a fine marinade in the pan. This should be brushed back over the slices from time to time. It is best to let the slices thaw and marinate 6 to 8 hours or overnight. When they are completely thawed, divide each slice into two steaks with a sharp, heavy knife. (You'll find that the cross-sections of breast and backbone will split easily.)

Have a good, hot bed of coals going in the barbecue. Arrange steaks in toasting racks, brush with basting sauce (¼ pound butter, ½ cup dry white wine, salt, and pepper). Broil about 8 inches from the fire for around 10 minutes on each side. Turn them a couple of times during the cooking, and brush with more butter-wine mixture. Don't let steaks dry out.

Serve them up, one to a person, with remainder of the basting sauce heated and spooned over each serving.

Broiled Baby Turkey

Split turkey, broil over medium coals for 45 to 60 minutes, depending on size. Baste regularly with a sauce made of ½ cup butter, 1 tablespoon curry powder, and ½ cup apple cider.

Spit-Barbecued Duckling

4 to 5-pound duckling
½ cup orange juice
¼ cup soy
1 teaspoon honey
½ teaspoon monosodium glutamate
⅛ teaspoon pepper

Truss duckling compactly and spit it from just in front of the tail (through the bone), diagonally to a point near the apex of the wishbone (again through the bone). Spit-roast the duckling 1½ to 2 hours over a medium to low barbecue fire. Baste frequently with sauce made by combining orange juice, soy, honey, monosodium glutamate, and pepper; heat sauce on the side of the grill and brush it warm on the bird. Using poultry shears, cut duckling into quarters to serve. Serves 4.

Broiled Wild Mallard Duck

1 mallard duck (2 to 3½ pounds)
1 cup prepared French dressing
1 teaspoon dry mustard
2 teaspoons Worcestershire
2 teaspoons grated orange peel
1 teaspoon grated lemon peel

Split duck up backbone with poultry shears. Place breast side down on meat cutting board and break down breast bones by pressing with another board or by pounding gently with a meat tenderizing mallet. Mix the sauce ingredients together and use it to baste the duck liberally. Insert the duck in a hinged wire grill and broil over hot coals until done to taste (about 10 to 15 minutes each side, according to taste), basting it at least once more while cooking. Divide duck at breastbone into two portions and serve. Serves 2.

Barbecued Duck

2 or 3 young ducks, quartered
1 cup sherry
⅓ cup honey or brown sugar
1 tablespoon soy
1 teaspoon grated fresh ginger (or powdered)
1 teaspoon dry mustard
Sesame seeds

Select lean, meaty young ducks. Trim off all excess fat possible. Pour marinade made of sherry, honey, soy, ginger, and mustard over the quartered duck and let stand several hours, or overnight, in refrigerator. Place on grill over bed of coals and barbecue until done, about 10 to 15 minutes on each side, according to taste.

Baste duck with remaining marinade during cooking. Sprinkle with sesame seeds before serving to 4 to 6 persons.

Charcoal Broiled Rabbit

1 cup salad oil
1 tablespoon celery seed
1 teaspoon paprika
2 teaspoons fresh thyme or ½ teaspoon dried thyme
½ teaspoon each salt and garlic salt
2 tablespoons lemon juice
1 young rabbit (2 to 2½ lbs.), cut in serving-size pieces

Mix together salad oil, celery seed, paprika, thyme, salt, garlic salt, and lemon juice. Pour over rabbit pieces and allow to marinate at least 1 hour. Slowly broil meat over charcoal about 30 minutes, or until tender. Turn frequently and baste often with remaining marinade. Serves 4.

Broiled Venison Steaks

For those who prefer venison rare, this is venison at its best. Have steaks cut thick — never less than 1 inch, preferably 1½ inches. Rub with garlic, if you wish; brush with olive oil or butter, and broil over hot coals 8 to 14 minutes, depending on the thickness of the steak and rareness desired. If steaks have been cut thinner than 1 inch, pan-broil them, searing them quickly on both sides in a heavy, very hot frying pan or griddle.

Barbecued Venison Chops

A flavorful butter and a spicy basting sauce lend their goodness to venison.

1 tablespoon dry mustard
1 tablespoon grated onion
2 tablespoons minced parsley
½ cup (¼ pound) butter, soft but not melted
6 venison chops, cut 1 inch thick
½ cup lemon juice
½ cup chili sauce
1 teaspoon salt

Blend mustard, onion, parsley, and butter thoroughly. Shape into a small roll and chill until firm. Barbecue chops on a grill about 12 inches above glowing coals. Brush chops frequently with mixture of lemon juice, chili sauce, and salt; turn only once. Cook until done to your taste — 8 to 14 minutes for rare. Remove to heated platter and place a slice of spiced butter roll on each chop. Garnish with fresh herbs. Serves 6.

Grains & Pastes

THIS FOOD CATEGORY offers two kinds of dishes: the grains and pastes that are prepared as an accompaniment to meat, and those that are prepared to perform as the main dish.

Most of the rice dishes and a few of the pastes fall into the first category. A stock-enriched pilaff, garlic-buttered noodles, and steamed, toasted, or fried rice, are supporting dishes to meats, and are seasoned with the meats in mind. They often provide the appealing casserole dish to round out a menu — and they are special favorites to serve as accompaniments to meats, poultry, or game from the barbecue.

In the second group sauces take on a highly important role. The size and shape of the *pasta* determines the type of sauce that goes with it. In general, large macaroni demands a robust gravy; tender strands ("long goods") are complimented by a delicate sauce. Hence, you will find the wide lasagne in our Lasagne Napoli not at all overwhelmed by beef, mushrooms, tomato sauce, spinach, and three kinds of cheese; and in Bavette with Green Sauce you will find the lacelike bavette keeping an easy balance with herb-flavored oil and cheese.

In this chapter of cooking, the foreign touch is again felt strongly. Rice in canna leaves shows Hawaiian influence; green rice and Nasi Goreng have Far Eastern overtones; and the paste dishes certainly cannot be separated from Italian cooking.

Orange Rice

Designed to flatter ham or poultry — rich with the sweet sharpness of orange.

3 tablespoons butter
⅔ cup sliced celery
2 tablespoons chopped onion
1½ cups water
2 tablespoons grated orange peel
1 cup orange juice
1¼ teaspoons salt
1 cup uncooked rice

Melt butter in a heavy saucepan with a cover; add celery and onion; and cook, stirring occasionally, until tender and light brown. Stir in water, orange peel and juice, and salt; then bring to a boil. Add rice, cover, and steam over low heat for 20 to 25 minutes, or until rice is tender. Serves 6.

Wild Rice with Mushrooms

1 cup uncooked wild rice, well washed
1 teaspoon salt
Water
½ pound fresh mushrooms, sliced
2 tablespoons butter
4 strips bacon, finely chopped
2 cups finely sliced celery
2 medium sized onions, chopped
1 large green pepper, chopped
5 tablespoons olive oil
½ cup tomato juice

Cook rice until tender (about 20 minutes) in enough boiling salted water to cover. Drain thoroughly. Turn into a greased 2-quart casserole. Meanwhile, sauté mushrooms in butter. In another pan, fry chopped bacon until crisp; add celery, onions, and green pepper; sauté until vegetables are limp. Stir mushrooms, the bacon-vegetable mixture, olive oil, and tomato juice into cooked wild rice. Bake in a moderate oven (350°) until liquid is absorbed, about 30 minutes. Serves 8 to 10.

Nasi Goreng

3 cups uncooked rice
6 cups water
3 teaspoons salt
1 cup (½ pound) butter
½ teaspoon very finely minced dry red chili peppers
¾ cup finely chopped salted peanuts
½ cup finely chopped onions
1½ cups cubed cooked ham or 1 can (12 oz.) luncheon meat cut in ½-inch cubes
1 pound medium sized prawns (20 to 25 count), cooked, shelled, and cleaned
Salt to taste

Cook rice in boiling salted water until tender but not mushy. Melt butter in a small saucepan and stir in chili peppers (they should be almost powdery). Add peanuts and onions and cook slowly for 5 minutes. Pour over the rice and add the cubed meat and prawns. Toss together carefully with 2 forks. Taste for seasoning. Set aside to season and blend flavors. Place over low heat just before serving time; toss occasionally to prevent scorching. Serves 8.

Green Rice in Canna Leaves

The flavors of curry, onion, and parsley steam into rice within tight leaf-packets.

1 cup uncooked rice
3 tablespoons chopped green onions
⅛ teaspoon curry powder (more, if desired)
3 tablespoons butter
⅓ cup toasted slivered almonds
1 teaspoon salt
⅓ cup finely chopped parsley
1 pimiento, chopped (optional)
12 to 14 medium sized canna leaves
¼ cup water

Cook rice according to directions on package just until tender; drain. Slowly cook onions with curry in butter about 5 minutes. Combine with rice and add almonds, salt, parsley, and pimiento. Spoon rice mixture, hot or cold, into each leaf. Fold, using envelope wrap, and place in a baking pan (packets may be stacked). Pour water in bottom of pan. Cover and bake in a hot oven (400°) for 25 minutes. Makes 5 to 6 servings.

Golden Toasted Rice

This gives the rice a pleasant nuttiness.

1 cup uncooked rice
2 tablespoons butter
1 can (11 oz.) consommé
½ cup hot water
3 or 4 green onions
1 to 3 tablespoons soy

Toast the rice by spreading the grains in a heavy pan and heating in a moderate oven (350°) until lightly browned.

Melt butter in a heavy pan with a tight fitting cover; add rice and cook it slightly, stirring constantly. Pour in hot consommé and water, stir once, cover, and turn heat to the lowest possible point. Let rice steam for 25 minutes, or turn into a casserole, cover, and bake in a moderate oven (350°) for 30 minutes.

Stir in finely sliced green onions and tops and soy. Remove from heat, put on the cover again, and let stand a few minutes to blend the flavors and partially cook the onion. Serves 4.

Oriental Rice

3 tablespoons butter
⅛ teaspoon curry powder
3 cups cooked rice
⅓ cup finely chopped parsley
1 teaspoon salt
¼ cup finely chopped peanuts or toasted almonds

Melt butter, add curry powder, and blend. Combine with rice. Season with parsley, salt, and chopped peanuts. Place in casserole or baking pan. Heat in a moderate oven (350°) for 20 to 25 minutes. Serves 6.

Sour Cream Pilaff

3 cups chicken stock or 3 tablespoons chicken stock base dissolved in 3 cups hot water
1 tablespoon lemon juice
1½ teaspoons salt
¼ teaspoon pepper
½ bay leaf
½ cup (¼ pound) butter
1½ cups uncooked rice
1 can (3 or 4 oz.) mushroom slices, or stems and pieces, drained
½ pint (1 cup) commercial sour cream
Chopped chives or parsley

Place chicken stock, lemon juice, salt, pepper, bay leaf, and ¼ cup of the butter in the top of a double boiler; heat over direct heat until stock starts to simmer. Add rice, cover, then cook over boiling water for 35 minutes, or until rice is tender and all of the liquid is absorbed. Remove bay leaf; stir in the remaining ¼ cup butter, well drained mushrooms, and sour cream. Heat through. Sprinkle with chopped chives or parsley for a more colorful dish. Serves 6.

Macaroni with Ricotta Cheese

1 pound macaroni
Boiling salted water
¼ cup melted butter
1 pound Ricotta cheese
½ cup milk
½ teaspoon salt
¼ cup grated Parmesan cheese

Cook macaroni until barely tender. Drain and mix with melted butter. Blend the Ricotta cheese with milk and salt. Mix with the macaroni, cover, and cook very slowly for 5 minutes. Serve from a heated bowl, and sprinkle with the Parmesan cheese. Serves 6 to 8.

Barley Pilaff

½ cup (¼ pound) butter
1¾ cups pearl barley
2 medium sized onions, chopped
2 medium cans (4 oz. each) sliced or button mushrooms
1 cup mushroom liquor and water
4 cups chicken stock or 6 chicken bouillon cubes dissolved in 4 cups boiling water
½ cup toasted slivered almonds (optional)

Melt half the butter in a heavy frying pan. Pour in the barley and cook slowly until it turns a golden brown, turning it frequently; spoon into large buttered casserole. Put 2 tablespoons more of the butter into the frying pan; add chopped onions and sauté until clear; add to the barley. Melt the remaining 2 tablespoons butter; add drained mushrooms (reserving liquid) and sauté for 5 minutes; add to barley and onion.

Add enough water to reserved mushroom liquor to make 1 cup liquid and combine with the chicken stock. Pour 2 cups of the liquid over the barley. Cover tightly and bake 45 minutes in a moderate oven (350°); add 2 more cups of liquid and stir; bake, covered, another 45 minutes. Stir in remaining cup of liquid and bake, covered, 30 minutes longer. You might add ½ cup of toasted slivered almonds when you stir in the last cup of liquid. Serves 8 to 10.

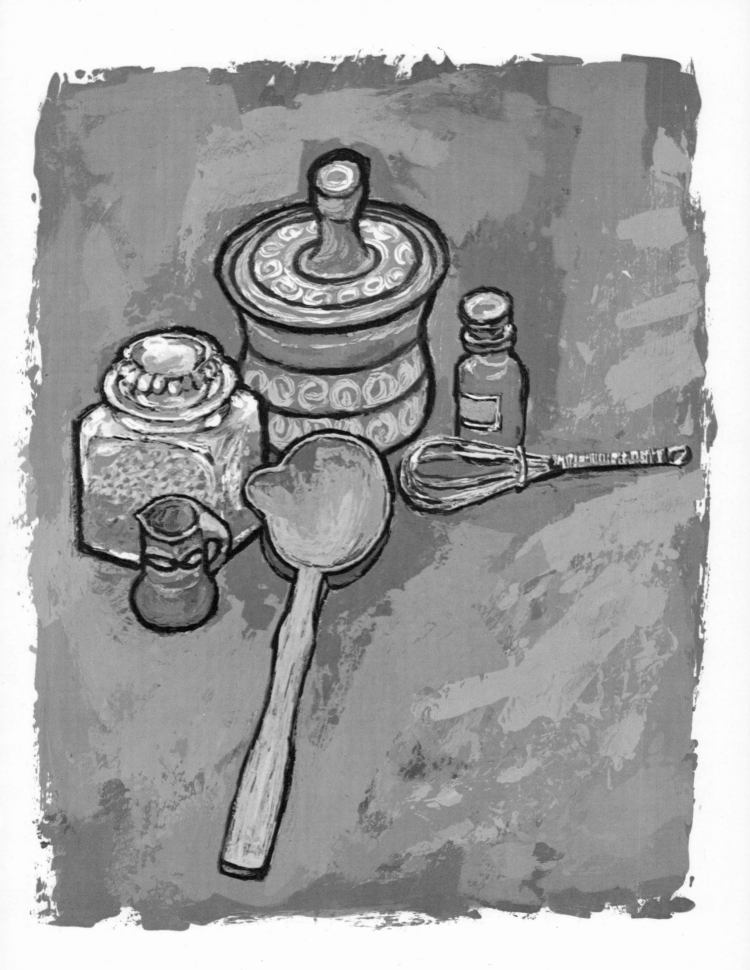

Swiss Fried Noodles

1 package (8 oz.) egg noodles
Boiling salted water
5 tablespoons butter
¼ cup grated Sap Sago cheese

Cook noodles in boiling salted water until tender; drain. Melt 2 tablespoons of the butter in a frying pan. Spread noodles evenly in pan and brown on one side. Turn upside down onto a plate. Melt the remaining butter and return noodles to brown the other side. With a spatula slide noodles onto a chop plate and sprinkle with cheese. Cut in wedges to serve. Serves 8.

Noodles Romanoff

1 package (8 oz.) egg noodles
Boiling salted water
1½ cups large curd cottage cheese
1 clove garlic, minced or mashed
1 teaspoon Worcestershire
½ pint (1 cup) commercial sour cream
3 green onions, finely chopped
¼ teaspoon Tabasco
½ cup grated Parmesan cheese

Cook noodles in boiling salted water until tender; drain. Combine cooked noodles, cottage cheese, garlic, Worcestershire, sour cream, green onions, and Tabasco. Turn into a buttered casserole; sprinkle grated cheese over the top. Bake in a moderate oven (350°) for 25 minutes. Serves 8.

Noodles Alfredo

1 pound narrow noodles or fettucini
Boiling salted water
½ cup (¼ pound) butter
⅓ cup grated Parmesan cheese
⅓ cup grated Swiss cheese
½ cup hot heavy cream

Cook the noodles in boiling salted water until barely tender. Drain and dress immediately with the butter, which has been melted and is still very hot, and the Parmesan and Swiss cheeses. Mix with a fork and spoon, lifting the noodles high so that the steam will escape. When each noodle is well coated with cheese, pour heated cream over the noodles, mix lightly, and serve at once to 6 persons.

Bavette with Green Sauce

1 large clove garlic
1½ teaspoons salt
1 cup fresh basil
¾ cup fresh parsley
¾ cup olive oil
1 cup grated Jack cheese
½ pound bavette or vermicelli
Boiling salted water

Mash garlic with salt. Gradually add basil and parsley and crush to a paste, pouring in olive oil as you crush. Blend in cheese. (All the mashing can be done in a blender.) Cook bavette in boiling salted water until tender; drain. Mix sauce with hot bavette. Serves 4.

Polenta

Coarsely ground cornmeal, simmered to a mush called *polenta,* takes the place of pasta in those parts of Italy which grow no wheat.

1½ cups cornmeal
4 cups water
1 teaspoon salt
Grated Parmesan cheese
Butter

Cook cornmeal in water, seasoned with salt, until thick, about 20 minutes. Stir often to prevent lumps. Remove from heat and allow to cool. Grease a shallow baking dish well and sprinkle with grated cheese. Drop the polenta by the spoonful into the dish. Dot each mound of polenta with butter and sprinkle with grated cheese. Heat in a moderately hot oven (375°) for 15 minutes before serving. (If desired, stir Parmesan cheese into hot polenta and serve without reheating in oven.) Serves 6.

Bucati with Anchovy Sauce

This sauce was created to use on *bucati,* a pasta that is larger than the thread-like *bavette,* but smaller than spaghetti. You could use either vermicelli or spaghetti.

½ cup (¼ pound) butter
1 clove garlic, minced or mashed
1 small tin (2 oz.) anchovies, chopped
½ pound bucati
½ cup grated Parmesan cheese

Melt butter in frying pan. Add garlic and anchovies. Fry over very low heat, stirring frequently, until the anchovies have almost disintegrated. Cook bucati in boiling water (no salt!). Then pour the sauce over and sprinkle with grated cheese. Serves 4.

Macaroni Oyster Loaf

1 cup uncooked elbow macaroni
Boiling salted water
1½ cups milk
1 cup (¼ pound) shredded Cheddar cheese
1 cup soft bread crumbs
¼ cup (4 tablespoons) butter
2 tablespoons each minced chives, parsley, and green pepper
1 teaspoon each lemon juice and Worcestershire
½ teaspoon each salt and dry mustard
⅛ teaspoon each black pepper and nutmeg
3 eggs, well beaten
1 jar (12 oz.) fresh small Pacific oysters (about 10 to 12 oysters)
Watercress for garnish

Cook macaroni in boiling salted water until tender; drain. Heat milk and cheese until cheese melts; add crumbs, butter, chives, parsley, green pepper, lemon juice, Worcestershire, salt, dry mustard, pepper, and nutmeg. Stir in beaten eggs and drained macaroni.

Turn half of mixture into a 9 by 5-inch buttered loaf pan and cover with oysters; top with the remaining macaroni mixture. Bake in a moderately slow oven (325°) for 50 minutes, or until set and golden brown. Unmold on a hot platter and garnish with sprigs of watercress. Serves 6.

Macaroni Loaf

2 cups cooked macaroni (approximately 1 cup uncooked)
1 can (4 oz.) pimiento
1 green pepper
2 cups milk
2 cups soft bread crumbs, well packed
2 cups grated Cheddar cheese
4 eggs
½ teaspoon salt
¼ cup (4 tablespoons) melted butter
1 can (3 oz.) chopped mushrooms

After cooking the macaroni in boiling salted water, drain and cool before running through the fine blade of your food grinder. Put the drained pimiento and seeded green pepper through the grinder also.

Mix together milk, bread crumbs, cheese, slightly beaten eggs, salt, melted butter, and drained mushrooms. Add ground macaroni, pimiento, and green pepper. Turn into a well buttered 9 by 5 by 3-inch loaf pan. Bake in a moderate oven (350°) for 50 to 60 minutes, or until set. Turn out of pan and cut into 6 to 8 slices.

Bowknots with Sour Cream Sauce

¼ cup (4 tablespoons) butter
1 large onion, chopped
½ pound fresh mushrooms, sliced
1 cup commercial sour cream
1½ teaspoons paprika
1 teaspoon salt
⅛ teaspoon pepper
½ pound macaroni bowknots
Boiling salted water

Melt butter in frying pan, add onion, and fry until browned. Remove onion. Sauté mushrooms in the same butter until tender. Stir in sour cream, onions, paprika, salt, and pepper, and bring just to the boiling point. Cook bowknots in boiling salted water. Pour sauce over bowknots. Serves 4 to 6.

Lasagne Napoli

1 medium onion, finely chopped
1 clove garlic, minced or mashed
2 tablespoons olive oil or salad oil
1 pound ground chuck
1 can (3 or 4 oz.) sliced mushrooms
1 can (8 oz.) tomato sauce
1 can (6 oz.) tomato paste
2 teaspoons salt
1 teaspoon oregano
¾ cup water
2 eggs
1 package (10 oz.) frozen chopped spinach, thawed
1 cup cream style cottage cheese
⅓ cup grated Parmesan cheese
1 package (12 oz.) lasagne, cooked in boiling salted water and drained
1 package (8 oz.) American cheese slices, cut in strips

In a medium-size frying pan lightly brown onion and garlic in 1 tablespoon of the oil; add ground chuck, and break apart; cook until brown. Blend in mushrooms (including mushroom liquid), tomato sauce, tomato paste, 1 teaspoon of the salt, oregano, and water; simmer 15 minutes. Meanwhile, mix 1 of the eggs with the spinach, cottage cheese, Parmesan cheese, remaining 1 tablespoon oil, and 1 teaspoon salt. Beat the second egg slightly and toss with cooked lasagne. Pour half the meat sauce in an oblong baking pan (about 9 by 13 inches) and cover with a layer of half the lasagne. Spread all the spinach mixture over lasagne. Complete layers with remaining lasagne and meat sauce. Cover and bake in a moderate oven (350°) for 45 minutes. Remove cover and arrange strips of American cheese on top; bake 15 minutes longer. Serve hot. Makes 6 to 8 servings.

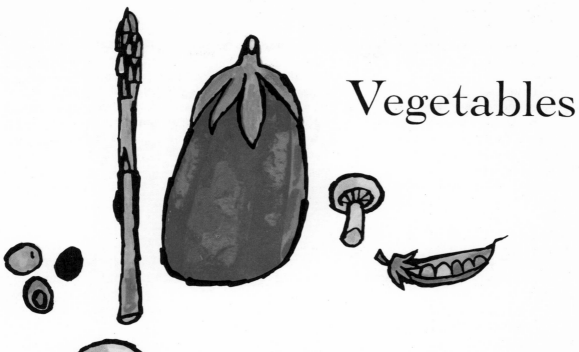

Vegetables

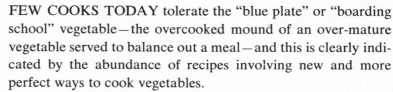

FEW COOKS TODAY tolerate the "blue plate" or "boarding school" vegetable—the overcooked mound of an over-mature vegetable served to balance out a meal—and this is clearly indicated by the abundance of recipes involving new and more perfect ways to cook vegetables.

Each year, vegetables seem to earn more and more respectful treatment. They are bathed in butter, they are cooked with herbs, they are simmered in wine, they are topped with sauces of all kinds. Everything from the humble onion to the delicate mushroom finds its way—successfully—into a pie.

Perhaps the biggest break-through in vegetable cookery has come through the widespread appreciation for the Oriental way: the near-waterless cooking that takes asparagus, cauliflower, cabbage, to the just-tender-crisp stage. The frozen food industry, too, has done much to raise our expectations of the vegetable dish; eating peas in December, or green beans in March, we are no longer in the least surprised to find peak-of-the-season flavor.

Most of all, however, vegetables owe their ever-increasing place in the sun to the hundreds of cooks who see them for what they are: a challengingly rich crop of textures and flavors and colors. To such a cook, no vegetable is a standby. Peas and corn, artichokes and eggplant—each is worthy of careful cooking, a thoughtful blending of seasonings, special menu companions.

Artichoke Barigoule

The wine-flavored cooking sauce simmers down to become a dipping sauce.

6 artichokes
6 tablespoons olive oil
1 onion, chopped
2 cloves garlic, minced
1 carrot, chopped
1 tablespoon minced parsley
½ teaspoon rosemary
1 cup dry white table wine

Trim artichokes. Place in saucepan with olive oil, onion, garlic, carrot, parsley, and rosemary. Cover and cook, shaking pan a few times, until onion is golden. Add wine; cover and cook until artichokes are tender, about 40 minutes. Serve with sauce in pan. Serves 6.

Artichoke Pie

Pastry for 2-crust pie
2 packages frozen artichoke hearts
¼ cup minced onion
2 teaspoons minced parsley
5 tablespoons butter
2 tablespoons flour
1 cup (½ pint) light cream
1 tablespoon tarragon vinegar

Prepare a 2-crust pastry. Cook artichoke hearts according to directions on the package. Line an 8-inch pie pan with half of the pastry. Trim pastry and seal edge to rim of the pan. Add the drained artichoke hearts; sprinkle with onion and parsley. Dot with 3 tablespoons of the butter, top with crust (rolled thicker than usual so it won't break), and cut to fit top of the pie. Lightly press top crust to rim of bottom crust, but *do not seal edges*. Bake in a hot oven (425°) for 10 minutes; reduce heat to moderate (350°) and continue cooking 20 to 25 minutes longer, or until crust is brown.

Just before time to serve pie, melt the other 2 tablespoons of butter and blend in flour and cream; cook until thick, stirring constantly. Then stir in the vinegar, drop by drop. Lift upper crust carefully and pour sauce over the artichoke hearts. Replace top and serve at once. Makes 6 servings.

Artichoke Hearts in Wine

12 small artichokes
½ cup olive oil or salad oil
½ cup dry white table wine
2 cloves garlic, minced or mashed
½ teaspoon salt
Dash of pepper

Cut slice off top of each artichoke, then cook in boiling salted water for 25 minutes, or until almost tender; drain. Pull off all tough outer leaves, and cut off the stem so that only the hearts of the artichokes remain. Cut hearts in half lengthwise and scrape out choke.

Combine olive oil and wine in a heavy saucepan with a tight fitting cover. Add garlic, salt, pepper, and the artichoke hearts. Cover and simmer, turning occasionally, for 30 minutes or until artichokes are thoroughly done. Serves 4.

Cheese-Stuffed Artichokes

Cut off stem and 1½ to 2 inches of artichoke top, pull off the tough outer leaves; hold artichoke under fast running cold water so leaves will loosen, spread apart.

Using fingers, force leaves apart. Scrape out fuzzy choke. Stuff Cheddar or American cheese between leaves and in center of artichoke (cut cheese in ½-inch squares ¼ inch thick). Place on rack, steam 40 minutes, or until tender.

Creamed Asparagus, Parmesan

If you prefer not to bake this, stir the Parmesan into the cream sauce and pass the sauce as an accompaniment.

2½ pounds fresh asparagus
¼ cup (4 tablespoons) butter
2 to 3 tablespoons chopped green onions
¼ teaspoon curry powder
½ teaspoon salt
⅓ cup flour
2 cups milk (or use 1⅔ cups milk with ⅓ cup dry white table wine)
⅓ cup grated Parmesan cheese

Wash, trim, and cut the asparagus into diagonal slices (about ⅔ inch long). Cook in boiling, salted water until tender-crisp. Meanwhile melt butter; add onions, curry, and salt; and cook for a few minutes. Stir in flour. Slowly add the milk, and cook and stir until mixture boils and thickens. Add the drained cooked asparagus. Turn into a shallow baking dish or into individual baking dishes. Sprinkle with the cheese and bake in a hot oven (400°) for 15 to 20 minutes. Makes 5 or 6 servings.

Asparagus Chinese Style

2 pounds fresh asparagus
¾ cup chicken stock
1 tablespoon cornstarch
1 tablespoon cold water
2 tablespoons soy
1 clove garlic, minced or mashed
Salt and pepper to taste
2 tablespoons olive oil or salad oil

Wash asparagus well and snap off lower stalks. Cut diagonally in very thin slices. Heat chicken stock to boiling and stir in a mixture of the cornstarch, water, and soy; stirring constantly, cook until thickened. Add garlic and salt and pepper to taste. Sauté sliced asparagus in hot oil for 2 minutes. Pour over sauce and stirring constantly, cook 1 minute longer. Serve at once. Serves 6.

Asparagus with Crumb Sauce

½ cup (¼ pound) butter
1 cup fine dry bread crumbs
1 teaspoon finely chopped onion
1 teaspoon salt
¼ teaspoon pepper
½ teaspoon dry mustard
2 hard cooked eggs, finely chopped
2 pounds cooked asparagus spears

Melt butter in a heavy frying pan; stir in crumbs and onion and cook over low heat until crumbs are golden brown. Add salt, pepper, and dry mustard. Just before serving, stir in chopped eggs. Serve hot over hot cooked asparagus. Makes 6 servings.

Asparagus with Baked Eggs

1 pound asparagus
3 tablespoons salad oil or olive oil
4 tablespoons finely chopped green onions and tops
1 cup water
1 teaspoon salt
¼ teaspoon pepper
6 eggs
½ cup grated Parmesan cheese
1 tablespoon finely chopped parsley

Wash asparagus; dry with paper toweling; cut in 1-inch pieces. Heat oil in a large frying pan; sauté asparagus and onions in oil until asparagus is limp and onions are clear. Pour in water; add salt and pepper; cover pan and simmer for 10 minutes. Remove cover; break eggs into a saucer, one at a time, then slide out over the top of asparagus, being careful not to break the yolks. Sprinkle grated cheese and parsley over eggs.

Bake, uncovered, in a moderately hot oven (375°) for 10 minutes, or until eggs are as set as you wish. Serves 6.

Herb Green Beans

Here an herb butter brings rich flavor overtones to fresh green beans.

1 pound fresh green beans
Boiling water
¼ cup (4 tablespoons) butter
½ cup minced onion
½ clove garlic, minced
¼ cup minced celery
½ cup minced parsley
1 teaspoon fresh rosemary or ¼ teaspoon of the dried herb
1 teaspoon fresh basil or ¼ teaspoon of the dried herb
¾ teaspoon salt

Snip ends from beans, then cut them diagonally into 2-inch pieces. Cook in about 1 inch of boiling water in a covered pan for 15 to 20 minutes, or just until tender. Meanwhile melt butter in a small pan; add onion, garlic, and celery and cook about 5 minutes. Add parsley, rosemary, basil, and salt; cover and simmer for 10 minutes. Just before serving, toss the herb-flavored butter with the drained beans. Serves 4.

Deviled Green Beans

Try this flavorful side dish with barbecued or roasted meat.

1 medium sized onion, chopped
1 clove garlic, minced
½ green pepper, chopped
2 canned pimientos, sliced or chopped
3 tablespoons butter
2 teaspoons prepared mustard
1 can (8 oz.) tomato sauce
1 cup (¼ lb.) shredded Cheddar cheese
1 package (10 oz.) frozen cut green beans

Sauté onion, garlic, green pepper, and pimientos in butter until onions are limp. Stir in mustard, tomato sauce, and cheese. Cook frozen beans in a small amount of salted water until just tender. Combine beans and sauce; turn into a greased 1-quart casserole. Bake in a moderate oven (350°) for 25 minutes, or until cheese is melted. Serves 4.

Green Beans Béchamel

This is rich. Serve it with the plainest of meats.

2 pounds green beans
2 cups Béchamel sauce
½ cup slivered almonds
½ cup freshly grated Parmesan cheese
½ cup cracker crumbs
¼ cup melted butter

Lightly cook the beans, either whole or cut French style; drain, and arrange in a flat, well buttered baking dish.

Make Béchamel sauce, following recipe on page 120. Cover beans with sauce and sprinkle with the slivered almonds. Over this, strew a mixture of the cheese, cracker crumbs, and melted butter. Put under the broiler until crumbs are nicely browned. Serves 8.

Lima Beans with Apples

1 pound (2½ cups) dried lima beans
2 quarts (8 cups) water
1 teaspoon salt
2 large onions, sliced
3 tablespoons bacon drippings or salad oil
¼ teaspoon turmeric
½ teaspoon allspice
¼ teaspoon pepper
1 teaspoon salt
2 tart apples, peeled, cored, and chopped

Wash beans; place in a heavy kettle with the water; cover, bring to a boil, and simmer for 2 minutes. Remove from heat and let soak 1 hour. Add salt, bring to a boil, and simmer for 1 hour. In a heavy frying pan, sauté the onions in the bacon drippings until golden brown. Add the turmeric, allspice, pepper, salt, and apples. Stirring, continue cooking until apples are barely tender. Stir in 1 cup of the bean liquid and the drained beans and continue cooking for 10 minutes. Serves 10 to 12.

Limas and Mushrooms in Cream

1 package (10 oz.) frozen lima beans, or 2 cups shelled fresh green lima beans
½ pound sliced fresh mushrooms, or 2 cans (4 oz. each) sliced mushrooms, drained
1 tablespoon butter
⅓ cup light cream
Salt and pepper to taste

Cook lima beans until tender; drain. Lightly brown mushrooms in butter. Combine lima beans and mushrooms in casserole; add cream, salt, and pepper. Cover and heat in moderate oven (350°) until heated through, about 15 minutes. Serves 4.

Chinese Stirred Broccoli

1 bunch broccoli (1½ pounds)
1 large clove garlic, mashed or minced
1 tablespoon minced candied or preserved ginger or 1½ teaspoons minced green ginger
1 tablespoon peanut oil
4 tablespoons water
¼ teaspoon monosodium glutamate
1 tablespoon soy

Separate broccoli tops from stems; save stems to use another time. Divide tops into small flowerets. In a large frying pan, sauté garlic and ginger in the oil until lightly browned. Add broccoli tops; stir and toss, then add water, monosodium glutamate, and soy. Cover and steam for 5 to 7 minutes, or until broccoli is just barely tender. Serve at once. Serves 4.

Sun-Gold Sprouts and Onions

4 cups water
2 teaspoons salt
2 teaspoons sugar
1 pound small white boiling onions
1 pound Brussels sprouts, washed and trimmed
1 medium sized carrot, thinly sliced
2 tablespoons butter
Freshly ground pepper

Season water with salt and sugar, add onions and simmer for 15 minutes; drop in sprouts and carrot and continue cooking for 10 minutes, or until sprouts are tender. Drain, add butter, and sprinkle with freshly ground pepper. Serves 6.

Creamy Cabbage

6 cups shredded cabbage
¼ cup chopped green onions
½ cup water
⅛ teaspoon salt
1 small package (3 oz.) cream cheese
½ teaspoon celery seed
1 to 2 tablespoons butter

Cook the cabbage with onion, water, and salt until it is tender-crisp, about 7 minutes; drain. Cube the cream cheese and add to the cabbage with celery seed and butter. Toss lightly. Makes about 4 servings.

Red Cabbage Supreme

1 head red cabbage, 3 to 4 pounds
2 tablespoons bacon drippings or
   butter
1 large onion, sliced
2 tart apples, peeled and sliced
2 tablespoons vinegar
1 cup water
3 tablespoons dry white table wine
½ to 1 teaspoon sugar
1 teaspoon salt

Wash cabbage and discard the outer leaves. Slice the whole head into thin shreds. In a large pan, heat the bacon drippings or butter. Add the cabbage, onion, apples, vinegar, water, and 2 tablespoons of the wine. Cover and cook over low heat until tender but still slightly crisp, about 30 minutes. Just before you remove the vegetable from the heat, add the sugar, salt, and the remaining 1 tablespoon wine. Serve immediately. Makes 6 to 8 servings.

Lemon Carrots and Apples

6 medium sized carrots, thinly sliced
1 large apple, peeled and sliced
2 tablespoons butter
1 teaspoon salt
1 teaspoon grated lemon peel
3 tablespoons water
½ cup shredded Cheddar cheese

Arrange carrot and apple slices in alternate layers in saucepan. Dot with butter; sprinkle with salt, grated lemon peel, and water. Cover and steam 20 minutes or until tender. Sprinkle with shredded cheese before serving. Makes 4 servings.

Carrots in Wine Sauce

The everyday carrot has an exotic side. Wine sauce emphasizes the natural sweetness of the carrot.

8 medium sized carrots, scraped and
   sliced
   Water
1 teaspoon salt
¼ cup minced onion
½ clove garlic
1 tablespoon butter
1 tablespoon flour
½ cup undiluted canned consommé
¼ cup dry white table wine
   Salt and pepper to taste

Cover and steam carrots for 10 minutes in a small amount of water with the 1 teaspoon salt; drain. Sauté onion and garlic in melted butter until golden brown; then discard garlic. Stir flour into sautéed onions, then gradually stir in consommé and wine; cook, stirring constantly, until thickened. Add cooked carrots to the sauce; cover and reheat until bubbly. Season to taste with salt and pepper. Serves 6.

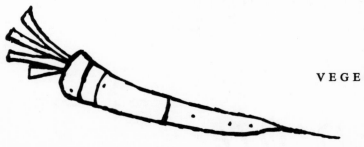

Celery Hearts with Spiced Tomato Sauce

4 whole celery hearts
1 teaspoon salt
¾ cup water
1 clove garlic
¾ cup catsup
2 tablespoons salad oil
1 tablespoon vinegar
2 teaspoons celery salt

Wash celery hearts; trim off ragged leaves. Tie a string around the top of each heart. Cook hearts in boiling salted water 15 to 20 minutes, or until tender. Drain; remove strings. Arrange cooked celery on a hot serving platter.

While celery is cooking, prepare sauce by rubbing a bowl generously with garlic, leaving pieces of about ½ clove garlic in the bowl. Pour in catsup, salad oil, and vinegar. Season with celery salt, and mix well. Spoon sauce over each celery heart before serving. Serves 4.

Fiesta Corn

¼ cup (4 tablespoons) butter
2 cups fresh corn cut off the cob
½ cup chopped green pepper
½ cup chopped pimientos
½ cup stuffed green olives, sliced
¼ cup chopped parsley
4 tablespoons flour
1 teaspoon salt
1 teaspoon pepper
2 cups milk
3 eggs, slightly beaten
1 cup shredded Cheddar cheese

In a large frying pan, melt the butter. Add the corn, green pepper, pimientos, green olives, and parsley. Sauté together for 2 minutes; cover and cook for 10 minutes. Blend in flour, salt, and pepper; gradually add milk, and cook, stirring, until thickened. Gradually stir the hot vegetable mixture into beaten eggs. Blend in the cheese. Turn into a buttered 2-quart casserole. Set the casserole in a pan of water and bake in a moderate oven (350°) about 25 minutes. Makes about 8 servings.

Western Corn Soufflé

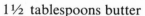

1½ tablespoons butter
4 tablespoons flour
2 cups milk
1 teaspoon dry mustard
½ teaspoon salt
1 cup (¼ pound) shredded Cheddar cheese
1 cup cooked corn kernels
3 tablespoons chopped green pepper
1 tablespoon butter
3 eggs, separated

Melt the 1½ tablespoons butter in saucepan, stir in flour, add milk, and cook until thick, stirring or beating to blend. Add mustard, salt, and cheese, and stir until well blended. Mix in corn. Fry green pepper in the 1 tablespoon butter until limp and add to mixture. Stir in slightly beaten egg yolks, then fold in stiffly beaten egg whites. Turn into buttered 1½-quart casserole, set in a pan of hot water, and bake in moderate oven (350°) for 45 minutes, or until set. Makes 6 servings.

Stuffed Eggplant

2 large onions, chopped
4 tablespoons olive oil or salad oil
2 cloves garlic, minced or mashed
1 medium sized carrot, finely chopped
4 stalks celery, chopped
½ cup chopped parsley
4 mint leaves
1 cup canned tomatoes
1 teaspoon salt
¼ teaspoon pepper
1 medium sized eggplant
2 tablespoons uncooked rice

Cook onions in the oil until lightly browned. Add garlic, carrot, celery, parsley, mint, tomatoes (do not drain these), salt, and pepper; cook until tender, about 30 minutes. Meanwhile, slice a lid from top of eggplant, and with a spoon, scoop out pulp; sprinkle inside lightly with salt. Chop the eggplant pulp and add to the cooked vegetables; continue cooking until eggplant is tender; stir in the rice.

Stuff eggplant with vegetable mixture; set lid on the top and secure with toothpicks. Place eggplant in a deep casserole or baking dish; cover dish with a lid or piece of foil. Bake in moderately slow oven (325°) until tender, about 1½ hours. Cut in slices and serve. Serves 6.

Eggplant Casserole

1 large eggplant
1 large onion, sliced
½ cup shredded sharp Cheddar cheese
½ teaspoon Worcestershire
2 small cloves garlic, minced
10 soda crackers, crushed
½ cup light cream
 Salt and pepper to taste
1 tablespoon butter

Peel and cut eggplant into 1-inch cubes. Add onion and cook in a small amount of boiling, salted water until tender; drain. Mix with cheese, Worcestershire, garlic, cracker crumbs, and cream. Season to taste with salt and pepper. Spoon into a greased casserole and dot with butter. Bake in a moderate oven (350°) for 15 minutes. Serves 4 to 6.

Party Onions

1 pound small onions
1 cup water
1 tablespoon brown sugar
1 teaspoon salt
¼ teaspoon paprika
 Pepper to taste
2 tablespoons chopped or slivered
 blanched almonds
¼ cup (4 tablespoons) butter
2 tablespoons flour
1 teaspoon Worcestershire

Pour boiling water over onions, let stand a few minutes, then drain and peel. Combine water, brown sugar, salt, paprika, and pepper, and bring to a boil. Add onions; cover and simmer for 30 minutes, or until onions are tender. Drain off liquid and save. Place onions in a greased 1½-quart casserole. Brown almonds in the butter; add flour and brown lightly. Stir in the liquid left from cooking the onions, cook until slightly thickened, then add Worcestershire. Pour over onions. Cover and bake in a moderately hot oven (375°) for 25 minutes. Serves 6.

Onion-Sour Cream Pie

Rich biscuit dough made from 1½ cups flour
7 medium sized baking onions
¼ cup (4 tablespoons) butter
2 eggs
1 cup (½ pint) commercial sour cream
1 teaspoon salt
⅛ teaspoon pepper

Line an 8-inch-square or round pan with biscuit dough; chill. Slice onions and sauté in butter until clear; spread over biscuit dough. Beat eggs slightly and blend in sour cream, salt, and pepper; pour over onions. Bake in a very hot oven (450°) for 10 minutes; reduce heat to moderate (350°) and continue baking 45 minutes longer, or until filling has set. Serves 8.

Peas with Lemon-Mint Butter

The lemon mint butter is also good on small onions or a combination of peas with tiny whole carrots. You can make it ahead and store it in the refrigerator.

½ cup soft butter
1 tablespoon lemon juice
¼ teaspoon grated lemon peel
2 to 3 tablespoons finely chopped fresh mint

Cream the butter with lemon juice and peel; add the mint. Melt the flavored butter generously over hot cooked peas just before you serve them.

Green Peas with Celery and Ripe Olives

The large surface area of an electric frying pan is ideal for preparing this colorful tender-crisp vegetable combination quickly — it also keeps vegetables at serving temperature.

2 cups celery, sliced at an angle into 2-inch pieces
2 tablespoons salad oil
2 packages (10 oz. each) frozen peas broken apart or partly thawed
About 20 large pitted ripe olives, cut in half lengthwise
½ teaspoon salt
¼ teaspoon pepper

Set controls of electric frying pan at low temperature (225°). Cover and cook celery in oil for 10 minutes; shake occasionally. Add peas; cover and continue cooking at same temperature for 5 or 6 minutes longer, shake several times. Stir in olives, salt, and pepper. Set temperature at warm and serve from electric frying pan. Serves 6 to 8.

Chinese Peas and Bean Sprouts

2 pounds Chinese (edible pod) peas
1 pound fresh bean sprouts
1 large onion
½ green pepper
2 stalks celery
1 slice raw ham, cut ¼ inch thick
2 tablespoons soy
1 tablespoon cornstarch
1 cup water
½ teaspoon salt

Remove tips and strings from peas; if pods are large, cut them in half. Mix peas and bean sprouts. Cut onion, green pepper, and celery into small pieces (don't chop). Cut ham, including fat, into thin strips. Put ham into large kettle and fry a few minutes to bring out fat.

Add onion, green pepper, and celery, and cook until they are wilted slightly. Add the mixed peas and bean sprouts, cover, and cook for 10 minutes, or until wilted. Mix together the soy, cornstarch, water, and salt; pour over vegetables and cook a few minutes longer, stirring occasionally. Serves 8 to 10 as a vegetable accompaniment, 6 as a main dish.

Green Peppers Florentine

6 large green peppers
4 tablespoons (¼ cup) olive oil
1 teaspoon wine vinegar
½ teaspoon sugar
3 tablespoons capers
2 tablespoons chopped ripe olives
¼ teaspoon oregano, crushed
   Salt and pepper

Wash peppers, cut in half, and remove seeds and veins; slice peppers lengthwise in strips ¼ inch wide. Sauté pepper strips in olive oil for 10 minutes, or until limp; stir in wine vinegar, sugar, capers, chopped olives, and oregano. Season with salt and pepper to taste. Simmer, uncovered, for 20 minutes to blend flavors. Serve hot or cold. Serves 12.

Peppers Stuffed with Sour Cream and Macaroni

6 green peppers
   Boiling salted water
2 cups cooked elbow macaroni
1 egg
1 cup (½ pint) commercial sour cream
2 teaspoons prepared mustard
¼ teaspoon salt
1 tablespoon grated onion (optional)
¼ pound (1 cup) shredded sharp Cheddar cheese

Cut tops off peppers and remove seeds; parboil in salted water for 3 minutes; drain. Stand green peppers in baking pan, then stuff with half of macaroni. Beat egg slightly, then mix with sour cream, mustard, salt, and onion. Pour half of sour cream mixture over macaroni and sprinkle with half of the shredded cheese. Spoon remainder of macaroni into peppers, pour in remaining sour cream mixture, and sprinkle with remaining cheese. Bake in a moderate oven (350°) for 30 minutes. Serves 6.

Cheese-Puffed Potato Casserole

Here's a way to make potatoes extraordinary.

4 eggs, separated
4 cups well seasoned mashed potatoes
1 cup shredded sharp Cheddar cheese
2 teaspoons each finely chopped onion and finely chopped green pepper
½ teaspoon celery salt
Salt
Paprika

Beat egg yolks with mashed potatoes until well mixed. Stir in cheese, onion, green pepper, celery salt, and salt to taste. Just before you are ready to bake, beat egg whites until they form soft peaks and fold into potato mixture. Spoon lightly into a well greased casserole (about 7 by 13 inches), sprinkle with paprika and bake in a moderately hot oven (375°) for 25 minutes. Makes about 6 servings.

Potato and Mushroom Pie

Serve this pie — mashed potatoes, and mushrooms cooked in butter — with barbecued meats.

Pastry for 2-crust pie
½ pound sliced mushroom caps
¼ cup (4 tablespoons) butter
2 cups seasoned mashed potatoes
1 egg, slightly beaten

Line a 9-inch pie pan with one-half of the pastry. Sauté mushrooms in butter for 5 minutes. Combine with mashed potatoes and put in a pastry-lined pan. Top with remaining pastry, seal edges, slash top, and brush with slightly beaten egg. Bake in a hot oven (425°) for 10 minutes. Reduce temperature to moderate (350°) and continue baking 20 to 25 minutes or until crust is brown. Makes 6 servings.

Potatoes in Green Sauce

This way of cooking potatoes is a traditional Basque recipe.

4 medium-large potatoes (good boiling potatoes that do not cook apart easily)
Salted water
1 medium onion, chopped (about ½ cup)
1 clove garlic, minced or mashed
½ cup finely chopped parsley
3 tablespoons salad oil
1½ cups broth or water (or use half broth and half water)
¾ teaspoon salt

Peel and cut the potatoes into ¼-inch-thick slices; cover with salted water and let stand while preparing the sauce. Cook the onion, garlic, and parsley in the oil until the vegetables are soft, about 15 minutes. Add the drained potatoes; cook a few minutes, stirring gently so as not to break them. Add the broth and salt. Bring to a boil, lower heat; cover and cook slowly until the potatoes are done. Correct seasoning if necessary. Makes 4 to 6 servings.

Pecan-Orange Sweet Potatoes

The sweet and sour glaze of brown sugar is delicious on oven-baked sweet potatoes.

8 cooked medium sized sweet potatoes
2 oranges, peeled and thinly sliced
2 tablespoons cornstarch
1 cup brown sugar, firmly packed
½ teaspoon salt
2 tablespoons grated orange peel
¼ cup (4 tablespoons) butter
2 cups orange juice
½ cup pecan halves

Peel, then slice sweet potatoes crosswise into 1-inch-thick slices. Arrange potato slices and the orange slices in alternate layers in a 1½-quart casserole. Combine the cornstarch, brown sugar, and salt; add orange peel and butter. Pour in orange juice, and stirring, cook over low heat until smooth and thickened. Pour sauce over the potato and orange layers; top with pecan halves. Bake in a moderate oven (350°) for 30 minutes, or until heated through and glazed. Serves 8.

Yams Cointreau

The orange-flavored liqueur gives a refreshing tang to mashed sweet potatoes.

4 large yams or sweet potatoes
  Boiling water
¼ cup (4 tablespoons) Cointreau
¼ cup (4 tablespoons) butter
1 teaspoon salt
⅛ teaspoon pepper

Scrub sweet potatoes; drop into boiling water to cover, cover pan, and cook for 30 to 40 minutes, or until tender when pierced with a fork. Drain, cool enough to handle, and peel. Mash sweet potatoes; blend in Cointreau, butter, salt, and pepper, and beat until fluffy. Serves 4 to 6.

Spinach Supreme

Here is a dressed-up, speedy version of creamed spinach, with sesame seeds and almonds supplying a novel texture.

2 packages (12 oz. each) frozen chopped spinach or 1½ pounds fresh spinach, washed and finely chopped
  Boiling salted water
1 can (10½ oz.) cream of mushroom soup, undiluted
  Salt and pepper to taste
  Dash of garlic salt
2 tablespoons toasted sesame seeds
¼ cup sliced almonds

Cook frozen or fresh spinach in a small amount of boiling salted water just until tender, about 5 minutes; drain very thoroughly. Mix in the mushroom soup, salt and pepper to taste, garlic salt, sesame seeds, and half of the sliced nut meats. Turn into a buttered 1-quart casserole, and sprinkle the remaining nut meats on top. Bake in a moderate oven (350°) for 20 minutes, or until bubbly and nuts are golden brown. Makes 4 servings.

Fresh Tomato Soufflé

Grated cheese coats the sides of the dish and flavors this vegetable soufflé.

5 tablespoons butter
½ cup grated Parmesan cheese
2 medium sized tomatoes, peeled
2 tablespoons flour
1 cup milk
3 tablespoons tomato purée
½ teaspoon salt
¼ teaspoon pepper
3 egg yolks
5 egg whites

Butter the bottom and halfway up the sides of a 1½-quart baking dish with 1 tablespoon of the butter. Coat with 2 tablespoons of the cheese.

Core and remove seeds and juice from tomatoes. Chop tomatoes and cook, uncovered, in 2 tablespoons of the butter until juice evaporates, about 10 minutes.

Melt remaining butter and blend in flour. Add milk gradually; cook, stirring until thick and smooth. Combine and stir in remaining cheese, tomato purée, salt and pepper, and well beaten egg yolks. Cook a minute or so longer, stirring constantly until the consistency of mayonnaise. Remove from heat. Beat the egg whites until they form peaks that are stiff, but not dry.

Gently fold in tomato-cheese mixture, adding it in 2 parts. Turn ⅓ of the mixture into baking dish, and spoon the cooked tomatoes into the center, being careful not to let them touch sides of the dish. Pour in remaining soufflé mixture. Bake in hot oven (400°) 20 to 25 minutes, or until soufflé feels set in the center when touched lightly with your finger. Makes 4 servings.

Tomato Sauté

Tomatoes keep their shape surprisingly well during the long, slow cooking.

1 cup fine dry bread crumbs
1 or 2 cloves garlic, minced or mashed
3 tablespoons chopped parsley
2 tablespoons olive oil or salad oil
½ teaspoon salt
⅛ teaspoon pepper
½ teaspoon dry mustard
5 unpeeled ripe firm tomatoes
3 tablespoons olive oil or salad oil

Combine the bread crumbs, garlic, parsley, the 2 tablespoons olive oil, salt, pepper, and dry mustard. Cut the tomatoes in half crosswise. Heat the 3 tablespoons olive oil in a large frying pan. Place tomato halves in the frying pan with cut sides down, and sauté on medium heat for about 5 minutes. Carefully turn tomatoes over and spread about 1 tablespoon of the crumb mixture on each. Turn heat low and cook slowly (uncovered) for about 45 minutes. Makes 4 to 6 servings. (These tomatoes should be quite moist, but if they seem to be drying out, set the cover on the pan for a short time.)

Crisp Zucchini Sticks

3 medium sized zucchini
  Salt, pepper, and flour
1 egg
1 tablespoon milk
  Fine cracker crumbs
3 tablespoons butter
  Lemon juice

Wash but do not peel zucchini; slice off ends. Cut into lengthwise sticks about ½ inch thick. Sprinkle with salt and pepper and roll in flour. Dip in mixture of the slightly beaten egg and milk; roll in crumbs. Fry in heated butter or oil until lightly browned and crisp on all sides, about 5 to 6 minutes. Sprinkle each stick with lemon juice. Serves 6.

Zucchini Slippers

This recipe, we're told, is from Turkey, where it is called "little slippers." You can serve it as a luncheon main dish or as a meat accompaniment. Zucchini slippers can also be sliced after baking and served on toothpicks for appetizers.

6 zucchini, about 7 inches long,
  straight, and well filled out
  Boiling salted water
2 eggs, well beaten
1½ cups shredded sharp Cheddar
  cheese
½ cup small curd cottage cheese
2 tablespoons chopped parsley
½ teaspoon salt
  Dash pepper

Cut off ends and scrub zucchini well; cook them whole in boiling, salted water to cover for about 12 minutes, or until they are tender but still firm. Remove the squash from the water and cut each one in half lengthwise. Scoop out the center pulp and invert each "slipper" to drain briefly. Meanwhile mix together the eggs, Cheddar, cottage cheese, parsley, salt, and pepper. Fill each zucchini shell with the cheese mixture and arrange in a greased baking dish. Bake uncovered in a moderate oven (350°) for 15 minutes. Then turn oven to 450° for 5 minutes, or until the cheese topping is browned. Serves 6.

Baked Squash with Blueberries

The tart juiciness of blueberries counteracts the bland flavor and rather dry texture of acorn squash. If you wish to use banana squash instead of acorn squash, peel squash, dice, then bake with the same blueberry mixture.

4 acorn (Danish) squash
1 container (12 oz.) frozen
  blueberries
½ apple, finely diced
6 tablespoons brown sugar
8 teaspoons butter

Cut squash in half lengthwise and remove seeds. Place in a pan that you can cover. Spoon partially thawed blueberries into each squash half; add a few pieces of apple. Sprinkle the brown sugar over the berries and squash and place 1 teaspoon of butter in the center of each squash. Pour ½ cup water into the pan, cover, and bake in a moderately hot oven (375°) for 45 minutes; remove cover and bake 15 minutes longer. Serves 8.

Sauces

THE GREAT WIDE WORLD of sauces is treated with highest respect in the following pages. But this is a subject that cannot be contained within one chapter. Throughout this book you'll find dozens of sauce recipes printed right along with the specific dishes they enhance. Here we deal with some special sauces for meat, fish, poultry, eggs, and vegetables.

Built into every good sauce recipe is a statement of intentions — a plan that relates the sauce to the dish it accompanies. Once the over-all strategy is determined, minor excursions into subtle taste variations follow naturally.

The basic sauces establish the over-all plan. White sauce with additions becomes curry sauce, egg sauce, cheese sauce, mushroom sauce. Béchamel, another basic white sauce, points toward fish dishes when fish stock is the basic ingredient, or toward poultry and eggs when you use chicken stock. Espagnole, the basic brown sauce, points in the direction of various meats, depending on additions of olives, dill, wine, tomato, mushrooms. Hollandaise, too, can travel in several directions: add whipped cream and it is Mousseline Sauce, the juice of a small orange and grated rind and it is Maltaise Sauce.

The building and use of sauces is not a haphazard thing. It is motivated by the logical affinities of taste, and it carries ordinary dishes subtly into the class of memorable food experiences.

Béchamel Sauce

Starting with this basic recipe, you can add or substitute liquids or seasonings to make the six sauces that follow.

¼ cup (4 tablespoons) butter
4 tablespoons flour
1 cup rich chicken stock
1 cup (½ pint) light cream
Salt and grated nutmeg to taste

Cook the butter and flour together for 2 to 3 minutes to remove the flour's raw taste. Stir in chicken stock and cream; stirring constantly, cook until smooth and thick. Season with salt, nutmeg. When serving with fish, substitute fish stock for chicken stock. Makes 2 cups sauce.

ANCHOVY SAUCE
(Any white fish, salmon)

Substitute 2 cups fish stock (made from trimmings) for the chicken stock and cream in the basic recipe. When smooth, add a dash of cayenne, 6 chopped anchovies, 1 tablespoon lemon juice, 1 tablespoon minced parsley, and anchovy paste to taste.

ARTICHOKE SAUCE
(Chicken, veal, brains, sweetbreads, fish)

Combine 1 cup Béchamel sauce with the bottoms of 2 large cooked artichokes cut in small pieces. Put in blender; run until smooth. Heat, then season with 1 teaspoon lemon juice, 1 tablespoon sherry, and salt to taste.

AURORA SAUCE
(Eggs, chicken, sweetbreads)

Combine 2 cups Béchamel sauce with ½ cup tomato purée, and 1 tablespoon of paprika. Heat.

EGG SAUCE
(Salmon, or other poached fish)

Combine 1 cup Béchamel sauce — made with fish stock instead of chicken stock — with 2 finely chopped hard cooked eggs. Heat; add 1 tablespoon minced parsley.

MUSHROOM SAUCE
(Veal chops, calf's liver, chicken, ham)

Cook ½ cup chopped onions and 1 cup chopped mushrooms in 1 tablespoon butter in a covered pan until vegetables are wilted and juicy. Combine with 1 cup Béchamel sauce, heat, and add 1 teaspoon minced parsley.

MORNAY SAUCE
(Fish, shellfish, vegetables)

Combine 1 cup Béchamel sauce with 2 tablespoons grated Parmesan cheese, 2 tablespoons shredded Swiss cheese, and a dash of cayenne. Heat just until cheese is melted.

Espagnole Sauce

You can build up a whole repertoire of sauces from this basic recipe for brown sauce.

1 cup diced, lean, cooked ham
1 cup chopped onions
½ cup sliced celery
½ cup sliced carrot
2 large tomatoes, peeled and chopped
¼ cup (4 tablespoons) butter
¼ cup (4 tablespoons) flour
1 quart beef stock
1 herb bouquet (parsley, bay, thyme)
½ cup sherry

Cook the ham, onions, celery, carrot, and tomatoes in the butter until vegetables are soft; stir in flour and cook 2 minutes. Pour in the stock (may use 1 quart water and 6 bouillon cubes or equivalent in canned bouillon) and herb bouquet. Simmer gently for 1 hour. Remove herb bouquet and add sherry; cool. Skim off fat and refrigerate or freeze. Makes 5 cups of sauce.

CAPER SAUCE
(Tongue, boiled beef, corned beef)

Heat 1 cup Espagnole sauce with 1 tablespoon each capers and tarragon vinegar.

SAUCE CHASSEUR
(Game of all kinds)

Cook 2 tablespoons chopped shallots or green onions in 4 tablespoons butter. Add ½ cup tomato sauce or catsup, 1 cup Espagnole sauce, 1 small can (2 or 3 oz.) sliced mushrooms, 2 tablespoons lemon juice, 2 teaspoons minced parsley, and a dash of cayenne. Heat and serve.

CHERRY SAUCE
(Tongue, poultry, ham, fresh pork)

Cook 2 tablespoons chopped shallots or green onions in 2 tablespoons butter for 3 minutes. Combine with 1 cup Espagnole sauce and 1 cup drained pitted dark, sweet cherries. Heat and serve.

SAUCE COLBERT
(Kidneys, veal chops, rabbit, beef, or lamb)

Heat together 1 cup Espagnole sauce, 2 to 3 tablespoons lemon juice, 1 bouillon cube, ¼ cup (4 tablespoons) butter, 1 teaspoon minced parsley, and salt and cayenne to taste.

SAUCE DIABLE
(Turkey, beef ribs, chicken, or other meats)
Cook together 1 cup dry white table wine, 2 tablespoons chopped onion, small piece of bay leaf, and pinch of thyme until liquid is reduced one-half. Combine with 1 cup Espagnole sauce, 1 tablespoon prepared mustard, 2 tablespoons wine vinegar, and a little cayenne. Heat and serve with any of the listed meats, which have been cooked, dipped in a mixture of melted butter and vinegar, rolled in fine crumbs, and grilled.

SAUCE DUXELLES
(Broiled chicken, stuffed tomato, eggplant, calf's liver, chicken livers)
Chop ½ pound of fresh mushrooms and cook in ¼ cup (4 tablespoons) butter for 3 minutes. Add 1 cup dry white table wine and cook until liquid is reduced one-half. Combine with 1 cup Espagnole sauce, 2 tablespoons tomato catsup, 1 teaspoon lemon juice, and 1 tablespoon chopped parsley. Heat and serve.

GARLIC SAUCE
(Roast lamb, pork, or goose)
Cook 1 cup peeled garlic cloves in water to cover. When tender, drain, rinse with cold water, and drain again. Combine with 1½ cups Espagnole (or pan gravy), season with salt, and cook, mashing the garlic slightly. Serve hot.

HORSE-RADISH SAUCE
(Boiled or corned beef, roast beef, tongue)
Combine 1 cup Espagnole sauce with 1 tablespoon each chopped parsley, chopped green olives, grated horse-radish, and lemon juice. Heat.

SAUCE AUX FINES HERBES
(Chicken, veal, omelet)
Cook 1 tablespoon chopped mushrooms and 1 tablespoon chopped shallots or green onions in 1 tablespoon butter. Combine with 1 cup Espagnole sauce, 1 tablespoon minced parsley, 1 teaspoon minced fresh tarragon or 1 teaspoon fresh marjoram (or both), and 3 tablespoons sherry. Heat.

MADEIRA SAUCE
(Veal, chicken, shrimp)
Heat 1 cup Espagnole sauce with ½ cup sautéed sliced mushrooms and ¼ cup Madeira wine.

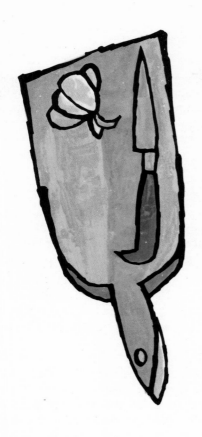

SAUCE PIQUANT
(Game, venison, lamb, liver)
Cook together ¼ cup chopped onion, ¼ cup vinegar, and 1 tablespoon butter until liquid is absorbed. Combine with 1 cup Espagnole sauce, 1 tablespoon capers or chopped pickles, and 2 teaspoons chopped parsley. Serve hot.

PORT WINE SAUCE
(Goose, duck, ham)
Combine 1 cup Espagnole sauce, 1 cup port, 1 tablespoon prepared mustard, and salt and Tabasco to taste. Heat.

RAISIN SAUCE
(Ham, tongue, game)
Heat 2 tablespoons golden raisins in 4 tablespoons sherry until they are plump. Combine with 1 cup Espagnole sauce, 3 tablespoons currant jelly, 1 tablespoon lemon juice, and salt and pepper. Serve hot.

SAUCE ROBERT
(Pork, roast beef)
Cook 1 cup chopped onions in 2 tablespoons butter until wilted. Add 1 cup Espagnole sauce and 1 tablespoon tarragon vinegar. Heat.

White Wine Sauce

3 tablespoons butter
3 tablespoons flour
1 cup (½ pint) light cream
⅓ cup dry white table wine
1 chicken bouillon cube
¼ teaspoon marjoram
   Salt to taste

(Chicken or turkey)
Cook butter with flour for 3 minutes. Add all other ingredients. Stirring, cook until thick and smooth. Serve hot.

Red Wine Sauce

½ cup chopped onion
3 tablespoons butter
1 teaspoon flour
1 cup dry red table wine
1 clove garlic, mashed
1 tablespoon tomato purée

(Steaks, chops, hamburgers)
Sauté onion in butter until lightly browned. Stir in flour, cook another minute, then add wine, garlic, and tomato purée. Simmer 15 minutes and serve hot.

Mint or Savory Sauce

(Lamb, mutton)
Combine ½ cup vinegar with ½ cup finely chopped mint, or summer savory, and 1 tablespoon sugar. If desired, put in the blender before heating. Simmer 5 minutes; serve hot or cold.

Beurre Noir

½ cup vinegar
  Piece of bay leaf
½ cup (¼ pound) butter
1 tablespoon minced parsley

(Brains, sweetbreads, mushrooms, fried eggs)
Boil vinegar with bay leaf until it is reduced one-half. Cook butter until it is deep brown. Remove bay leaf from vinegar and combine with butter. Add parsley, and serve hot.

Green Onion Sauce

1 bunch green onions
1 cup (½ pound) butter
2 tablespoons tarragon vinegar

(Broiled meats or fish)
Chop onions, including the tender part of the green leaves; sauté in ½ cup (¼ pound) of the butter until soft. Add vinegar and remove from heat. Cut the other ½ cup of the butter in pieces, and add, a piece at a time, to onion mixture. Beat after each addition. When the butter is melted, serve at once.

Raisin Almond Sauce

3 tablespoons butter
3 tablespoons flour
1½ cups consommé
½ cup raisins
½ cup slivered blanched almonds
½ cup sherry
¼ teaspoon cloves
1 tablespoon lemon juice

(Ham, smoked tongue, smoked turkey)
Cook butter with flour for 2 minutes. Add consommé, raisins, almonds, sherry, cloves, and lemon juice. Cook until thick; serve hot.

Horse-Radish Apple Sauce

(Pork, goose, turkey)
Combine 2 cups tart apple sauce with ½ cup prepared bottled horse-radish. If fresh horse-radish is used, add 2 tablespoons vinegar. Serve cold.

Curry Sauce

1 cup chopped onion
1 cup chopped tart apple
¼ cup shortening
1 clove garlic, crushed
2 (or more) tablespoons curry powder
¼ cup catsup
2 cups rich stock (chicken, beef, or fish)
2 tablespoons lemon juice
Salt to taste

(Cooked lamb, veal, chicken, or seafood)
Cook onion and apple in shortening until onion is transparent. Add garlic, curry powder, catsup, stock, and lemon juice. Salt to taste; thicken slightly if desired. Heat the cooked food to be served in this sauce.

Rémoulade Sauce

1 cup mayonnaise
2 or 3 chopped shallots or green onions
2 minced anchovy fillets
1 teaspoon chopped capers
1 chopped gherkin (not a sweet one)
1 tablespoon minced parsley

(Shrimp, salmon, other fish, raw cauliflower, other raw vegetables)
Combine all ingredients thoroughly. A little chervil or tarragon can be added if desired. Serve cold.

Orange Ginger Sauce

1 cup orange juice
¼ cup each vinegar, sugar, and sherry
2 tablespoons soy
1 tablespoon each shredded fresh ginger and slivered orange peel (no white membrane)
2 tablespoons melted butter
2 tablespoons cornstarch

(Spareribs, short ribs, pork chops, broiled chicken)
Mix together all ingredients, and cook, stirring, until the sauce becomes thick and clear, about 15 minutes.

Cucumber Sauce

1 cucumber, peeled and grated
½ teaspoon salt
2 tablespoons vinegar
1 cup (½ pint) commercial sour cream
Freshly ground pepper
1 tablespoon minced green onion or chives

(Baked or poached salmon, other fish, tomatoes)
Mix cucumber with salt, and allow to stand in the refrigerator for 1 hour or longer. Drain thoroughly and combine with the remaining ingredients. Add more salt if necessary. Serve cold.

Ten-Second Hollandaise Sauce

3 egg yolks
1½ tablespoons lemon juice
¾ cup butter, melted
1 tablespoon hot water
½ teaspoon salt
　Dash of cayenne
1 teaspoon prepared mustard

(Broccoli, asparagus, other vegetables)
Let egg yolks and lemon juice stand (separately) at room temperature for at least 2 hours before using. Melt butter. Heat blender container with hot running water. Leave 1 tablespoon hot water in the bottom. Add egg yolks and turn on blender. Pour in melted butter in a steady stream. (This takes about 5 seconds.) Toss in salt, cayenne, mustard, and, finally, the lemon juice. Stop the blender. Serve at once. Makes 2 cups sauce.

(Since this sauce is not cooked but is only heated by the warmth of the butter and the blender container, it will not curdle. You can reheat leftover sauce in the top of a double boiler over hot but not boiling water; stir until smooth.)

Sauce Mousseline

(Veal, chicken breasts, sweetbreads, other delicate-flavored meats and fish)
Combine equal amounts of Hollandaise and whipped cream. Season with a little lemon juice. (Mayonnaise may be used instead of Hollandaise.)

Cumberland Sauce

(Mutton, duck, venison, other game)
Cut the very outside peel of an orange into pin-like slivers and cook in water for 5 minutes; drain. Add a 6-ounce glass of red currant jelly, the juice of 1 small orange, a dash of cayenne, 1 teaspoon lemon juice, and 1 cup port wine. Heat until the jelly melts; serve hot.

Sour Cream Sauce

½ cup chopped onion
3 tablespoons butter
3 tablespoons flour
2 cups (1 pint) commercial
　sour cream
　Salt to taste

(Veal, chicken, baked potatoes, any cold cooked meat)
Sauté onion in butter until wilted. Stir in flour; cook 2 minutes, then add sour cream and salt. Heat very gently. Parsley, capers, chopped pickles, mushrooms, or chopped olives may be added for variation. Serve hot.

Eggs & Cheese

FEW FOODS CAN COMPETE with the egg in versatility. Eggs are present at almost any meal in an amazing number of forms, often veiled in a cake or rich sauce.

But given the spotlight eggs may appear as a creamy omelet with its endless variety of fillings and sauces that give it special flavor, heartiness, or elegance—or as a fragile puffy soufflé. And you never can tell what surprise may hide beneath a baked egg.

Eggs and cheese move into beautiful companionship in many dishes, and for that reason we have allowed them association in this chapter. A creamy cheese sauce does wonderful things to a baked egg, and a cheese soufflé can be a culinary triumph.

In addition to the ways cheese is used in fine cooking, it offers many taste discoveries, served as is. Almost every famous cheese of the world is represented in today's market. The slicing cheeses of the Scandinavians, Dutch, and Swiss are particularly well keyed to sliced cold meats and rye and pumpernickel breads. Try Emmentaler Swiss and Gruyère; Norwegian kuminost, or Tilsit; Danish Samsöe or Port Salut; Dutch Edam or Gouda.

Cheese, sour French bread, and a robust red wine can make a fine meal. Experiment with pungent Italian Gorgonzola, Brick, Muenster, the sharpest Cheddar you can find. Contrast these with the mellower cheeses—fresh but rugged Monterey jack, Italian Fontina, creamy-rich Western Teleme.

Basic Omelet

Here is our recipe for the perfect omelet — tender and golden, firm but delicate outside, smooth and creamy inside. A properly made omelet is a delicacy in itself, but for some delicious fillings that qualify it for a luncheon or supper entrée, refer to the collection on the pages that follow.

Basic proportions to tuck away in your memory are: 1 teaspoon of water for each egg used, a little salt, and a dash of pepper. As a general rule, you can plan to serve one person a three-egg omelet as an entrée, or a one or two-egg omelet as a side dish or dessert. (An omelet larger than six-egg size is awkward to handle; it is more efficient to make several small omelets.)

Break eggs for one omelet into a bowl; add water, salt, and pepper. Beat vigorously with a fork or a wire whip for about 30 seconds, or until yolks and whites are blended. In an omelet pan, heat butter (1 teaspoon per egg) on medium high heat until it bubbles, browns ever so slightly, and gives off a rich, nutlike odor. Pour beaten eggs all at once into heated pan. They should begin to set and turn opaque around the edges almost immediately. Slide pan rapidly back and forth on the burner, keeping omelet in motion and free from the bottom of the pan to avoid browning and sticking.

As soon as bottom of the omelet begins to set, slip a thin-bladed spatula well under the edges and let the uncooked eggs flow into contact with center of the pan. (This lifting, along with frequent shaking, causes the rippled surface and irregular edges that are characteristic of a good omelet.) Don't worry about tearing the omelet as you lift the edges; the fresh supply of liquid egg soon mends the damage. Your omelet is done when the egg no longer runs freely but the top still looks liquid and creamy. If you're going to add a filling (see recipes that follow), do so now. Spoon filling (2 teaspoons filling per egg) directly in line with the handle. Hold omelet pan with your right hand and tilt pan sideways, lifting right side off the heat. With your left hand, use spatula to guide omelet as you fold the right side (about ⅓) over the center. Holding the omelet over a hot serving dish or platter, shake the pan and ease with the spatula until the omelet begins to slip out. With· a quick downward flick of the wrist, let the folded section of the omelet neatly fall over its extended edge on the hot plate. The omelet continues to cook even as you carry it to the table for immediate consumption.

Artichoke Omelet

Cover and simmer until tender 1 cup finely chopped artichoke hearts in 3 tablespoons butter. (To prepare fresh artichokes, remove tough outer leaves from small artichokes, trim off thorny tip, peel stem, and cut artichokes in half. Remove any fuzzy choke center. Rinse artichokes in water mixed with lemon juice; drain. If you use frozen artichoke hearts, just let them thaw.) Season with salt to taste. Add ¼ teaspoon crushed tarragon, if desired. Add 2 tablespoons artichoke mixture to a 3-egg omelet before you cook it, or fill omelet with 2 tablespoons of the mixture. Fold and serve with remaining artichokes. Serves 1.

Gorgonzola Cheese and Black Walnut Omelet

Prepare a 3-egg omelet; omit salt and substitute sherry for water. Fill omelet with 2 tablespoons crumbled Gorgonzola cheese (or blue cheese) and 2 teaspoons chopped black walnuts. Serves 1.

Avocado and Tomato Omelet

½ cup cubed ripe avocado
1 medium sized tomato, peeled, seeded, and diced
2 teaspoons lemon juice
¼ teaspoon garlic salt
⅛ teaspoon curry powder
2 three-egg omelets (add another ⅛ teaspoon curry powder to the omelet mixture)
Avocado slices (optional)

Combine avocado, tomato, lemon juice, garlic salt, and curry powder. Toss lightly. Fill each omelet with 2 tablespoons filling. Serve with remaining filling and garnish with additional avocado slices. Serves 2.

Green Chili and Jack Cheese Omelet

1 tablespoon finely chopped green chili
1 tablespoon cubed soft Jack cheese
2 tablespoons shredded sharp Cheddar cheese
2 three-egg omelets

Lightly mix the chili, Jack cheese and Cheddar cheese. Fill each omelet with 2 tablespoons of the mixture. Fold, then top with more shredded sharp Cheddar cheese, if desired, and melt cheese quickly under the broiler. Serves 2.

Sherried Shrimp Omelet

½ cup minced fresh mushrooms
1 tablespoon minced green onion
3 tablespoons butter
1 cup small whole cooked and
    shelled shrimp
1½ tablespoons flour
¾ cup light cream
¼ cup sherry
2 three-egg omelets

Simmer mushrooms and onion in butter until mushrooms are cooked. Add shrimp. Stir in flour. Gradually add cream, and cook until thickened. Blend in sherry. Fill each omelet with 2 tablespoons of the shrimp mixture. Serve with remaining sauce. Serves 2.

Specialty Sausage Omelet

Remove casings from specialty sausages such as Italian chorizo or Portuguese linguisa, or other favorite sausage. Crumble or chop sausage. Heat or cook but do not brown. Add to uncooked omelets 2 teaspoons sausage for each egg; or use to fill omelets. Cook whole sausages to serve alongside omelet, if you like.

Fresh Strawberry Omelet with Sour Cream

Sweeten sliced fresh strawberries to taste, or use thawed frozen strawberries. If you wish, add ¼ teaspoon sugar per egg before mixing omelet. Fill omelet with 2 teaspoons strawberries for each egg used. Fold and top with dollops of sour cream, dust with powdered sugar, and pass under a hot broiler just long enough to set sour cream. Garnish with whole strawberries.

Smoked Salmon and Cream Cheese Omelet

2 chopped green onions and tops
1 package (3 oz.) chopped smoked
    salmon
2 tablespoons butter
1 package (3 oz.) cream cheese
2 three-egg omelets

Simmer onions and salmon in butter for 2 or 3 minutes. Cut cream cheese in cubes and add; stir until melted. Fill each omelet with 2 tablespoons sauce; serve with remaining sauce. Serves 2.

Cream-Poached Eggs au Gratin

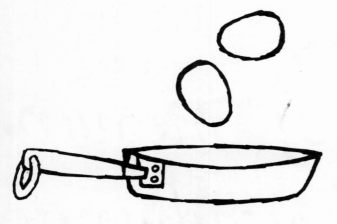

Heat 2 cups table cream in a frying pan; season with ½ teaspoon salt. Poach eggs in cream a few at a time so eggs are not crowded. Put poached eggs on buttered rounds of toast or toasted English muffins; sprinkle with grated Parmesan cheese and place under the broiler until lightly browned. Heat the cream remaining in the frying pan and pour around the eggs before serving.

Garnish each plate with crisp Canadian bacon slices and avocado (optional), and serve with toasted English muffins and preserves of your choice.

Eggs Mexican

For a festive brunch, serve these eggs on crisp tortillas, with colorful sauce.

1 avocado, peeled and sliced
2 tablespoons lemon juice
1 medium sized onion, minced
1 small clove garlic, mashed
2 green peppers, finely chopped
2 small hot pickled peppers, minced
½ teaspoon chili powder
⅓ cup tomato catsup
1 tablespoon each butter and lard
4 tortillas
4 eggs
Salt and pepper to taste
4 garlic link sausages, sliced
2 tablespoons shredded sharp
Cheddar cheese

Sprinkle avocado with lemon juice; chill. For the sauce combine onion, garlic, green peppers, hot peppers, chili powder, and catsup; set aside. In a frying pan, melt butter and lard; fry tortillas until light brown on both sides; set each on a heated plate. Fry eggs; season with salt and pepper. Set one egg on each tortilla; brown the sausages.

Garnish each plate with avocado on one side, sausage on the other; spoon sauce over egg; top with cheese. Serve at once with extra toasted, buttered tortillas. Makes 4 servings.

Scrambled Eggs and Oysters

4 eggs
Salt and pepper
3 tablespoons commercial sour cream
1 can (7¾ oz.) oysters, drained, or 1
cup fresh Pacific or Olympia oysters
2 teaspoons butter
1 teaspoon very finely chopped chives

Beat eggs lightly and season with salt and pepper to taste. Stir in sour cream. If oysters are large, cut into bite sized pieces, then stir into the eggs. Melt butter in a medium sized frying pan; pour in egg mixture and cook slowly, stirring occasionally, until eggs are set. Sprinkle with chives before serving. Serves 2.

Chinese Style Scrambled Eggs

Serve these eggs with steamed rice, soy, and a salad made of Chinese cabbage and bean sprouts mixed with a sweet mustard dressing.

6 eggs
6 teaspoons mayonnaise
¼ cup (4 tablespoons) butter
½ cup chopped green pepper
½ cup chopped onion
½ cup sliced celery
   Freshly ground pepper

Beat eggs and mayonnaise together thoroughly. Melt butter; add green pepper, onion, and celery. Sauté until golden. Pour over the egg mixture and cook over low heat, stirring occasionally, until eggs are set. Do not salt. Grind pepper over eggs just before serving. Serves 4. You can add sautéed chicken livers or lamb kidneys along with the eggs.

Scrambled Eggs with Clam Chowder

6 eggs
1 can (10½ oz.) tomato base clam
   chowder
½ teaspoon salt
⅛ teaspoon pepper
2 tablespoons butter

Beat eggs just until yolks and whites are mixed. Stir in clam chowder, salt, and pepper. Melt butter in a heavy frying pan over low heat, pour in egg mixture, and scramble slowly. Serves 4.

Scrambled Eggs Diablo

These unusual scrambled eggs make a festive but quick dish for breakfast or luncheon.

8 eggs
2 canned green chili peppers
1 teaspoon salt
¼ teaspoon freshly ground pepper
½ pound (8 oz.) processed sharp
   Cheddar cheese
2 tablespoons butter
   Additional minced green chili
   peppers

Beat the eggs just until the yolks and whites are blended. Wash chili peppers, remove seeds, drain, and then chop finely; stir into beaten eggs, and add salt and pepper. Shred the cheese. Melt butter in a large frying pan and pour in the egg mixture. Cook slowly, lifting the eggs from the bottom by slipping a spatula underneath.

When the eggs are barely set, sprinkle with the cheese, cover, and turn heat as low as possible. Let cook just until cheese is melted and eggs are set, about 3 minutes. Serve immediately with a small side dish of minced green chili peppers for those who are especially fond of them. Makes 4 servings.

Scrambled Eggs on Muffins

8 eggs
½ can (10½ oz.) cream of mushroom soup
¼ cup milk
½ teaspoon salt
⅛ teaspoon pepper
2 tablespoons chopped pimiento
¼ cup (4 tablespoons) butter
4 English muffins, torn in half
8 slices processed cheese, sharp or
  mild according to taste

Slightly beat eggs; stir in mushroom soup, milk, salt, pepper, and pimiento. Melt butter in a heavy frying pan, add egg mixture, and cook over low heat until eggs are just set, stirring occasionally.

While eggs are cooking, toast split English muffins. Spoon scrambled eggs on muffins, top with cheese, and broil until cheese melts. Serves 8.

Eggs Baked in Mushroom Sauce

1 pound small mushrooms
¼ cup (4 tablespoons) butter
3 tablespoons flour
2 cups milk
1 bouillon cube dissolved in 1 tablespoon hot water
1 tablespoon grated onion
  Salt and pepper to taste
6 eggs

Wash and slice mushrooms, stems and all. Sauté in butter for 5 minutes. Stir in flour, milk, bouillon, onion, salt, and pepper. Cook, stirring, until thick. Pour into individual shallow ramekins or a baking dish; sauce should be 1 inch deep. Drop eggs into sauce, slipping a spoon under each egg so that it will sink slightly into the sauce. Bake in a moderate oven (350°) until eggs are consistency desired. Serves 6.

Bacon and Egg Pie

Prepare pastry for a 2-crust pie. Line a 9-inch pie pan with half of the pastry, cover with 5 to 8 whole slices cooked bacon. Carefully break 5 eggs on top of the bacon, leaving yolks whole. Sprinkle with salt and pepper, and top with 5 more slices of cooked bacon. Cover with remaining pastry (which has been pricked or slashed), seal edges, and bake in a hot oven (425°) for 30 to 35 minutes or until brown. Serve hot or cold. Makes 5 or 6 servings.

Eggs Mornay

Swiss cheese and Parmesan cheese give a piquant flavor to hard cooked eggs.

12 hard cooked eggs
 1 small can (4½ oz.) liver pâté
 3 cups thin cream sauce (3 cups milk,
   3 tablespoons flour, 3 tablespoons
   butter)
   Salt and pepper
 ½ cup grated Swiss cheese
 ½ cup grated Parmesan cheese

Cut eggs in half lengthwise. Remove yolks and blend together with the liver pâté; stir in 2 tablespoons of the cream sauce and salt and pepper to taste. Stuff eggs with the egg yolk mixture; arrange eggs in a flat baking dish. Add the Swiss cheese and half of the Parmesan cheese to the remaining cream sauce. Stirring, cook over low heat until cheese melts. Pour sauce over eggs; sprinkle with the remaining Parmesan. Heat under the broiler until bubbly and brown.

Eggs Vinaigrette

Serve these with cold salmon, or on a tray of cold meats.

6 tablespoons olive oil or salad oil
3 tablespoons vinegar
½ teaspoon salt
1 small clove garlic, cut in half
1 tablespoon each minced gherkin,
   parsley, green pepper, chives
12 hard cooked eggs

Combine oil with vinegar, salt, garlic, gherkin, parsley, green pepper, and chives; refrigerate until thoroughly chilled. Remove the garlic and beat until thick. Just before serving cut the hard cooked eggs in half lengthwise, and arrange on serving dish. Pour over the vinaigrette sauce.

Cheese Custard Pie

Toast points form a crisp, brown crust around this cheese custard pie.

 2 tablespoons butter, softened
 6 slices bread, crusts removed
 2 egg yolks
1½ cups milk
 ½ teaspoon salt
 ½ teaspoon dry mustard
 ½ teaspoon paprika
 1 teaspoon Worcestershire
 ½ pound (2 cups) shredded sharp
   Cheddar cheese

Butter bread on one side; cut in half to form triangles. Fit half of bread triangles around the sides of a 9-inch pie pan, arranging them so tips of triangles stick up beyond rim of pan. Fit remaining bread, buttered side down, into bottom of pan. Slightly beat egg yolks and milk together; stir in salt, mustard, paprika, Worcestershire, and cheese; pour mixture into bread-lined pan. Bake in a moderate oven (350°) for 30 minutes. Serves 6.

Cheese Pimientos with Mushroom-Bacon Sauce

1 small package (3 oz.) softened
   cream cheese
1 cup grated Parmesan cheese
2 tablespoons milk
2 eggs, beaten
1 teaspoon prepared mustard
½ teaspoon salt
   Dash each black pepper and Tabasco
2 cans (4 oz. each) whole pimientos

Mash cream cheese until smooth. Mix in Parmesan cheese, milk, eggs, mustard, salt, pepper, and Tabasco. Drain pimientos. Fill pimiento shells with cheese mixture; arrange in greased shallow baking dish. Bake in a moderate oven (350°) for 30 minutes or until set. Serve hot with Mushroom-Bacon Sauce. Serves 4.

Mushroom-Bacon Sauce

4 strips bacon
¼ pound fresh mushrooms, sliced, or
   1 can (6 oz.) sliced mushrooms,
   drained
   Butter
1 can (10½ oz.) cream of celery
   soup, undiluted
½ soup can milk

Cook bacon until crisp; drain, and crumble. Sauté mushrooms in butter. Add bacon, soup, and milk. Heat together.

Chili Pepper Soufflé

The layering with sliced green chili peppers and extra grated cheese gives an even distribution of flavor throughout this soufflé mixture.

2 tablespoons butter
3 tablespoons flour
¾ cup milk
¾ pound (3 cups) shredded Cheddar
   cheese
4 eggs, separated
½ teaspoon salt
   Dash of pepper
2 cans (4 oz. each) green chili
   peppers, thinly sliced
1 large can (1 lb. 13 oz.) tomatoes
   with purée

Melt butter, stir in flour, and blend until smooth. Add milk and cook until sauce is thick. Add 2 cups of the cheese and cook, stirring occasionally, until cheese is melted; remove from heat.

With a fork beat egg yolks with salt and pepper; slowly stir into sauce. Beat egg whites until stiff but not dry; slowly add cheese sauce to egg whites, folding together carefully. Turn half of the soufflé mixture into ungreased 1½-quart casserole. Sprinkle remaining cup of shredded cheese on this, then top with sliced green chili peppers, using about ⅔ cup (1¼ cans). Add remainder of soufflé mixture.

Bake in a moderately slow oven (325°) for 40 minutes, or until set. While soufflé is baking, simmer the tomatoes with the remainder of the chili peppers. Spoon tomato sauce over each serving of soufflé. Serves 6.

Cheese Cream Casserole

A bottom crust of crumbled bacon distinguishes this cheese custard.

8 slices bacon
½ pound (2 cups) shredded Swiss
  cheese
¼ pound (1 cup) grated Parmesan
  cheese
2 large eggs (or 3 small)
2 cups (1 pint) light cream
1 teaspoon salt
½ teaspoon nutmeg
  Dash of cayenne

Cook bacon until crisp and break into pieces. Sprinkle on the bottom of a not-too-deep 1½-quart greased casserole. Combine Swiss and Parmesan cheese, well beaten eggs, cream, salt, nutmeg, and cayenne; pour over bacon in casserole. Bake in a moderate oven (350°) for 35 minutes, or until set. Serves 4 to 6.

Swiss Fondue

A chafing dish or an earthenware or cast iron casserole placed over a warmer provides enough heat to cook the fondue. It is important to keep the heat low. If overcooked, the cheese gets stringy. Use imported Swiss cheese (called Emmentaler) or Swiss Gruyère to make a successful fondue.

1 clove garlic
2 cups dry white table wine
1 pound (16 oz.) Swiss or Gruyère
  cheese, coarsely shredded (4 cups)
3 tablespoons flour
  Salt and pepper to taste
  Dash of nutmeg
6 tablespoons kirsch (cherry brandy)
1 loaf sour dough French bread

Peel garlic and rub over the bottom of the earthenware casserole or the chafing dish. Pour in the wine and heat very slowly. Mix cheese with flour. When air bubbles rise to the surface of the wine, add a handful of cheese and flour mixture and stir constantly with a fork until cheese is melted. Continue to add handfuls, making sure each is completely melted before you add another. Stir constantly. When cheese mixture is smooth and starts to bubble lightly, add salt and pepper to taste and a dash of nutmeg. Slowly pour in the kirsch, stirring constantly until blended.

Cut bread into bite-sized pieces so each piece has at least one side of crust. Spear bread with a fork, going through the soft part first and securing the points in the crust. This way you are less likely to lose the bread when you dip into the fondue. Take turns dipping. If the fondue becomes too thick, pour in a little warm white wine. Serves 8.

Cheese Enchiladas

Whole ripe olives are a surprise in each tortilla roll.

2 cans (10 oz. each) Spanish red chili sauce
1 dozen tortillas
4 hard cooked eggs, finely chopped
4 cups (1 lb.) shredded sharp Cheddar cheese
1 large onion, finely chopped
1 can (4½ oz.) pitted ripe olives, drained

Heat chili sauce in a large frying pan; bring to a boil; simmer for 5 minutes. Dip each tortilla in hot sauce; lay on a plate, and spread across the tortilla's center a spoonful each of chopped egg, shredded cheese, chopped onion. Top with 2 or 3 ripe pitted olives. Roll tortilla and secure with a toothpick. Arrange stuffed tortillas in a baking dish; pour over any remaining sauce. Sprinkle remaining cheese over top; garnish with rest of olives. Bake in a moderate oven (350°) for 15 minutes, or until cheese melts and the sauce is bubbly. Makes 6 servings.

Deviled Ham Rabbit

The combination of ham and cheese is joined by mushroom soup in this quickly prepared luncheon or supper main dish. Ham and mushroom flavors blend with cheese.

1 can (10½ oz.) mushroom soup
¼ cup evaporated milk
½ pound package processed sharp Cheddar cheese
1 small can (2½ oz.) deviled ham
1 teaspoon Worcestershire
1 teaspoon prepared mustard
Dash of pepper
Salt to taste
4 slices bread, toasted and cut in half diagonally

In a saucepan mix together mushroom soup and milk, and heat. Add cheese that has been cut or broken into small pieces, and stirring occasionally, heat until cheese melts. Stir in deviled ham, Worcestershire, mustard, pepper, and salt to taste. If you are not serving immediately, heat mixture in top of a double boiler and keep hot over hot water. Serve over toast points in individual casseroles. Serves 4.

Shrimp Tomato Rabbit

1 can (8 oz.) tomato sauce
½ cup light cream
1½ cups shredded American cheese
Salt, pepper, and paprika to taste
1 cup cooked shrimp
1 teaspoon curry powder

Mix the tomato sauce and cream together, and heat in a double boiler over hot water or in your chafing dish. Blend in the cheese and seasonings to your taste. When mixture is smooth and cheese has melted, add the shrimp and curry powder. Serve over steamed rice to 4 persons.

Breads, Pancakes, Sandwiches

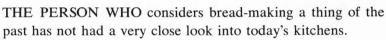

THE PERSON WHO considers bread-making a thing of the past has not had a very close look into today's kitchens.

For in spite of the wide variety of high quality specialty breads now on the market, hundreds of recipes continue to testify to the fact that the occasional luxury of home-made bread is very much valued.

For anyone who has childhood recollections of the Saturday morning aroma of bread in the oven, or who remembers the taste of the chewy-crisp crust of still-hot bread, this fact is both heartening and understandable.

The cook might explain the appeal of bread-making in another way. There are countless women who bake bread for no other reason than its soul-satisfying qualities—getting hands into the dough, and slapping it, punching it down, waiting for it to double and then double again. And it is certainly true that in the shaping, flavoring, decorating involved, bread-making allows a great creative scope.

In reading this collection of recipes for yeast breads, quick breads, coffee cakes, muffins, another pattern emerges: there is a very apparent season-awareness. Here you find fancy breads for Christmas, coffee breads for Easter. You find nut breads that tell of fall harvests, dried fruit breads designed to carry into winter an abundant summer crop.

Prune Bread

2 cups boiling water
2 cups dried prunes, pitted and coarsely chopped
2 teaspoons soda
2 tablespoons melted butter
1¼ cups sugar
1 egg
1 teaspoon vanilla
4 cups flour
2 teaspoons baking powder
1 teaspoon salt
1 cup chopped walnut meats

Pour boiling water over chopped, uncooked prunes; add soda, and allow to stand. Mix butter, sugar, and egg thoroughly; stir in vanilla. Sift flour, measure, and sift again with baking powder and salt. Add to creamed mixture alternately with water from prunes. Stir in prunes and nut meats. Spoon into two 9 by 5-inch greased loaf pans. Bake in a slow oven (300°) for 1 hour, or until the bread is golden brown. Makes 2 loaves.

Pineapple Nut Bread

2¼ cups flour
¾ cup sugar
3 teaspoons baking powder
½ teaspoon soda
1 teaspoon salt
1 cup bran cereal
1 egg, beaten
1½ cups crushed pineapple, undrained
3 tablespoons melted butter
¾ cup chopped walnut or pecan meats

Sift flour, measure, then sift again with sugar, baking powder, soda, and salt into a mixing bowl. Stir in cereal, beaten egg, pineapple, and melted butter, and mix just until blended. Fold in nut meats. Turn into a greased 9 by 5-inch loaf pan. Bake in a moderate oven (350°) for about 1 hour and 15 minutes, or until a toothpick inserted in the center comes out clean. Let cool slightly before slicing. Makes 1 large loaf.

Flatbread

These fragile, thin, crisp rounds are excellent to serve with salads and soups.

2 cups flour
½ cup yellow cornmeal
½ teaspoon salt
¼ cup (4 tablespoons) butter
⅔ cup warm water

Sift flour, measure, then sift again with the cornmeal and salt. Mix in the butter until crumbly. Stir in ⅔ cup warm water; chill. Form chilled dough into balls the size of large marbles. Roll out into paper-thin rounds about 4 inches in diameter. Bake on an ungreased cooky sheet in a moderately hot (375°) oven for 5 minutes, or until very lightly browned. Cool; then store in a tightly covered can. Makes 90 wafers.

Apricot Nut Loaf

The tangy flavor of apricots dominates in this quick loaf bread that stays moist and fresh for a long time.

¾ cup dried apricots
  Lukewarm water
½ cup raisins
1 orange (juice and rind)
  Boiling water
⅔ cup sugar
2 tablespoons melted butter
1 egg
2 cups flour
2 teaspoons baking powder
1 teaspoon salt
1 teaspoon soda
½ cup chopped walnut meats
1 teaspoon vanilla

Cover apricots with lukewarm water and let stand for 30 minutes; drain. Force apricots, raisins, and one-half of the orange rind through medium blade of food chopper. Add enough boiling water to orange juice to make 1 cup and pour into ground fruit. Mix in sugar and butter. Beat egg and stir in. Sift flour, measure, then sift again with baking powder, salt, and soda into apricot mixture. Mix thoroughly. Add nut meats and vanilla. Spoon into a well-greased 5 by 9-inch loaf pan. Bake in a moderate oven (350°) for 1 hour or until a toothpick inserted in the center comes out clean. Cool thoroughly on rack before slicing. Makes 1 loaf.

Tea Bread

Jasmine tea, spices, almonds, and fruit peels and juices give this quick bread an unusual flavor and a delightful fragrance.

¼ cup (4 tablespoons) butter
¾ cup brown sugar, firmly packed
1 egg
1 teaspoon each grated lemon and
  lime peel
1 tablespoon grated orange peel
3 cups flour
½ teaspoon salt
¼ teaspoon each cinnamon and ginger
1 teaspoon each baking powder and
  soda
¾ cup tangerine or orange juice
½ cup steeped jasmine tea
½ cup coarsely chopped blanched
  almonds

Cream butter and brown sugar; beat in egg and grated peels. Sift flour, measure, then sift again with salt, cinnamon, ginger, baking powder, and soda. Add dry ingredients to the creamed mixture alternately with the tangerine juice and tea. Stir in almonds. Spoon into greased 9 by 5-inch loaf pan. Bake in a moderate oven (350°) for 50 minutes, or until lightly browned and a toothpick when inserted in the center comes out clean. Cool on rack; cut in thin slices. Makes 1 loaf.

Mincemeat Coffee Cake

½ cup (¼ pound) butter
1 cup sugar
2 eggs, well beaten
2 cups flour
2 teaspoons baking powder
¼ teaspoon salt
1 teaspoon lemon extract
⅞ cup milk (1 cup, less 2 tablespoons)
1 cup mincemeat
¼ cup chopped walnut meats
2 tablespoons melted butter
2 tablespoons brown sugar
1 teaspoon cinnamon

Cream butter and sugar together; stir in well beaten eggs. Sift flour, measure, then sift again with baking powder and salt. Add lemon extract to milk, and stir into creamed mixture alternately with dry ingredients. Combine mincemeat and nut meats. Spread ⅔ of batter in greased 8-inch spring form pan. Dot with ⅔ of the mincemeat mixture, distributing it over the batter by the teaspoonful. Cover with remaining batter and dot with rest of mincemeat. Sprinkle with melted butter, brown sugar, and cinnamon. Bake in a moderate oven (350°) for 45 minutes. Serve hot.

Jiffy Coffee Cake

"Jiffy" because you don't have to cream the sugar and shortening and it has a quick broiled topping.

1⅓ cups flour
4 teaspoons baking powder
1 teaspoon salt
1⅓ cups quick cooking rolled oats
Grated peel of 1 large or 2 medium sized oranges
⅔ cup brown sugar, firmly packed
2 eggs
1 cup milk
⅔ cup melted butter

Sift flour, measure, then sift again with baking powder and salt into a bowl. Mix in rolled oats, grated orange peel, and brown sugar. Beat eggs slightly, add milk and melted butter, and pour into well in center of dry ingredients; stir just enough to moisten. Spread batter in a greased 9-inch-square baking pan. Bake in a hot oven (400°) for 30 minutes.

Meanwhile, combine topping ingredients and spread over baked cake. Place cake under the broiler for 3 minutes, or until topping is bubbly. Serve hot.

Topping

½ cup brown sugar, firmly packed
2 tablespoons melted butter
¼ cup drained crushed pineapple
2 tablespoons each chopped maraschino cherries and walnut meats

Cinnamon Sour Cream Coffee Cake

This creamy coffee cake is baked in a tube pan and has a cinnamon-nut layer in the middle as well as on top.

1 cup (½ pound) butter
1¼ cups sugar
2 eggs
½ pint (1 cup) commercial sour cream
2 cups flour
½ teaspoon soda
1½ teaspoons baking powder
1 teaspoon vanilla
¾ cup finely chopped walnut meats combined with 1 teaspoon cinnamon, 2 tablespoons sugar

In the large bowl of your electric mixer, combine the butter, sugar, and eggs. Beat until the mixture is light and fluffy. Blend in the sour cream. Sift flour, measure, and sift with soda and baking powder into the creamed mixture; add vanilla. Blend well. Spoon half of the batter into a 9-inch tube pan which has been buttered and floured (batter will be quite thick). Sprinkle half of cinnamon-nut mixture over batter. Spoon in remaining batter and top with rest of nut mixture. Place in a cold oven, set oven to moderate (350°), and bake about 55 minutes. Cut pieces in pan to serve warm or cool. Makes 8 to 10 servings.

Danish Coffee Crescents

¾ cup butter
⅓ cup flour
1½ packages yeast, active dry or compressed
¼ cup warm (not hot) water
1 cup milk
¼ cup sugar
1 egg, slightly beaten
3½ cups sifted flour
1 teaspoon salt

Cut butter into flour, using pastry blender. Pat into a ball, then flatten out in a 9-inch square on a baking sheet; put in freezer 20 minutes.

Sprinkle yeast into warm water; stir until dissolved. Scald milk; add sugar and cool until lukewarm; mix in dissolved yeast and egg. Put flour and salt in mixing bowl. Add yeast and milk mixture and beat until smooth. Turn out on a floured board and roll out into a 9 by 18-inch rectangle. With spatula lift butter mixture onto half the dough. Fold over dough and roll out. Fold over ⅓ of dough from the left, then ⅓ from the right, and roll out. Repeat twice more. Refrigerate ½ hour. Roll out dough ⅛ inch thick; cut into 3-inch triangles; roll and shape into crescents. Place on greased baking sheet. Let rise 45 minutes. Bake in a very hot oven (450°) for 15 minutes. Makes 36.

Golden Sour Cream Twists

These elegant bread twists have crunchy crusts— — inside, they're flaky tender.

1 cup melted shortening (may be part butter)
1 cup (½ pint) commercial sour cream
1 teaspoon each salt and vanilla
1 package yeast, active dry or compressed
1 whole egg
2 egg yolks
3½ cups flour
1 cup sugar with 1 teaspoon cinnamon

Combine the shortening, sour cream, salt, and vanilla (mixture should be lukewarm). Crumble or sprinkle in the yeast. Combine whole egg and egg yolks and beat until creamy; blend into yeast mixture. Sift flour, measure, and blend into yeast mixture. Place in a greased bowl, cover with damp cloth, and refrigerate 2 hours. Mix sugar and cinnamon and spread on your board. Roll dough into a rectangle (15 by 18 inches), turning so both sides are coated with sugar. Fold over 3 times as you would a letter. Repeat rolling and folding 3 times or until sugar is used up. Roll into a rectangle about ¼ inch thick and cut into 1 by 4-inch strips. Twist strips, lay on greased baking sheet. Bake in moderately hot oven (375°) 15 minutes. Cool. Makes 24.

Bohemian Almond Triangles

Almond paste goes between the butter-rich layers of these yeast triangles.

¼ cup milk
2 teaspoons sugar
1 cake yeast
3 egg yolks
1 cup (½ pint) light cream
3 cups flour
2 tablespoons sugar
1 teaspoon salt
½ cup (¼ pound) butter
½ pound almond paste
Melted butter

Scald milk, add the 2 teaspoons sugar, and cool to lukewarm. Soften yeast in lukewarm milk mixture. Beat egg yolks until thick and blend in cream. Sift flour, measure, then sift again with the 2 tablespoons sugar and the salt. With a pastry blender or two knives, cut butter into flour until pieces are about the size of large peas. Combine the yeast and egg mixtures; stir into flour mixture, making a soft dough. Cover and store in the refrigerator overnight.

Turn out on a lightly floured board, divide in half; roll out in two equal-sized portions about ⅓ inch in thickness. Spread almond paste over one piece of dough and lay second piece of dough on top. With a sharp knife, cut in 2½-inch triangles. Place on a greased baking sheet, brush lightly with melted butter, and set in a warm place to rise until almost doubled in bulk. Bake in a moderate oven (350°) for 18 minutes, until golden brown. Makes 20 rolls.

Stollen

This recipe is a large one, but you can freeze this fruit-filled Christmas bread. Make the loaves ahead of time to give as gifts or to serve during the holidays.

8 cups sifted flour
1 pound soft butter
3 packages yeast, active dry or compressed
¾ cup warm (not hot) water
1 quart milk, scalded, then cooled to lukewarm
4 well beaten eggs
4 cups white sugar
1¼ teaspoons salt
1 pound chopped walnut meats, or other nut meats as desired
1 teaspoon nutmeg
About 1½ cups flour
1 pound fruit mix (or less if desired)
1¼ pounds seedless raisins

Blend the 8 cups flour and butter as if you were making pie crust. Dissolve yeast in the warm water. Combine flour and butter mixture, milk, yeast, eggs, and sugar. Set in a warm place to rise until about double in bulk (will take about 2 hours). Then add salt, nut meats, and nutmeg. Mix part of the 1½ cups flour with the fruit mix and raisins so the individual fruits don't stick together. Add them to the batter; then add more flour as necessary to make the batter stiff.

Let rise again about 2 hours until double size. Put in loaf pans and let rise again. Bake in a moderate oven (350°) about 1 hour, or until done. Serve hot or cold. Makes 5 medium sized loaves.

Holland Twists

1 cup milk
⅓ cup sugar
1 teaspoon salt
1 package yeast, active dry or compressed
3 cups flour
2 eggs
⅓ cup melted butter
1 teaspoon grated lemon peel
1 tablespoon lemon juice
Melted butter

Scald milk, add sugar and salt, and cool to lukewarm. Soften yeast in lukewarm milk mixture. Sift flour, measure, then gradually beat half of the flour into yeast mixture. Cover with cloth and set in a warm place to rise until full of bubbles (about 1 hour). Beat eggs slightly and stir into soft dough with the ⅓ cup melted butter, lemon peel, and lemon juice. With a large spoon gradually beat in the remaining flour, blending until smooth. Place in a greased bowl and smooth top with salad oil, cover with cloth and let rise in a warm place until almost doubled in bulk.

Turn out of bowl onto lightly floured board, knead lightly, and roll out to about ⅓ inch in thickness. Brush with melted butter and fold over in thirds — total width of dough should be 6 inches. With a sharp knife, cut into ¾-inch strips. Twist and bring ends together to form a circle. Place on a greased baking sheet, brush lightly with melted butter, and let rise 30 minutes. Bake in a hot oven (400°) for 20 minutes, or until golden brown. When cool, spread with powdered sugar frosting made by blending a small amount of orange juice into 1 cup powdered sugar until right consistency for spreading. Makes 18 twists.

Basic White Bread

Here is a basic recipe for bread with interesting variations. Cheese and bacon bread is particularly good with eggs. Raisin bread, nut bread, fruit bread, and cinnamon bread, each distinct in texture and flavor, can be made by adding to the basic dough.

2 packages yeast, active dry or
  compressed
½ cup warm (not hot) water
3 tablespoons butter
1½ cups milk
1½ cups cold water or potato water
9 cups flour
3 tablespoons sugar
3 teaspoons salt

Cheese and Bacon Bread

1 pound (4 cups) grated sharp
  Cheddar cheese
6 slices crumbled crisp bacon

Raisin or Nut Bread

½ cup melted butter
6 tablespoons sugar
1 cup raisins or nut meats

Fruit Bread

½ cup melted butter
6 tablespoons sugar
1 egg, beaten
½ cup each chopped candied lemon
  peel, orange peel, and citron
½ cup glacéed cherries
½ cup nut meats

Cinnamon Bread

½ cup melted butter
6 tablespoons sugar
½ cup sugar
4 tablespoons softened butter
1 tablespoon cinnamon
½ teaspoon nutmeg
1 teaspoon water

Sprinkle or crumble yeast into warm water and stir until dissolved. Drop butter into the milk and heat until scalding. In a large bowl, combine scalded milk and 1½ cups cold water; stir in yeast. Sift flour and measure. Sift 3 cups of the flour with the sugar and salt into the milk and yeast mixture; beat until smooth. Add ingredients needed for any one of the variations described below, then add the remaining 6 cups flour, and mix well.

Turn out dough on a lightly floured board; knead until smooth and elastic, about 10 minutes. Place dough in a large greased bowl, cover, and set in a warm place to rise. When nearly doubled in bulk, punch down and turn out on a lightly floured board. Knead lightly for 1 minute. Divide dough in 3 parts and form 3 loaves. Place in greased 9 by 5-inch pans, and allow to rise until nearly doubled in bulk. Bake in a moderately hot oven (375°) for 1 hour. Remove loaves from pans and butter the crusts; cool on a wire rack. Makes 3 medium sized loaves.

To make Cheese and Bacon Bread, Raisin or Nut Bread, or Fruit Bread, simply mix the added ingredients to the basic dough after you have mixed in 3 cups of the flour.

To make Cinnamon Bread, add the ½ cup melted butter and the 6 tablespoons sugar to the basic dough after mixing in 3 cups of the flour. Mix together the ½ cup sugar, 4 tablespoons butter, cinnamon, and nutmeg. Before the last rising, divide dough into thirds; pat each part into an oblong. Spread with the sugar mixture; sprinkle water over each piece of dough. Roll into loaves and place in pans for second rising.

Rye Bread

This bread has a light texture for one containing rye flour. Instant mashed potato simplifies the preparation.

1 package yeast, active dry or compressed
½ cup warm (not hot) water
1½ teaspoons anise seed
1½ teaspoons caraway seed
2 cups water
3 tablespoons instant mashed potato
1 tablespoon butter
¼ cup (4 tablespoons) molasses
¼ cup (4 tablespoons) brown sugar
1½ teaspoons salt
2 cups rye flour
4 cups all-purpose flour (approximately)
Salad oil

Sprinkle yeast into the ½ cup warm water and stir until dissolved. Add anise and caraway seeds to the 2 cups water, and heat water to boiling. Pour ¾ cup of the boiling water and seeds into a mixing bowl, add the instant potato, and quickly stir with a fork until the potato mixture is smooth. Stir in the remaining hot water and seeds, the butter, molasses, brown sugar, and salt; let cool to lukewarm.

Add the dissolved yeast to potato mixture and mix well. Gradually stir in the rye flour, beating until smooth. Sift all-purpose flour, measure, then gradually stir in enough flour to make a soft dough. Mix thoroughly. Turn out dough on a lightly floured board and knead for 10 minutes, using as little additional flour as possible to keep dough from sticking to the board. Place dough in a large bowl and lightly grease the top with oil; cover and set in a warm place to rise.

When dough is nearly doubled in bulk (about 2½ hours), punch down, then let rise again. When almost doubled in bulk for the second time, punch down dough and turn out on a lightly floured board. Knead dough slightly, divide in half, and shape into loaves. Place in 2 greased 9 by 5-inch loaf pans, brush tops with oil, and allow to rise until nearly doubled in bulk. Bake in a hot oven (400°) for 10 minutes; reduce heat to moderately slow (325°), and continue baking 50 minutes longer, or until loaves are nicely browned. Makes 2 medium sized loaves.

Swedish Orange Rye Bread

This crusty rye bread has a distinct orange tang.

Rinds from 2 oranges
Boiling water
1 package yeast, active dry or compressed
¼ cup warm (not hot) water
1½ cups lukewarm water
¼ cup molasses
⅓ cup sugar
1 teaspoon salt
2 tablespoons shortening
2½ cups rye flour
2½ cups all-purpose flour

Cook orange rinds in boiling water until tender; drain. With a spoon scoop out and discard the white portion, then finely chop outer peel. Sprinkle or crumble yeast into the ¼ cup warm water, and stir until dissolved.

Using a large mixing bowl, mix together orange peels, the lukewarm water, molasses, sugar, salt, dissolved yeast, and shortening. Sift flours, measure, and sift again; gradually add them, and beat until smooth. Knead lightly and let rise until almost doubled in bulk. Shape into 2 loaves and place in 9 by 5-inch loaf pans. Let rise until almost doubled in size. Bake in a moderately hot oven (375°) for 40 minutes. Makes 2 loaves.

Oatmeal Bread

Cooked oatmeal keeps this dark bread moist for several days.

1 package yeast, active dry or compressed
½ cup warm (not hot) water
2 cups water
1 cup rolled oats
½ cup molasses
2 tablespoons butter
2½ teaspoons salt
½ cup cold water
7 cups flour (approximately)
6 tablespoons non-fat dry milk
   powder
1 cup very finely chopped filbert
   meats
1 cup raisins

Soften yeast in the ½ cup warm water and set aside. Bring the 2 cups of water to a boil and gradually pour in rolled oats, stirring constantly for 1 minute; add molasses, the butter, and salt; stir until butter is melted. Stir in the ½ cup cold water and let stand until lukewarm. Sift flour, measure, then sift powdered milk with half the flour. Stir yeast into cool oatmeal; gradually beat in flour sifted with powdered milk, then enough more flour to make a soft dough. Add nut meats and raisins and mix well. Turn out on a lightly floured board, cover dough, and let rest 10 minutes. Knead thoroughly, using as little additional flour as possible. Place dough in a large greased mixing bowl, cover, and set in a warm place to rise. When nearly doubled in bulk, punch down and turn out on a lightly floured board. Divide into 3 parts and form into loaves.

Place in 3 greased 9 by 5-inch loaf pans, cover tops with a thin coating of salad oil, and allow to rise until nearly doubled in bulk. Bake in a hot oven (425°) for 10 minutes, reduce heat to moderate (350°) for 45 minutes, or until loaves are nicely browned. Makes 3 medium sized loaves.

Whole Wheat Bread

This soft, whole wheat dough requires no kneading. You simply spoon it into loaf pans and smooth out the tops. When it is baked, the crust is thick and crisp.

2 packages yeast, active dry or compressed
3 cups warm (not hot) water
1 tablespoon sugar
4 cups all-purpose flour
5 cups stone ground whole wheat flour
1 tablespoon salt
2 tablespoons sugar

Soften yeast in ½ cup of the warm water; combine with the remaining 2½ cups warm water and 1 tablespoon sugar in a large bowl. Sift all-purpose flour, measure, and gradually beat into yeast mixture. Cover with a cloth and set in a warm place to rise for about 1 hour. Mix whole wheat flour with salt and the 2 tablespoons sugar; gradually stir into the soft dough after it has been rising for 1 hour, mixing thoroughly with a large spoon. If dough gets too thick to beat, gradually stir in a little warm water. Cover with a cloth and set in a warm place to rise for 45 minutes.

Grease three 9 by 5-inch loaf pans; spoon dough into pans only until they are half full. Smooth down tops with a spoon dipped frequently in hot water. Cover and set in a warm place to rise until almost doubled in bulk. Bake in a hot oven (400°) for 20 minutes; reduce heat to moderate (350°) for 40 minutes longer, or until loaves are browned. Makes 3 medium sized loaves.

Cottage Cheese Pancakes

3 eggs
1 cup sieved small curd cottage cheese
2 tablespoons salad oil
¼ cup (4 tablespoons) flour
¼ teaspoon salt

Beat eggs until light and stir in cottage cheese and oil. Sift flour and salt into the cheese mixture; mix thoroughly. Spoon 4-inch circles of batter onto a lightly greased hot griddle. Bake on both sides until golden brown. You may make these pancakes the night before, fill them with applesauce, then reheat them in a 350° oven 15 minutes. Makes 8 pancakes.

Norwegian Pancakes

¾ cup flour
1 tablespoon sugar
1 cup (½ pint) commercial sour cream
4 eggs
1 cup small curd cottage cheese
Butter

Sift flour with sugar into a bowl. Spoon in sour cream; blend thoroughly. Beat eggs until very light; fold into flour mixture along with cottage cheese. Bake on a lightly buttered griddle until golden brown on both sides. Makes 36 pancakes about 3 inches in diameter.

Baked German Pancake

This is a grand one-pancake meal. A large oven can handle two such giant pancakes for a supper for two. Or you can bake two giant pancakes, and cut each in half to serve four persons for dessert. Traditionally, this pancake is served with melted butter, a squeeze of lemon juice, and a dusting of powdered sugar. But why not try some variations — sliced almonds, browned with butter and sugar; a fluffy honey-butter topping; pan-glazed cinnamon-spiced apple slices.

3 eggs
½ cup flour
½ teaspoon salt
½ cup milk
2 tablespoons melted butter

Using a French whip or fork, beat eggs until blended. Sift flour, measure, and sift again with salt. Add flour and salt to eggs in 4 additions, beating after each addition, just until mixture is smooth. Add milk in 2 additions, beating slightly after each. Lightly beat in melted butter. Generously butter bottom and sides of unheated 9 or 10-inch heavy frying pan. Pour batter into frying pan and bake in a very hot oven (450°) for 20 minutes. Reduce oven temperature to 350° and bake 10 minutes more. Slip onto heated plate; serve immediately.

Almond Filling

¼ to ½ cup sliced almonds
2 tablespoons melted butter
¼ cup sugar

When pancake has baked 20 minutes, quickly sprinkle center with almonds, drizzle with melted butter, and sprinkle generously with sugar. Return to oven and bake remaining 10 minutes at 350°.

Swiss Honey Butter Topping

½ cup (¼ pound) soft butter
½ cup honey
½ cup whipping cream
1 teaspoon vanilla

Cream butter with honey. Slowly add whipping cream, beating continuously until mixture is fluffy. Add vanilla. Spoon over hot pancakes. Makes about 1½ cups.

Pan-Glazed Cinnamon Apple Slices

2 tablespoons butter
2 apples, peeled and sliced
2 tablespoons sugar
½ teaspoon cinnamon

Melt butter in small frying pan. Add apples. Sprinkle with sugar and cinnamon. Slowly cook over low heat, stirring occasionally until slices are glazed and tender. Spoon into center of baked pancake as you serve it.

Swedish Oven Pancake

3 strips bacon, cut up
1 cup flour
2 tablespoons sugar
¾ teaspoon salt
3 eggs
2 cups milk
½ pint (1 cup) whipping cream
1 jar (12 oz.) lingonberry preserves

In a large frying pan about 9 inches in diameter, sauté bacon until crisp (do not pour off drippings). Sift flour, measure, then sift again with sugar and salt. Beat eggs lightly with milk, stir into the dry ingredients, and mix until smooth.

Pour batter over crisp bacon and drippings in the frying pan and bake in a moderately hot oven (375°) for 30 minutes, or until set and golden brown. Cut in wedges and serve immediately with a berry-cream topping, made by whipping cream until stiff and folding in lingonberry preserves. (Instead of lingonberries, you can blend whole cranberry sauce into the whipped cream, or serve the pancake with assorted berry jams or jellies.) Serves 6.

Rice Griddle Cakes

These custard-like pancakes do not contain flour of any kind. The thickening comes from the rice which is cooked in milk until very tender. Serve with maple syrup, orange marmalade, or wild berry jelly at breakfast-time. Or drizzle hot honey-butter over them as a dinner accompaniment to ham.

½ cup uncooked white rice
3 cups milk
¼ teaspoon salt
2 teaspoons honey
4 eggs
¼ teaspoon salt

Combine rice, milk, the ¼ teaspoon salt, and honey in the top of a double boiler. Cook over boiling water, stirring occasionally, for 2 hours, or until the milk is absorbed and the rice is creamy. Beat eggs thoroughly and mix in the cooked rice and the ¼ teaspoon salt. Beat thoroughly. Drop spoonfuls of batter onto a medium hot, lightly buttered griddle. Bake slowly on both sides until golden brown. Makes 30 pancakes, 3 inches in diameter.

Fried Oyster and Bacon Sandwiches

1 small package (3 oz.) cream cheese
Salt and paprika to taste
½ teaspoon minced chives or green onion tops
8 slices bacon, cut in half
4 slices bread
6 tablespoons butter
2 pints fresh medium sized oysters
4 teaspoons cracker meal
¼ teaspoon each salt and paprika

Blend the cheese (warmed to room temperature) with salt and paprika to taste; add the chives; set aside. Fry bacon until crisp; toast bread and spread with the cheese mixture; keep bacon and toast warm. In a frying pan, melt butter, heat until frothy, and add oysters. Sprinkle them with cracker meal and the ¼ teaspoon salt and paprika; sauté until they're golden and plump and start to curl. Arrange oysters on the cheese-covered toast, and garnish each sandwich with 4 pieces of crisp bacon. Makes 4 servings.

Broiled Crab and Avocado Sandwiches

2 tablespoons flour
3 tablespoons butter
1½ cups light cream
Salt and pepper to taste
½ cup shredded Swiss cheese
2 tablespoons grated Parmesan cheese
Few grains cayenne
4 English muffins
Butter
1 pound crab meat
8 sandwich-size slices Cheddar cheese
1 large avocado

Blend flour and butter together in a saucepan; add cream and cook, stirring, until smooth and thickened. Season with salt and pepper. Add cheeses and cayenne and stir until cheese melts.

Split English muffins, butter, then toast. Put a spoonful of sauce on each muffin. Arrange crab meat over sauce. Place a square of Cheddar cheese on the crab; then top with a slice of avocado, and spoon the rest of the sauce over all. Brown quickly under the broiler so that avocado is not overheated. Makes 8 open-faced sandwiches.

Steak Sandwiches, Italian Style

For a light dinner, try these open-faced steak sandwiches and a big green salad.

4 half-inch-thick slices French or Italian bread
Butter
1½ pounds beef tenderloin, cut in 4 slices ¾ inch thick
Salt and pepper
½ cup port wine
2 tablespoons whipping cream

Brown bread in butter on both sides in a heavy skillet. At the same time, in another skillet, brown meat for about 3 minutes on each side. Season with salt and pepper, and keep warm by placing on top of the bread. Stir port into pan in which meat was browned, and cook until wine is reduced one-half. Stir in cream and simmer 1 or 2 minutes, stirring constantly. Pour sauce over sandwiches on plate. Makes 4 open-faced sandwiches.

Croque Monsieur

This grilled sandwich, served with a green salad, is a supper favorite in France; try it for lunch, too.

Shred Swiss cheese and mix with enough heavy cream to make it the consistency of slightly softened butter. For each sandwich, place a slice of boiled ham on a slice of firm textured white bread (available in small loaves, heavier than regular bread), thickly spread cheese mixture on ham, top with another slice of bread and grill in butter.

Cheese Fondue Sandwich Bake

1 pound jack or Cheddar cheese, cut in 8 slices
16 slices buttered bread
1 can (4 oz.) green chili peppers
4 eggs
2 cups milk
½ teaspoon salt

Place cheese slices on 8 of the bread slices. Remove seeds from chilis and coarsely chop; sprinkle chilis over each slice of cheese. Cover sandwiches with the remaining bread slices. Cut sandwiches into quarters, then arrange in layers in a shallow baking dish. Beat eggs slightly; scald milk, then stirring, pour gradually into eggs; add salt. Pour egg mixture over sandwiches and let them stand at least 4 hours in the refrigerator. Bake in a moderately slow oven (325°) for 30 minutes, or until custard is set. Serves 6 to 8.

Ham and Egg Supper Sandwich

1 loaf French bread
⅓ cup soft butter
1 tablespoon finely chopped parsley
⅓ cup soft butter
½ teaspoon prepared mustard
12 slices boiled ham
Melted butter
8 eggs
½ cup light cream
Salt to taste
1 tablespoon finely chopped fresh herbs (chives, rosemary, oregano)
½ cup cream

Trim top and bottom crusts from bread, cut in half lengthwise. Spread one half with parsley butter, made by creaming ⅓ cup soft butter with the finely chopped parsley. Spread mustard butter on the second half (make it by creaming together ⅓ cup soft butter and the prepared mustard). Place both slices, buttered side up, on a baking sheet, and heat in moderate oven (350°) for 15 minutes.

Meanwhile, lightly brown boiled ham slices in a small amount of melted butter, and roll each loosely. Beat eggs slightly; add cream, salt to taste, and herbs. Scramble eggs in a small amount of melted butter. Spoon eggs on parsley buttered bread, and sprinkle with additional chopped herbs, if desired. Place ham roll-ups on mustard-buttered bread. Arrange on a platter and garnish with crisp greens and pickle slices. Cut each half loaf into 6 pieces. Serve open-face, or put ham and egg pieces together in a closed sandwich. Serves 6.

Special Picnics

THE PICNIC MENUS we remember best were highly repetitive and reassuring. There was plenty of cold fried chicken, potato salad, pickles, several kinds of bread, oranges, bananas, cold lemonade, cake, and watermelon. If we built a fire, there would be weiners and baked beans.

This chapter does not belittle such ceremonial food.

Here, however, we divorce ourselves from the expected and report the discovery that food which is generally associated with snow white linen, silver, candlelight, and faultless service tastes even better in forest shade beside a brook. Why not toast the scolding jay with champagne? Why not an epicurean picnic?

Preparation for such special events is but little more demanding than if menus were prosaic.

Your special picnic might be planned around a foreign theme—a Cantonese Picnic prepared over a *hibachi,* served in baskets on a straw table mat, and brought to a pleasant close with Chinese fortune or almond cookies, litchi nuts, and Chinese tea; or a Mexican Fiesta Picnic set against a gay Mexican cloth and featuring Taquitos and Chili Beans. Or it may be a picnic served on the tailgate of a station wagon en route to a football game or a week end in the snow.

It is to be noted that if a picnic is not on your calendar, the food ideas here are worthy of many backgrounds.

Elegant Trout Picnic

CHICKEN LIVER-MUSHROOM PÂTÉ

SESAME WATER CRACKERS

WINE POACHED TROUT

SALAD RELISH SKEWERS

MARINATED ASPARAGUS TIPS WITH LEMON

RUSSIAN RYE BREAD

BABA AU RHUM

Chicken Liver-Mushroom Pâté

Simmer for 5 minutes in 4 tablespoons butter: ½ pound fresh mushrooms, 1 pound chicken livers, 1 teaspoon each garlic salt and paprika, and ⅓ cup finely chopped green onion. Add ⅓ cup white table wine, $\frac{1}{16}$ teaspoon dill weed, and 3 drops Tabasco ; cover and cook slowly 5 to 10 minutes more. Cool, and sieve or whirl smooth in a blender. Blend in ½ cup (¼ pound) butter, and salt to taste. Pack in a jar or small crock and chill overnight. (Pâté will be thin before chilling.) Makes about 3 cups. Carry in an insulated bag. Serve with sesame water crackers.

Wine Poached Trout

Choose a pan that will hold 4 to 6 medium sized trout (with heads removed) flat on the bottom. In the pan bring to a boil 1¼ cups rosé or Chablis wine, 1¼ cups chicken broth, 1 teaspoon chicken stock concentrate, 2 tablespoons lemon juice, 1 teaspoon salt, and 1 small sprig fresh rosemary. Place trout in stock and poach gently for 5 to 10 minutes, or until fish flakes. Remove herb sprig; let trout cool in liquid. Carefully lift trout from stock and place on a wire rack on a tray; cover and chill thoroughly.

Meanwhile prepare glaze: Soften 1½ tablespoons (1½ envelopes) unflavored gelatin in 3 tablespoons white table wine. Strain stock; add gelatin and heat until dissolved. Chill until syrupy. Arrange slices of stuffed green olives in a row alongside the neck of each fish. Spoon aspic over all; coat 2 or 3 times, chilling between (and reusing aspic that drips on tray). Makes 4 to 6

servings. Carry trout to picnic on a well chilled tray wrapped in foil, or in an insulated bag wrapped individually in foil.

Salad Relish Skewers

On silver skewers place cherry tomatoes, pickled artichoke hearts, hors d'oeuvre pickled onions, and jumbo ripe olives stuffed with Cheddar cheese spread put through a pastry tube. Wrap in foil and carry to picnic in an insulated container. Bring along a cantaloupe or grapefruit with a thin slice of rind removed from one side to make it sit steady. Place fruit on a tray and plunge in skewers.

Baba au Rhum

Drain and save syrup from 1 or 2 cans (12 oz. each) rum cakes. Arrange cakes in a basket lined with clear plastic wrap, then wrap all in foil. (You might like to tuck in a few blossoms and leaves.) For each can of rum cakes, whip ½ cup cream and fold in rum syrup. Carry cream in a covered container in an insulated bag. Spoon on when ready to serve. Each 12-ounce can serves 4. Serve with coffee, freshly made or from a vacuum bottle.

Champagne Picnic

STRAWBERRIES WITH STEMS

PINK CHAMPAGNE IN ICE

CHICKEN BREASTS IN HAM

AVOCADO HALVES WITH GARLIC FRENCH DRESSING

HERB-BUTTERED BREAD

LEMON VELVET TARTS

Crystal, silver, and china emphasize the elegance of this menu. You must pack these fine pieces carefully, of course, with plenty of towels and tissue to protect them (or use a special hamper). Strawberries go in a chilled glass bowl with a few leaves silhouetted against the side. Champagne cools in an ice bucket or bag.

Chicken Breasts in Ham

Remove skin and bones from 4 large chicken breasts. Cut meat in strips about 1 inch wide. Dredge in a mixture of ½ teaspoon each garlic salt and paprika, ¼ teaspoon chili powder, and ¼ cup flour. Brown strips in 3 tablespoons butter. Add ⅔ cup chicken broth or white table wine, cover, and simmer for 20 minutes or until tender. Cool. Wrap each piece of chicken in strips of thinly sliced baked ham. Skewer with cocktail picks. Wrap and carry in a refrigerated container to the picnic. To serve, arrange chicken in a row down the center of a silver tray with avocado halves on one side and herb-buttered bread on the other. Garnish with watercress. Serves 4 to 6.

Avocado Halves with Garlic French Dressing

Cut ripe avocados in half, remove seed, but do not peel. Brush with lemon juice and put halves back together. Wrap in foil or clear plastic wrap; carry along garlic French dressing.

Herb-Buttered Bread

Spread slices of bread (the firm textured kind that resembles home-made bread) with this mixture: ½ cup (¼ pound) butter blended with ¼ teaspoon dill weed.

Lemon Velvet Tarts

Mix together 1⅓ cups sugar, 6 tablespoons cornstarch, and ½ teaspoon salt; stir slowly into 1½ cups boiling water. Cook and stir until thick. Place over boiling water; cook 15 minutes longer. Add 2 beaten egg yolks, blended with some of the hot mixture, and 2 tablespoons butter; cook 2 minutes more. Remove from heat. Stir in 1 teaspoon grated lemon peel, ⅓ cup lemon juice, and 1 teaspoon vanilla. Set aside 1 cup of this filling to cool.

Soften 1 envelope (1 tablespoon) unflavored gelatin in ¼ cup water; blend into hot mixture to dissolve. Add 1 cup whipping cream. Cool until mixture begins to set, then fold in 2 stiffly beaten egg whites. Spoon into 6 or 8 baked 4-inch tart shells; let stand until partially set. Top with reserved 1 cup filling. Chill until set. Serve tarts with a mint sprig in the center of each. Makes 6 to 8 servings. Pack in a box, chill, and carry to picnic.

Cantonese Picnic

SHELLFISH TIDBITS

BACON-WRAPPED CHICKEN LIVERS

CHINESE NOODLES

SWEET AND SOUR PORK

PICNIC FRIED RICE

CONDIMENTS: PRESERVED GINGER AND SOY

SLICED TOMATOES, CUCUMBERS, AND TURNIPS OR GREEN ONIONS

CHINESE COOKIES

CANDY

NUTS

SPARKLING APPLE JUICE

CHINESE TEA

For this unusual outdoor dinner, you need a picnic site where you can build a small campfire or set up a small portable barbecue or *hibachi*. The menu is surprisingly easy to prepare, in spite of its foreign quality.

For each member of the party, you need an inexpensive straw table mat. On it place a shallow basket, foil lined, to serve as a plate. Inside this basket place a smaller basket filled with dessert, a Chinese teacup, and two paper food containers filled with condiments.

Fold the mat over the baskets, and wrap the whole package in a sheet of Chinese gift paper or newspaper. Tie with colored ribbon and slip an inexpensive pair of chopsticks through the bow. (It's a good idea to bring forks, too!)

Guests eat the appetizers and sip the apple juice while you prepare the rest of the picnic food.

Be sure to keep the shellfish and chicken livers cool en route. Wrap them in foil and set the packages on ice cubes in a large mouthed vacuum-type container or jar. If you chill the apple juice in a large container filled with ice, you can place the foil packets right on top.

Shellfish Tidbits

Bring lobster chunks or crab legs and a dip made by combining equal parts soy and lime or lemon juice. You can eat the seafood cold, or skewer the bites of shellfish and grill them lightly over the coals.

Chicken Livers

If chicken livers are large, cut them in half. Place a chicken liver and a piece of water chestnut on half a strip of bacon, wrap, and skewer. You broil these over the coals, too.

Chinese Noodles

Lightly heat the canned crisp noodles, or eat them right from the can.

Sweet and Sour Pork

1½ pounds lean pork shoulder
  2 tablespoons salad oil or shortening
  1 medium sized can (1 lb. 4 oz.)
    pineapple chunks
 ⅓ cup vinegar
 ¼ cup brown sugar, firmly packed
  2 tablespoons cornstarch
 ½ teaspoon salt
  1 tablespoon soy
 ½ cup sliced onion
 ¾ cup sliced green pepper

It is best to prepare this attractive entrée entirely at home and reheat it at the picnic site.

Cut meat in strips about ½ inch wide and 2 or 3 inches long. Brown in hot oil; drain off any excess fat. Drain syrup from the pineapple, add enough water to make 1½ cups liquid, and combine with the vinegar, sugar, cornstarch, salt, and soy. Cook just until clear and slightly thickened. Add to meat; cover and simmer until tender, about 1 hour. Add pineapple chunks, onion, and green pepper; cook just until vegetables are crisp-tender. Serves 6.

Picnic Fried Rice

  3 slices diced bacon
  2 tablespoons minced green onion
  2 tablespoons minced green pepper
  3 cups cooked rice
  2 eggs
  1 tablespoon soy
 ½ teaspoon salt
 ¼ teaspoon pepper

In your kitchen measure all the ingredients for the fried rice, and pack together. It takes only about 10 minutes to prepare the rice over a small fire.

Cook bacon in a hot frying pan until almost crisp. Add onion and green pepper and cook slowly, about 5 minutes, or until vegetables are soft. Stir in rice, beaten eggs, soy, salt, and pepper. Cook and stir constantly until eggs are set. Serves 6.

Sliced Tomatoes, Cucumbers, and Turnips or Green Onions

Peel and slice vegetables at home; chill. To keep them cool, carry in a plastic bag inside an insulated bag.

Chinese Cookies, Candy, and Nuts

Fortune and almond cookies, Chinese candy, and litchi nuts are appropriate choices for this picnic.

Sparkling Apple Juice

Carry the bottled beverage in an iced container, or chill in a stream if one is close by.

Tea

Brew your favorite Chinese tea at the picnic spot.

Fiesta Picnic

TAQUITOS (MEXICAN SANDWICHES OR LITTLE TACOS)

SALSA DE TOMATILLO

CHILI BEANS

AVOCADO WITH LIME WEDGES

FRESH FRUIT

MEXICAN CHOCOLATE

This menu is appropriate for either luncheon or supper. Set the table at the picnic site with a gay Mexican cloth, or use inexpensive yardage in bright colors, and perhaps the paper napkins can have a Mexican or fiesta motif. Pack the food in a colorful woven Mexican basket. To prepare this menu, you need a picnic spot where you can build a small fire.

You can purchase both frozen and canned tortillas, or make your own with *masa* (moist ground cornmeal), *masa harina* (corn tortilla flour), or white flour. Bring either a frying pan or a metal toaster rack to heat the tortillas. Pack the other ingredients separately in plastic containers, or wrap each one in foil, so each person can get them handily when assembling his own Taquito.

Taquitos

 1 dozen tortillas
   Salad oil for frying
12 slices jack cheese
 2 tomatoes, thinly sliced
¼ cup finely chopped onion
12 slices chicken, turkey, ham, or other
   sliced meat
   Salsa de Tomatillo
   Shredded lettuce and radishes

Fry each tortilla in hot oil a few seconds. Or brush with oil on both sides, slip into a wire toaster rack, and heat on both sides over a picnic fire. Cover each hot tortilla with sliced cheese, tomato, onion, and chicken or meat. Spoon about 1 tablespoon Salsa de Tomatillo on each filled tortilla. Roll or fold over. Place on plates and garnish with shredded lettuce and radishes. Serve with remaining Salsa. Makes 1 dozen, enough to take care of 6 picnic appetites.

Salsa de Tomatillo

 1 tablespoon minced onion
 1 tablespoon salad oil
 1 can (10 oz.) tomatillo (Mexican
   green tomatoes), mashed
 1 teaspoon salt
½ teaspoon crumbled dried oregano
½ teaspoon chili powder (or more
   to taste)

Make this sauce the day before the picnic. Sauté onion in oil until clear. Add tomatillo. Season with salt, oregano, and chili to taste. Simmer 5 to 10 minutes, or until the flavors are blended. Makes 1 cup.

Chili Beans

Use canned chili beans or, if you prefer, refried beans. Heat and mash canned beans in a generous amount of heated oil. (Figure on using ½ cup oil to 2 cups cooked beans.)

Avocados with Lime Wedges

Bring well wrapped whole avocados. At the picnic cut in half lengthwise, and remove the seed. Serve ½ avocado per person and pass salt and lime wedges. (Remember to take spoons.)

Fresh Fruit

Bring any selection of fresh fruits that you wish —the small Mexican mangoes, red-skinned bananas, and oranges are particularly appropriate with this menu. You can arrange the fruit assortment in a basket for easy carrying to the picnic.

Mexican Chocolate

To each quart of chocolate milk (homemade or creamery), add 2 sticks cinnamon or 1 teaspoon ground cinnamon, and heat. Carry hot chocolate in a vacuum bottle or reheat at the picnic site. Shake or beat well to a froth before serving. One quart serves 4.

Beach Picnic

BROILED OYSTERS OR CLAMS MARINIERE

FRENCH BREAD   SHOESTRING POTATOES

CABBAGE SLAW

APPLE CRISP   COFFEE

When oysters and clams are in season, feature them at a beach barbecue. You'll need a camp stove or miniature barbecue, a frying pan or hinged broiler (one with narrow grills) for broiling the oysters, and a kettle for steaming the clams. A plastic container with a tight lid is fine for carrying the cabbage salad. You can buy the shoestring potatoes in cans. Pack individual servings of apple crisp, made from your own recipe, in paper cups that have lids.

Pan-broiled Oysters

Dip the shucked oysters in melted butter, then in fine crackers or bread crumbs. Sauté in small amount of butter in a hot frying pan just until well browned on each side, 3 to 5 minutes. (For charcoal-broiled oysters, arrange the crumb-coated oysters in a greased hinged broiler; broil over hot coals.) Serve with lemon wedges.

Clams Mariniere

With a brush thoroughly scrub about 5 pounds hard-shell clams. Place in a kettle with a tight cover. Combine ⅓ cup each finely chopped onion, celery, and parsley; add ½ teaspoon pepper. (Do this before you leave home.)

Sprinkle seasonings over clams. Cover tightly; cook until shells start to open, about 10 minutes. Add 4 tablespoons butter and ¼ cup bottled clam juice or white table wine. Cook another 5 to 10 minutes. Serve nectar in paper cups for a hot soup.

Soup and Salad Picnic

FRESH TOMATO SOUP

WHEAT CRACKERS

POTATO SALAD CAESAR

OPEN FACE SANDWICHES

CHOCOLATE CREAM CUPS

CHOCOLATE REFRIGERATOR COOKIES

Instead of relying completely on hampers for this picnic, you may want to anchor most of the food and serving pieces to a board with plastic clay. Tie the board hobo-fashion in a sturdy weave tablecloth to carry in your car.

Fresh Tomato Soup

Simmer 2 cups peeled, diced ripe tomatoes in 3 tablespoons butter for about 5 minutes; purée or sieve. Blend in 2 tablespoons flour, 1 teaspoon salt, and a dash of pepper. Bring to a boil, reduce heat, and cook 2 or 3 minutes; stir constantly. Add ¼ teaspoon soda and 1 cup light cream; cook until slightly thickened. Stir in ½ cup white table wine or chicken broth and heat to simmering. Pour into a vacuum bottle and carry to picnic. Serve as an opening course in cups to sip (Oriental tea cups are nice for this). Makes 4 to 6 servings.

Potato Salad Caesar

Beat together ½ cup salad oil, 1 teaspoon each Worcestershire and salt, ⅛ teaspoon each pepper and garlic powder, ¼ cup lemon juice, 1 egg, and ¼ cup minced green onion. Toss with 4 cups diced hot cooked potatoes; chill thoroughly. Spoon into a large, chilled salad bowl (use wood, if you have it). Top with 1½ to 2 quarts broken pieces crisp romaine. Cover with clear plastic wrap to carry to picnic. (Cold bowl and salad keep cool for several hours if kept in a shaded place.)

Carry along in individual containers: 2 cups croutons that have been tossed with 2 tablespoons melted butter and a pinch of garlic powder; ¼ cup each grated Parmesan and crumbled Roquefort cheeses; 6 or 8 chopped anchovies;

½ cup sliced pitted ripe olives. When ready to serve, combine all ingredients and toss. Makes 6 to 8 servings.

Open Face Sandwiches

Spread slices of your favorite bread with soft butter, top each with a thin slice of luncheon meat such as cooked salami, mortadella, or galantina; spread with more soft butter and cover with a thin slice of Swiss, provolone, or kuminost cheese. Cut with fancy-shape cutters. Arrange on a serving tray and cover with foil; chill. Carry to picnic on tray.

Chocolate Cream Cups

Prepare 1 package (3 oz.) chocolate or butterscotch pudding mix according to package directions using 1½ cups milk and ¼ cup Sherry for the liquid. Add ⅛ teaspoon salt and 1 teaspoon instant coffee powder. Cover and chill. Fold in ½ cup cream, whipped, and spoon into 6 or 8 individual serving cups (use crème pots, or paper cups with lids) and cover. Carry to picnic in an insulated bag along with a covered bowl of spiced cream topping to spoon on chocolate cream when ready to serve.

Spiced cream topping. Whip ½ cup cream; fold in 1 tablespoon sugar, ½ teaspoon instant coffee powder, and ⅛ teaspoon cinnamon.

Barbecue Picnic

HOT TOMATO BOUILLON

CHARCOAL BROILED STEAK, ORANGE MARINADE

TOASTED HAMBURGER BUNS

GRILLED PEPPERS

POTATO CHIPS

FRUIT BASKET OF PEARS AND GRAPES

HOT COFFEE

The soup can be carried in a vacuum bottle or heated on the spot while you wait for coals to glow in the *hibachi*. You could also use a camp stove to grill the steak and peppers in a frying pan.

Charcoal Broiled Steak, Orange Marinade

- 2 pounds skirt steak, sirloin, or top round
- 1 teaspoon salt
- Freshly ground pepper
- ¼ cup sugar
- 2 tablespoons vinegar
- 1⅓ cups fresh orange juice
- 2 teaspoons lemon juice
- ½ teaspoon dry mustard
- 2 beef bouillon cubes
- ½ cup whipping cream

If you intend to broil the steak over charcoal, cut it into bite-sized chunks and thread these on small bamboo or metal skewers. To prepare the meat for cooking quickly over a camp stove, cut steaks diagonally across the grain into thin (about ¼ inch) slices and about 2 inches long.

Rub meat with salt and pepper, and put in a polyethylene bag or a pan to marinate. Caramelize the sugar in a heavy skillet over low heat, stirring constantly. Add vinegar and orange juice; cook and stir until sugar dissolves again. Cool. Add lemon juice and mustard, and pour over steak pieces. Twist top of bag so it won't leak, or cover the pan; refrigerate overnight to marinate.

Before you leave home, pour off the marinade into a small pan, add bouillon cubes, and simmer until about half as much remains. Add cream, stirring rapidly so it doesn't curdle; remove sauce from heat. Cool and put into a container to carry to the picnic.

Reheat the sauce at the picnic spot while you wait for coals to form in the *hibachi*. Let each one broil his own skewered steaks over hot coals until done to his liking. (To cook steak on a camp stove, melt 3 or 4 tablespoons butter in a heavy frying pan; brown steak pieces 3 to 5 minutes per side; reheat orange sauce in the same pan.) Serve on toasted hamburger buns; spoon orange sauce over the meat.

Grilled Pepper

Cut 3 or 4 green or sweet red peppers lengthwise into 1-inch strips; weave several on each small bamboo skewer. Brush with olive oil and put in a container to carry to the picnic. To serve, grill lightly over charcoal, or sauté in frying pan with meat. Dress with a well seasoned French dressing, adding ½ teaspoon dry mustard to each ½ cup of the dressing. Serves 4.

Game Day Picnic

WIENER SCHNITZEL ON FRENCH ROLLS

HOT MUSTARD

CATSUP

HARD COOKED EGGS WITH CAPERS

GRAPE CLUSTERS

GRUYERE OR PORT SALUT

SALTINES

COFFEE

On game days an early start followed by a picnic near the stadium is a pleasant way to avoid heavy traffic and be assured of a parking place. If you have a station wagon, set up your picnic on its tailgate. Our menu features wiener schnitzel sandwiches, borrowed from the hearty Bavarian morning meal. Just add relish to sandwiches and lunch is ready to eat—all can be eaten as "finger food." You serve hot coffee from a vacuum bottle.

Wiener Schnitzel on French Rolls

1 pound veal round steak or 2 round
   steaks cut ¼ inch thick
   Salt and pepper
2 eggs, beaten
   Finely rolled bread crumbs or cracker
   crumbs
   Butter
4 French rolls

Trim outer layer of skin, fat, and bone from steaks and pound thin (about ⅛ inch). Cut large pieces into sections that will fit on French rolls. Season veal with salt and pepper, dip in egg, and coat well with crumbs. Melt enough butter just to cover bottom of the frying pan. Quickly brown a few pieces of veal at a time, adding more butter as needed. Drain cooked veal on absorbent paper and let cool.

Divide schnitzels among the 4 rolls and wrap in waxed paper or clear plastic wrap. Add hot mustard or catsup when you get to the picnic. Makes 4 generous servings.

Hard Cooked Eggs with Capers

Mash yolks of 4 hard cooked eggs, and mix with 1 teaspoon finely minced capers and 2 teaspoons liquid from jar of capers. Stuff the egg whites with yolk mixture and dot each half with several whole capers. Wrap individually. Makes 4 servings.

Cool-Weather Picnic

FINGER-FOOD SPARERIBS

HOT LIMA BEAN AND PEAR CASSEROLE

CELERY STICKS

GINGERBREAD WITH SUGAR GLAZE

COFFEE

This is a hearty picnic—one that would be welcome on an autumn or winter day. Include it in an excursion to gather dried plant material or Christmas greens, or to view fall color.

Finger-Food Spareribs

Cut 6 pounds lean spareribs into individual ribs and place in a large baking pan, lean side up. Bake in a hot oven (400°) for 30 minutes. Drain off fat and pour this sauce over ribs: Blend together 1 bottle (12 oz.) chili sauce, 2½ cups water, ½ teaspoon allspice, 2 teaspoons Worcestershire, 2 tablespoons brown sugar, 1 teaspoon salt, and 1 medium onion, chopped.

Continue cooking in a moderate oven (350°) for an additional 1 hour and 15 minutes, basting every 15 minutes. Drain ribs thoroughly on cake cooling rack and allow to cool. Refrigerate. Place in a covered container to carry to the picnic; serve as finger food with plenty of napkins. Makes 6 servings. (It's a good idea to include a big paper bag lined with waxed paper in your picnic hamper so you'll have a place to deposit all the bare spareribs.)

Hot Lima Bean and Pear Casserole

½ cup (¼ pound) butter
6 cups cooked and drained lima beans (about 1 pound uncooked dry limas) or 3 cans (15 oz. each) lima beans, drained
1 can (1 pound) pears, drained and chopped
¾ cup brown sugar, firmly packed

Dot a 2½ or 3-quart casserole or bean pot with half of the butter. Cover bottom of the casserole with 2 cups beans; top with half the pears and half of the brown sugar. Repeat layers, ending with the last 2 cups of beans; distribute remaining butter over top layer. Bake in a slow oven (275°) for 2 hours. Cover and wrap casserole in a thick layer of newspapers to hold heat until ready to eat. It will keep warm 3 to 4 hours. Makes 6 to 8 servings.

Gingerbread with Sugar Glaze

Make your favorite recipe of gingerbread, or use a mix and follow package directions. Frost gingerbread while it's still warm with 1 cup sifted powdered sugar blended with 1½ tablespoons milk, 1 tablespoon melted butter, and ½ teaspoon grated lemon peel. Carry to your picnic in the baking pan.

Roadside Smorgasbord

ASSORTED BREADS   BUTTER

COLD CUTS   CHEESE SLICES   SARDINES

WILTED CUCUMBERS

TANGY MACARONI SALAD

FRUIT COMPOTE

COOKIES   COFFEE

For that week-end day when you can't resist going out for a drive, this menu is easy to assemble. It starts with make-your-own, open face sandwiches, so take several kinds of bread and your favorite cold cuts, cheese, and sardines or tuna spread—all convenient to carry in plastic containers. The fruit compote—just big pieces of fresh fruit in fruit juice—also goes in a plastic container.

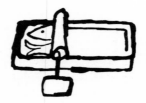

Wilted Cucumbers

Thinly slice 2 cucumbers; marinate in 3 tablespoons vinegar, ½ teaspoon salt, and a dash of pepper. Sprinkle chopped parsley or a little dill weed over the top, if you wish.

Tangy Macaroni Salad

　1 package (8 oz.) shell or elbow
　　macaroni
　　Boiling salted water
　1 can (1 lb.) garbanzos
　1 can (6 or 7 oz.) tuna, flaked
　1 medium sized dill pickle, chopped
　4 green onions, chopped
⅓ cup chopped parsley
　1 clove garlic, minced or mashed
　2 tablespoons capers, including liquid
　1 small bottle (2 oz.) stuffed olives,
　　halved, with their liquid
⅓ cup lemon juice
　　Dash of black pepper
　1 cup mayonnaise

Cook macaroni in boiling salted water until tender; drain. Add all other ingredients. Toss lightly. Add salt to taste, if needed. Chill until time to start on picnic. (Salad keeps well in refrigerator for a couple of days.)

Desserts

THERE IS NO more perfect finale to a splendid meal than the classic dessert of fresh fruit, served alone or in combination with a compatible cheese and an assortment of crackers. You'll find simple fruit desserts in this chapter — Strawberries Grand Marnier, Figs in Port — and more elaborate ones — a Tropical Fruit Float or Cantaloupe Alaska.

The cheese and fruit board is another way to serve fruits in season. Offer a selection — or offer one favorite cheese matched perfectly with one fruit. Try Provolone with Bartlett pears, sharp Cheddar with Jonathan apples, any blue cheese with Anjou or Bosc pears, Gouda with Delicious apples, or a soft, ripened cheese with sweet Ribier grapes.

A dessert should be light and refreshing if it follows a bounteous meal — and desserts other than fruit *can* fill this requirement. The flaky Walnut Cheese Sticks on page 185, or the delicate, moist Sour Cream Orange Cake on page 184 are gentling accompaniments to after-dinner coffee.

There are occasions, too, when dessert becomes the highlight and when a very special creation is called for. A light supper leads logically to the smooth, rich cheese cake on page 183. And if you entertain friends with a "dessert and coffee" party, you may wish to present an elegant Bittersweet Chocolate Tweed Cake, or a meringue-topped Strawberry Sundae Pie.

Cantaloupe Alaska

3 ripe cantaloupes, chilled
4 egg whites
Dash of salt
½ cup sugar
1 pint firm vanilla ice cream
2 tablespoons halved blanched
almonds

Cut cantaloupes in half and remove seeds; level base. Beat egg whites and salt until stiff; gradually beat in sugar until meringue is very stiff and glossy. Place cantaloupes on a cooky sheet; put 1 scoop vanilla ice cream in each half; spread stiff meringue over ice cream and melon; sprinkle with almonds. Bake in a pre-heated, very hot oven (500°) for 2 minutes, or until meringue is golden. Serve at once. Serves 6.

Figs in Port

Peel black figs and marinate them in port wine to cover for several hours. When you serve, pass sugar. This dish can also be served flaming.

Baked Papaya

Papaya baked with lime juice and ginger is an unusual hot fruit dessert. Try it also as an accompaniment to chicken or fish.

2 half ripe medium sized papaya
¼ cup (4 tablespoons) butter
2 tablespoons lime juice
½ teaspoon ground ginger
Cayenne (optional)

Cut papaya in half lengthwise and scoop out the seeds; place in a greased baking dish. Melt together the butter, lime juice, and ginger; spoon into the cavity of each papaya. Bake in a moderate oven (350°) for 30 minutes, or until tender, basting every 5 minutes with the butter mixture. Serve hot (with a dash of cayenne if you serve it as a meat accompaniment). Serves 4 with a half papaya apiece.

Peach-Cherry Jubilee

1 can (1 lb. 13 oz.) peach halves
1½ teaspoons vanilla
1 can (1 lb. 4 oz.) pitted dark
cherries
1 glass (10 oz.) currant jelly
½ cup brandy or kirsch
1 quart vanilla ice cream

Turn the peaches, with their syrup, into a pan; add vanilla. Bring to a boil, and simmer 2 or 3 minutes. Lift peaches from syrup to a bowl to take to the table. Drain cherries and put into a bowl.

At the table heat jelly in a chafing dish. Add cherries and peaches; spoon melted jelly over peaches as they heat through.

To flame the dessert, pour warmed brandy into center; light immediately. Serve over ice cream. Makes 6 or 7 servings.

Peaches with Sherry Cream

3 or 4 large fresh peaches
¾ cup sugar
2 cups water
1 teaspoon vanilla
2 egg yolks
¼ teaspoon salt
¾ cup sifted powdered sugar
⅓ cup sherry or ⅓ cup orange juice
   and ½ teaspoon grated orange peel
½ pint (1 cup) whipping cream
   Nutmeg

Peel, halve, and pit peaches. Bring sugar and water to a boil, then add peaches. Simmer until tender, about 5 to 10 minutes. Add vanilla. Chill until ready to serve. Beat egg yolks and salt until thick. Add sugar gradually, and continue beating until very thick and lemon colored. Add sherry. Whip cream until stiff, and fold into egg yolk mixture. Spoon over peaches and sprinkle with nutmeg. Serves 6 to 8.

Pears Baked in Wine

4 whole unpeeled pears (including
   stems)
4 whole cloves
1 cup dry red table wine
½ cup water
½ cup sugar

Pierce with a clove the blossom end of each pear. Put pears in a deep casserole (fruit may be placed on sides); add wine, water, and sugar. Cover and bake in a hot oven (400°) for about 30 minutes; baste occasionally. Uncover and continue cooking 15 to 20 minutes longer or until pears are quite tender; baste frequently. Serve hot or cold with wine sauce. Makes 4 servings.

Pineapple with Grapes

Cut ripe pineapples in quarters, leaving the leaves on. Carefully remove and dice flesh. Combine with seedless grapes (half the quantity of the pineapple), mix with sour cream sweetened with brown sugar, and pile into pineapple shells. Serves 4.

Pineapple in Gingered Sour Cream

1 can (1 lb. 13 oz.) pineapple chunks
1 cup (½ pint) commercial sour cream
1 tablespoon honey
1 tablespoon chopped candied or
   preserved ginger

Chill pineapple chunks. Drain pineapple, reserving syrup. Mix sour cream with honey, ginger, and enough pineapple syrup to make the sauce the consistency of heavy cream. Mix well and pour over the pineapple arranged in chilled sherbet glasses. Garnish with sprigs of mint. Serves 6.

Strawberries in Red Wine

Clean and hull 1 to 2 baskets of firm, ripe strawberries, leaving the berries whole. Sprinkle with about ¼ cup sugar, or to taste. Chill the berries until 1 hour before it is time to serve them. Pour over them 1 cup red table wine (claret or Burgundy) and chill until time to serve.

Strawberries Melba

For each serving, put a scoop of vanilla ice cream in a sherbet glass, top with sliced strawberries, and pour over raspberry purée. (To make purée, whirl a basket of raspberries in the blender or force through a sieve; sugar to taste.)

Strawberries Grand Marnier

Clean berries, sprinkle with sugar and Grand Marnier to taste, and chill. Line a glass bowl with about 2 inches orange or other flavored ice, and top with the berries. Sprinkle with more liqueur, if you wish.

Sour Cream Dip for Strawberries

½ pint (1 cup) commercial sour cream
1 teaspoon grated lemon peel
1 teaspoon lemon juice
½ cup powdered sugar

Beat sour cream, lemon peel, lemon juice and powdered sugar with a rotary beater until light. Place in a bowl and surround with whole strawberries whose stems and caps are still intact.

Tropical Fruit Float

2 cans (11 oz. each) mandarin oranges
1 can (1 lb. 4 oz.) pineapple chunks or tidbits
1 can (about 1 lb.) papayo or mango
1 to 1½ cups orange juice
1½ cups shredded or flaked coconut
1 quart vanilla ice cream

Drain fruit and cut papaya or mango into bite-sized pieces; combine all the fruits in bowl. Pour orange juice over the fruit; chill. Spread coconut in a shallow pan and place in a moderate oven (350°) for 5 to 7 minutes; stir or shake to toast evenly. Mound spoonfuls of firm vanilla ice cream in center of fruit. Use a ladle to serve. Pass the toasted coconut. Makes 6 to 8 servings.

French Pancakes

2 cups flour
2 tablespoons powdered sugar
Dash of salt
5 eggs
2 cups milk
2 tablespoons brandy
Butter

Sugar Coating

1 cup powdered sugar
1 tablespoon softened butter
½ teaspoon lemon juice
2 tablespoons brandy

Orange Sauce

½ cup (¼ pound) butter
2 tablespoons powdered sugar
6 cubes sugar
½ cup orange juice
¼ cup curacao
2 tablespoons B & B (Benedictine and brandy)
⅓ cup brandy

Sift flour, measure, then sift again with the 2 tablespoons powdered sugar and salt. Beat eggs until blended; add dry ingredients and stir until smooth. Gradually add the milk and the 2 tablespoons brandy; beat until smooth.

Heat a 7-inch frying pan and grease lightly with butter. Pour in 2 tablespoons of batter (a small gravy ladle is a handy measure), and roll pan quickly to spread batter. Brown quickly on each side. Lay pancakes on waxed paper, spread with the sugar coating, and roll up. Cover to keep warm.

To prepare sugar coating, cream together 1 cup powdered sugar and 1 tablespoon butter. Add lemon juice and the 2 tablespoons brandy; cream together until the coating is the consistency of butter icing.

For orange sauce, cream the ½ cup butter and 2 tablespoons powdered sugar; chill. Dissolve sugar cubes in orange juice. When ready to serve, melt the prepared sugar-butter mixture in a chafing dish over direct heat. Add the orange juice and sugar mixture and cook until reduced to one-half. Put water jacket, half filled with boiling water, under the pan. Place as many rolled pancakes in the pan as it will hold in one layer; spoon orange sauce over them. Mix together the curacao and the B & B; pour over pancakes. When hot, pour over warm brandy, light immediately, and spoon flaming sauce over pancakes until flame dies. Serve at once. Makes 20 pancakes; serves 10.

Strawberry Almond Pancakes

4 small packages (3 oz. each) cream cheese
¼ cup sugar
1½ tablespoons grated lemon peel
3 tablespoons lemon juice
16 French pancakes
2 cups sliced and sugared strawberries
1 tablespoon lemon juice
¼ cup slivered almonds
¼ teaspoon almond extract

Beat softened cream cheese with sugar, lemon peel, and lemon juice until light and fluffy. Put 2 tablespoons of the filling on each pancake and roll. Place, seam side down, in a shallow baking pan. Chill until serving time, then heat in a hot oven (400°) just until pancakes are hot.

Combine strawberries, lemon juice, almonds, and almond extract. Heat or not as desired (contrast of hot pancake and cold strawberries is very pleasant). Spoon over filled pancakes and serve at once. Serves 8.

Swiss Chocolate Puffs

16 tiny cream puffs, 1½ inches in diameter
½ cup light cream
6 ounces sweet chocolate or 1 bar (6 oz.) Swiss milk chocolate
1 pint vanilla ice cream
1 pint (2 cups) whipping cream

Make the tiny cream puffs from a cream puff mix (1 stick of the mix will make more than enough) or your own recipe.

For chocolate sauce, pour cream in the top of a double boiler. Break chocolate into chunks and add to cream; heat over boiling water until melted. Beat smooth.

At serving time split and fill each cream puff with a spoonful of firm ice cream. Drop puffs into whipped cream. Drizzle in the chocolate. Fold gently to marble. Heap in bowl. Makes about 8 servings.

Fried Crème Flambé

Crisp on the outside, richly soft within, this famous San Francisco dessert is served flamed with brandy.

1 pint (2 cups) whipping cream
¼ teaspoon salt
1-inch piece vanilla bean, split or ½ teaspoon vanilla
⅓ cup sugar
4 egg yolks
¼ cup cornstarch
¼ cup milk
  Minced almonds
2 eggs, slightly beaten
  Fine dry bread crumbs
¼ cup brandy

In the top of a double boiler, scald cream with salt, vanilla bean, and sugar. Beat egg yolks. Moisten cornstarch in milk, and add to the egg yolks. Add to the cream, put over hot water, and cook, stirring constantly, until thick and smooth.

Remove vanilla bean; pour mixture into a lightly greased 8-inch-square pan; chill. Cut into squares or oblongs, and roll in finely minced almonds. Dip into slightly beaten eggs; then roll in bread crumbs, and fry in deep fat (370°) until brown. Put on a fireproof dish and keep warm. To serve, pour on warmed brandy and light.

Coeur à la Crème

Surround the cheese mold with any fresh fruit.

1 large package (8 oz.) cream cheese
1 tablespoon powdered sugar
3 tablespoons whipping cream
½ teaspoon vanilla
  Powdered sugar

Let cream cheese soften to room temperature. Beat until light; add the 1 tablespoon sugar, cream, and vanilla, and beat until blended and fluffy. Pack mixture into a heart-shaped mold lined with dampened cheesecloth; chill 3 hours. Turn out on a platter and sprinkle with powdered sugar. Surround with any fresh fruit, such as strawberries, raspberries, Bing cherries, or peach slices. Serves 4 to 6.

Pumpkin Flan

1¼ cups sugar
3 cups thin cream, scalded
2 cups canned pumpkin
⅔ cup sugar
¼ cup rum, or rum flavoring to taste
6 whole eggs plus 2 egg yolks, slightly beaten
1 teaspoon each salt and cinnamon
¼ teaspoon ginger
½ teaspoon mace or nutmeg
¼ cup brandy for flaming (optional)
1 cup whipping cream

Slowly melt sugar in a heavy frying pan, stirring until it becomes a smooth, deep amber syrup. Pour into a well chilled, round-bottomed glass casserole (2 quart). Tip to coat sides, bottom of bowl; chill while you prepare custard.

Mix well all remaining ingredients; pour into the caramel-lined bowl. Set bowl in a pan of hot water, and bake in a moderate oven (350°) for about 1¼ hours, or until set. Cool at room temperature 30 minutes. Invert on plate; after 10 minutes lift off bowl. Flame if you wish; then serve with whipped cream. Serves 10 to 12.

Crème Brûlée, Amandine

1 pint (2 cups) whipping cream
7 egg yolks
1 teaspoon vanilla
⅓ cup brown sugar, firmly packed
⅛ teaspoon salt
½ cup toasted blanched almonds
¾ cup brown sugar, firmly packed

Scald cream in top of double boiler. Beat egg yolks until light colored and thick; add vanilla, the ⅓ cup brown sugar, and salt. Add the scalded cream. Return to double boiler and cook over hot water until smooth and about as thick as thin mayonnaise. Stir constantly so that it will be smooth, and do not overcook or it may curdle.

Chop toasted almonds very fine. (One easy way is to use a rotary grater; another is to chop in an electric blender.) Stir almonds into the custard and pour into an 8-inch round (1-quart) baking dish. Chill thoroughly.

Two hours before serving, sift remaining brown sugar in an even layer over the entire top of the custard. You should have an even layer of brown sugar about 3/16 to ¼ inch thick. Put under a preheated broiler and watch carefully until the sugar melts in an even glaze. It takes just a few seconds. (You can also use an electric charcoal starter for melting the sugar. Heat the lighter and hold it 3 or 4 inches from the topping, moving it as the sugar melts. In this way you have complete control of the situation and are less apt to overbrown the sugar.) Again chill the dessert. Serve by breaking the hard top crust with a spoon and giving each person some of this as well as the custard underneath.

Apricot-Almond-Coffee Trifle

One definition of a trifle: luxury upon luxury in a clear glass bowl. You can vary the flavor combination as you will, but this one is outstanding.

1 layer sponge cake (about ½ pound)
6 tablespoons sherry
2½ dozen almond macaroons (the crisp kind)
2 large cans (1 lb. 14 oz. each) peeled apricots
Soft Custard Sauce (below)
½ pint (1 cup) whipping cream
Powdered sugar
Almond extract
¼ cup diced toasted almonds

Place sponge cake in bottom of large bowl. Sprinkle evenly with 4 tablespoons of the sherry. Arrange about 12 of the macaroons over top of sponge cake layer. Sprinkle lightly with 1 tablespoon sherry. Drain apricots thoroughly; cut in half, and remove pits. Arrange half the apricot halves over macaroons. Arrange another layer of macaroons; sprinkle with the remaining tablespoon sherry; top with remaining apricots. Arrange additional macaroons to stand around the sides of bowl. Pour cooled sauce over contents in trifle bowl. Chill for at least 4 hours.

To serve, whip cream until stiff, sweeten and flavor to taste with powdered sugar and almond extract. Swirl on top of trifle. Garnish with toasted almonds stuck upright into cream. Makes 12 servings.

Soft Custard Sauce

4 egg yolks
2 cups (1 pint) light cream
4 tablespoons sugar
⅛ teaspoon salt
1 teaspoon vanilla
1½ teaspoons instant coffee powder

Beat together thoroughly egg yolks, cream, sugar, and salt. Place in top of double boiler, and cook over hot water, stirring until mixture coats a silver spoon. Strain custard, add vanilla and instant coffee powder, and allow to cool. Makes about 2 cups sauce.

Orange Marmalade Soufflé

4 egg whites
Pinch of salt
4 tablespoons sugar
4 tablespoons orange marmalade
Butter
Chopped toasted almonds
2 egg yolks
Pinch of salt
½ cup sugar
1 cup (½ pint) whipping cream
Brandy or Cointreau (optional)

Beat egg whites with salt until stiff; fold in the 4 tablespoons sugar and orange marmalade. Butter generously the top half of a 1½-quart double boiler and sprinkle with plenty of chopped toasted almonds. Carefully spoon in egg white mixture. Sprinkle more chopped almonds over the top. Cover and steam for 1 to 1½ hours. Turn out on serving dish and serve with the sauce made by beating the egg yolks with the salt and ½ cup sugar and folding in the whipping cream that has been beaten until stiff. The sauce may be flavored with brandy or Cointreau to taste. Serves 4.

Chocolate Soufflé

2½ ounces (2½ squares) unsweet-
    ened chocolate
½ cup sugar
5 tablespoons hot water
5 tablespoons butter
3 tablespoons flour
1 cup milk
½ teaspoon salt
4 egg yolks
5 egg whites
1 teaspoon vanilla

Melt the chocolate over hot water. Add ¼ cup of the sugar and the hot water, and stir until smooth. Make a roux of the butter and flour; gradually add milk, and bring slowly to a boil. Add chocolate mixture and salt. Cool slightly, then combine with the very well beaten egg yolks. Cool to lukewarm.

Beat egg whites until stiff; add remaining sugar gradually, beating until glossy. Add vanilla. Combine one-third of the whites very thoroughly with the chocolate mixture, then carefully fold in remaining whites. Pour into a buttered 2-quart soufflé dish and bake in a moderately hot oven (375°) for 25 minutes. This will give you a soufflé with a nice crusty bottom and sides, and a creamy interior — the way the French prefer their soufflés. If you prefer a firmer one, bake at 325° for about 40 minutes. Serves 8.

Chilled Fruit Pudding

A lemon-sharp sauce tops sweet, fresh fruits; a crumbly caramel sugar tops all.

1 cup sugar
3 tablespoons cornstarch
¼ teaspoon salt
1¼ cups water (may be part orange
    or pineapple juice)
1 egg, well beaten
⅓ cup lemon juice
½ teaspoon grated lemon peel
2 tablespoons butter
1 cup seedless grapes
1 cup sliced strawberries (fresh or
    frozen)
5 figs, sliced (fresh or dried)
3 peaches, peeled and sliced (fresh
    or frozen)
Caramel Crumbs (see below)

Blend together the sugar, cornstarch, and salt. Mix in water (or water and fruit juice). Stir while you bring to a boil, and cook 5 minutes, or until clear and thickened. Remove from heat and blend slowly with the beaten egg. Return to heat; cook about 1 minute longer. Add lemon juice, lemon peel, and butter. Cool. Arrange the fruits in layers in a casserole or in 8 individual serving dishes. Pour cooled lemon sauce over fruit. Sprinkle generously with Caramel Crumbs. Chill. Serves 8.

Caramel Crumbs

⅓ cup brown sugar, firmly packed
½ cup flour
¼ teaspoon salt
2 tablespoons butter

Mix together until crumbly brown sugar, flour, salt, and butter. Spread in a loose, thin layer on a baking sheet. Bake in a moderately hot oven (375°) about 10 minutes, or until crisp and golden brown.

Pear Crumble Pie

This open-faced fresh pear pie has a spicy sugar topping.

6 medium sized pears
½ cup sugar
1 teaspoon grated lemon peel
3 tablespoons lemon juice
9-inch unbaked pastry shell

Topping
½ cup each flour and sugar
½ teaspoon each ginger and cinnamon
¼ teaspoon mace
⅓ cup butter
½ pint (1 cup) whipping cream
flavored with sugar and vanilla

Peel, halve, core, and slice pears, and toss them lightly with the ½ cup sugar and the lemon peel and juice. Arrange in unbaked pastry shell. For the topping combine flour, sugar, ginger, cinnamon, and mace; cut in butter until crumbly. Sprinkle mixture over the pears. Bake in a hot oven (400°) for 45 minutes, or until the fruit is tender. Serve warm with flavored whipped cream. Serves 6.

Crunch Top Apple Pie

6 medium sized cooking apples
10-inch unbaked pastry shell
1 cup sugar
1 cup graham cracker crumbs
½ cup flour
½ cup chopped walnuts
½ teaspoon cinnamon
¼ teaspoon salt
½ cup (¼ pound) butter
½ pint (1 cup) whipping cream

Pare, quarter, core, and slice apples; arrange in unbaked pastry shell. Mix together sugar, graham cracker crumbs, flour, nut meats, cinnamon, and salt; sprinkle over apples. Melt butter and pour evenly over topping. Bake for 1 hour in a moderate oven (350°), or until apples are tender. Serve at room temperature or chilled. Decorate with the cream that has been beaten until stiff enough to put through pastry bag, or spoon the whipped cream on each serving. Serves 6 to 8.

Peach Sour Cream Pie

1 cup (½ pint) commercial
sour cream
¾ cup brown sugar, firmly packed
½ teaspoon salt
2 egg yolks, well beaten
2 tablespoons flour
9-inch unbaked pastry shell
2½ cups drained, sliced peaches

Blend together sour cream, sugar, and salt; stir in egg yolks. Sprinkle 1 tablespoon flour in bottom of pie shell. Arrange peach slices on top; sprinkle with remaining flour. Pour sour cream mixture over peaches. Bake in a hot oven (425°) for 10 minutes; reduce heat to moderate (350°) and continue baking for about 40 minutes longer. Serves 6.

Chocolate-Topped Rum Pie

1 envelope (1 tablespoon) unflavored gelatin
¼ cup cold water
4 eggs, separated
½ cup sugar
½ teaspoon salt
½ cup hot water
⅓ cup rum
½ cup sugar
  9-inch baked pastry shell
6 tablespoons butter
6 tablespoons powdered sugar
1½ squares unsweetened chocolate,
  melted
1 egg yolk

Soften gelatin in cold water. In the top of the double boiler, beat the 4 egg yolks slightly and stir in the ½ cup sugar and the salt; gradually stir in hot water. Cook over hot water, stirring constantly, until the mixture thickens. Remove from heat and mix in softened gelatin, stirring until dissolved. Cool slightly, pour in rum, and beat well. Chill until mixture starts to congeal.

Beat egg whites until stiff and gradually beat in the other ½ cup of sugar. Fold into the chilled rum custard. Spoon into baked pastry shell; chill until firm. Cream together the butter and powdered sugar until light and fluffy. Stir in melted chocolate. Add egg yolk and beat well. Spread on pie. Chill again. Serves 6.

Angel Pie

A tender baked meringue shell and tart lemon filling . . .

4 egg whites
½ teaspoon cream of tartar
  Pinch of salt
1 cup sugar

Beat egg whites until frothy, sprinkle in cream of tartar and salt, and beat until stiff. Beat in the sugar, 2 tablespoons at a time. The mixture should be glossy and stand in stiff peaks when all the sugar has been added. With the back of a tablespoon, spread meringue in a large, well-greased pie pan, pushing it high on the sides so that it resembles a pie shell. Bake in a slow oven (300°) for 40 minutes. Cool on a rack.

Filling

4 egg yolks
½ cup sugar
  Grated peel of 2 lemons
3 tablespoons lemon juice
½ pint (1 cup) whipping cream

Beat egg yolks and sugar in the top of double boiler until light. Stir in lemon peel and juice and cook over hot water until thick, stirring constantly. Chill. Whip cream and fold into chilled lemon mixture. Fill meringue shell with lemon filling; chill for several hours. Serves 6 to 8.

French Cherry Pie

You may want to add lemon juice or almond extract to the prepared cherry pie filling used in this easy but elegant pie. For another version, substitute prepared blueberry pie filling, with 1 tablespoon lemon juice, for the cherry pie filling.

1 small package (3 oz.) cream cheese
½ cup powdered sugar
½ teaspoon vanilla
1 cup whipping cream
  9-inch baked pastry shell
1 can (1 lb. 5 oz.) prepared cherry
  pie filling

Cream cheese, powdered sugar, and vanilla together. Whip cream and fold in carefully. Pour into pastry shell, spread evenly, cover with prepared cherry pie filling. Chill thoroughly before serving. Serves 6.

Chocolate Almond Bar Pie

12 pieces sweetened zwiebach
¼ cup (4 tablespoons) butter
¼ cup (4 tablespoons) sugar
¼ teaspoon cinnamon
 7 small (⅞ oz. each) chocolate
  almond bars
¼ cup blanched, toasted almonds
16 marshmallows
½ cup milk
  Pinch of salt
½ pint (1 cup) whipping cream

Roll zwiebach into fine crumbs and mix thoroughly with butter, sugar, and cinnamon. Pat into a 9-inch pie pan. Bake in a hot oven (400°) for 10 minutes. Cool. Put chocolate bars, almonds, marshmallows, milk, and salt in top of double boiler and melt over hot water. Cool thoroughly. Whip cream until stiff and fold in. Pour into baked shell. Chill until firm. If desired, sprinkle a slivered chocolate bar over the top. Serves 6.

Palm Springs Date Pie

 3 eggs
½ cup sugar
 1 cup dark corn syrup
¼ cup (4 tablespoons) melted butter
¼ teaspoon salt
 1 teaspoon vanilla
 1 cup finely chopped, pitted dates
  9-inch unbaked pastry shell
½ pint (1 cup) whipping cream

In the large bowl of your electric mixer, beat the eggs until light; add the sugar gradually, beating thoroughly. Beat in the corn syrup, butter, salt, and vanilla. Fold in dates. Turn into the pastry-lined pan and bake in a moderately hot oven (375°) for about 35 minutes, or until the filling is set and lightly browned. Remove from oven and serve with unsweetened whipped cream. Makes 6 to 8 servings.

Strawberry Sundae Pie

1¼ cups fine gingersnap cooky crumbs
1 tablespoon sugar
⅓ cup melted butter
1 package (1 lb.) frozen sliced
  strawberries
3 egg whites
  Dash each salt and cream of tartar
6 tablespoons sugar
1 quart vanilla ice cream

Combine cooky crumbs with the 1 tablespoon sugar and the melted butter. Press into a greased 9-inch pie pan. Chill several hours. Thaw strawberries, then drain.

Make meringue by beating egg whites with salt and cream of tartar until just stiff. Gradually add the 6 tablespoons sugar, beating after each addition until the mixture is glossy.

At serving time pack firm ice cream into crust; cover with drained berries. Spread with meringue, being sure it is sealed tightly to edge of pie. Set pie on a board, put into very hot oven (475°) for 3 to 5 minutes. Cut into wedges and serve immediately. Makes about 6 servings.

Walnut Tarts

½ cup (¼ pound) butter
½ cup brown sugar, firmly packed
¾ cup granulated sugar
4 eggs, well beaten
¼ teaspoon salt
¼ cup light corn syrup
½ cup whipping cream
1½ cups chopped walnut meats
1 teaspoon vanilla
  Pastry for 12 small tart shells
1 pint (2 cups) whipping cream

In the top of a large double boiler, cream butter with brown and white sugars until light and fluffy. Stir in beaten eggs, salt, corn syrup, and the ½ cup of cream. Place over boiling water and cook for 5 minutes, stirring constantly. Add walnuts and vanilla. Spoon into pastry-lined tart pans. Bake in a moderately hot oven (375°) for 20 minutes. Cool. Top with sweetened whipped cream. Makes 12 servings.

Brownie Mint Torte

3 egg whites
  Dash of salt
¾ cup sugar
½ teaspoon vanilla
¾ cup fine chocolate wafer crumbs
½ cup chopped walnut meats
½ pint (1 cup) whipping cream
  Sugar to taste
¼ cup crushed peppermint stick candy
1 square (1 oz.) unsweetened chocolate,
  shaved

Beat egg whites and salt until soft peaks form. Add the ¾ cup sugar, 1 tablespoon at a time, beating after each addition until glossy. Beat in vanilla. Fold in crumbs and nut meats. Spread in buttered 9-inch pie pan, piling meringue high at sides. Bake in slow oven (325°) 35 minutes. Let cool.

About 3 hours before you're ready to serve, whip cream until stiff; fold in sugar to taste, and crushed peppermint candy. Pile the peppermint cream into chocolate shell. Chill. Before serving, trim with curls of shaved chocolate. Serves 6.

Mosaic Fruit Cake

2 large eggs
⅔ cup brown sugar, firmly packed
1 teaspoon vanilla
1 teaspoon rum flavoring
3 tablespoons soft butter
½ cup all-purpose flour
½ teaspoon each baking powder and salt
2 cups whole candied cherries
1 cup large candied pineapple chunks (about 4 slices)
1½ cups pitted whole or halved dates
2 cups pecan halves or Brazil nuts

Beat eggs until light. Add sugar, vanilla, rum flavoring, and butter; continue beating until well blended. Sift flour and measure; sift with baking powder and salt into the first mixture. Mix to a smooth batter. Add the fruits and nuts. Blend with a spoon or your hands until well mixed — batter will barely coat fruit mixture. Turn into a well greased 9-inch square pan; distribute batter evenly. Bake in a moderately slow oven (325°) for 40 to 45 minutes.

Let cake stand in pan until partially cool; turn out on cake rack to cool thoroughly before storing. Age the cake at least 4 days before cutting. Cut in thin slices or in 1-inch squares. It is easier to get perfect slices if you freeze the cake and cut it while hard. The slices defrost in a very short time. Makes about a 3-pound fruit cake square.

Date Cake

This freezes exceptionally well. For a freshly baked flavor, warm the frozen cake; serve with whipped cream or ice cream.

1 cup pitted dates, cut in sixths
1 cup water
½ teaspoon soda
½ cup (¼ pound) butter
1 cup sugar
2 eggs
1½ cups all-purpose flour
1 teaspoon baking powder
½ teaspoon cinnamon
¼ teaspoon salt
1 teaspoon vanilla

Place dates in a bowl. Bring water to a boil in a saucepan, add soda, stir until dissolved, pour over dates, cool.

Cream together butter and sugar. Add eggs, one at a time; beat well. Sift flour with baking powder, cinnamon, and salt, and add to creamed mixture alternately with the water poured off the dates; beat well after each addition. Stir in dates and vanilla. Spread in a well greased 9-inch-square pan. Bake in a moderate oven (350°) for 40 minutes. When cake is cool, cover with date and walnut frosting.

Frosting

Boil together 1 cup water and ½ cup each brown sugar and white sugar for 10 minutes. Add ½ cup finely cut dates, ½ cup butter, and ½ cup walnut meats, chopped. Continue cooking until thick. Pour over cool cake.

Chocolate Almond Cake

1 cup shortening
2 cups sugar
4 eggs, separated
¾ cup cold mashed potatoes
2 cups all-purpose flour
1 teaspoon each salt, cinnamon, and
    powdered cloves
1 cup ground sweet chocolate
½ cup milk
1 cup finely ground almonds

Cream shortening and sugar until light. Blend in beaten egg yolks; mix in mashed potatoes. Sift flour, measure, then sift again with salt, cinnamon, cloves, and chocolate. Add dry ingredients alternately with milk, mixing until smooth. Mix in ground nut meats (grind in a nut grinder or chop very fine), and fold in stiffly beaten egg whites. Turn into a lightly greased 10-inch tube pan. Bake in a moderate oven (325°) for 1 hour and 10 minutes. Cool thoroughly on wire rack. Makes 12 to 16 servings.

Bittersweet Chocolate Tweed Cake

Chocolate-specked, velvet-smooth, it's unreservedly rich and elegant.

½ cup (¼ pound) butter
½ cup sugar
2 cups cake flour
3 teaspoons baking powder
    Pinch of salt
1 cup milk
1 teaspoon vanilla
3 squares (1 oz. each) unsweetened
    baking chocolate
2 egg whites
½ cup sugar

Cream together thoroughly butter and sugar. Sift flour, measure, and sift with the baking powder, and salt. Add dry ingredients to creamed mixture alternately with milk combined with vanilla — beginning and ending with dry ingredients. After each addition beat until smooth. Finely grate chocolate. Blend into batter. Beat egg whites until foamy; add the ½ cup sugar, a tablespoon at a time; beat until stiff. Carefully fold into batter.

Pour into three 8-inch round layer cake pans, or two 9-inch pans, greased and floured. Bake in a moderate oven (350°) for 20 to 25 minutes, or until toothpick inserted in center comes out clean. Cool slightly. Turn layers out of pans; cool thoroughly on wire racks. Frost between layers and on top and sides with this frosting:

Frosting

¾ cup soft butter
3 egg yolks
2¼ cups sifted powdered sugar

Beat together butter and egg yolks. Blend powdered sugar into butter and egg mixture until smooth.

Chocolate Topping

½ package (6 oz. size) semi-sweet
    chocolate chips
2 tablespoons water

Melt chocolate chips in top part of double boiler. Add water and stir until smooth. Pour over top of cake, allowing a small amount to drip down sides of cake.

Cherry Angel Cake

10-inch angel food cake
2 cans (1 lb. each) pitted Bing
  cherries
1 package (3 oz.) cherry flavored
  gelatin
¼ cup sherry
1 pint vanilla ice cream
¼ cup toasted slivered almonds
¼ cup red currant jelly
½ teaspoon grated orange peel
1 cup (½ pint) whipping cream
  Toasted slivered almonds

Cut a 1-inch layer from top of cake, remove and save. Cut out center of remaining part of cake, leaving a 1-inch outside shell. Fill bottom (to 1-inch depth) with pieces of cake you have removed from center.

Drain cherries; save syrup and heat it. Dissolve gelatin in hot cherry syrup. Remove from heat and add sherry. Add vanilla ice cream, stirring until melted. Chill until thickened but not set. Fold one-half of the cherries into thickened gelatin mixture along with the ¼ cup toasted slivered almonds. Spoon into cake shell. Replace cake top; refrigerate overnight.

Over very low heat, melt jelly; add grated orange peel and remaining cherries. Stir carefully, just to glaze cherries. Cool. At serving time, fill cake center with glazed cherries. Swirl sweetened whipped cream over top of cake, around cherry center; sprinkle with a ring of additional toasted, slivered almonds. Serves 12.

Elegant Cheese Cake

Crumb Layer

1 cup zwieback crumbs
2 tablespoons sugar
¼ teaspoon cinnamon
3 tablespoons melted butter

Cake Layer

3 large packages (8 oz. each) cream
  cheese, softened
½ teaspoon salt
3 tablespoons light rum or 1 tablespoon vanilla
4 egg whites
1 cup sugar

Sour Cream Topping

2 cups (1 pint) commercial
  sour cream
2 tablespoons sugar
⅛ teaspoon salt

Mix together the crumbs, sugar, cinnamon, and melted butter. Press into the bottom of an 8 or 9-inch spring form pan in an even layer.

Cream cheese, salt, and rum together until soft and creamy. Beat the egg whites until they form soft peaks, then gradually beat in the sugar to make a meringue. Fold egg white mixture into the cheese until well blended. Turn into the spring form pan. Bake in a moderate oven (350°) about 25 minutes. Remove from oven; increase oven temperature to 450°. Combine sour cream with sugar and salt; spread over top of cake. Return to oven for 4 to 5 minutes, until cream is set. Remove from oven and cool until cold. Remove sides from pan. Serves 12.

Persimmon Almond Cake

You won't detect the persimmon flavor in this very light, ground almond cake, but the fruit pulp makes the cake very moist.

½ cup (¼ pound) butter
1¼ cups sugar
2 eggs
2 cups cake flour
1½ teaspoons baking powder
¼ teaspoon salt
½ teaspoon soda
1 cup sieved persimmon pulp
¼ cup sour milk or buttermilk
1 cup ground, unblanched almonds
Powdered sugar (optional)

Cream butter and sugar together until light and fluffy. Add eggs, one at a time, and beat until smooth. Sift flour, measure, then sift again with baking powder, salt, and soda. Add dry ingredients alternately with persimmon pulp and sour milk to the creamed mixture, mixing until smooth. Stir in ground nut meats. Pour into a greased 10-inch tube pan. Bake in a moderate oven (350°) for 50 minutes, or until a toothpick inserted in the cake comes out clean. Cool. Slice and serve plain or dust with powdered sugar. Serves 12.

Lemon or Cinnamon Crunch Cake

1½ cups sugar
⅓ cup water
¼ cup light corn syrup
1 tablespoon sifted baking soda
⅛ teaspoon oil of lemon or a few drops oil of cinnamon
1 10-inch sponge or chiffon cake
1 pint (2 cups) whipping cream
¼ cup powdered sugar
⅛ teaspoon lemon extract (lemon crunch cake) or ½ teaspoon vanilla (cinnamon crunch cake)

Combine sugar, water, and corn syrup in a heavy saucepan. Cook over moderate heat, stirring occasionally, until syrup reaches very hard-crack stage (300° on candy thermometer). Remove from heat at once and quickly stir in soda and oil of lemon or cinnamon. Stir until blended and turn out onto a buttered 8 by 12-inch shallow baking pan. Let cool. Crush into crumbs.

Split cake into 4 layers. Whip cream until stiff; flavor with powdered sugar and appropriate flavoring. Spread half the cream between layers and remainder on top and sides. Sprinkle crushed candy generously on top and sides. Serves 14 to 16.

For Coffee Crunch Cake, add 3 teaspoons instant coffee to syrup mixture before cooking, and flavor whipped cream with 1 teaspoon instant coffee.

Sour Cream Orange Cake

1 cup sugar
½ cup (¼ pound) butter
2 eggs
½ pint (1 cup) commercial sour cream
1 teaspoon soda
1 cup ground raisins
1 medium sized orange, ground
2½ cups cake flour

Cream together sugar and butter; beat in eggs, sour cream, soda, raisins, and orange which has been put through the food chopper (include all the juice). Sift and measure flour and add to batter, blending well. Turn batter into a greased and flour-dusted 9-inch-square baking pan; bake in a moderate oven (350°) for 35 minutes or until cake begins to pull away from edge of pan. Serve warm or cold. Top with whipped cream, if desired. Makes 8 to 10 servings.

Walnut Cheese Sticks

½ pint (1 cup) creamed cottage cheese
1 cup (½ pound) butter
2 cups flour
¼ cup (4 tablespoons) butter, melted
¾ cup brown sugar, firmly packed
¾ cup finely chopped walnut meats

Blend cottage cheese and butter together with a fork. Sift flour, measure, and sift again into the butter mixture, and blend until dough holds together. Roll out on a lightly floured board until ⅛ inch thick. Spread dough with melted butter, then sprinkle with brown sugar and nut meats. Cut into triangles 3 inches wide at the base. Beginning at the base of the triangle, roll dough into sticks. Place on a greased baking sheet, with the point side on the bottom, and bake in a hot oven (400°) for 20 minutes, or until golden brown. Makes 3 dozen cookies.

Cream Wafers

1 cup (½ pound) butter
2 cups flour
½ cup whipping cream
   Granulated sugar

Filling

¼ cup (4 tablespoons) butter
2 cups sifted powdered sugar
1 egg yolk
1 teaspoon vanilla

Cream butter until light and fluffy. Sift flour, measure, then add it alternately with the cream to the butter, mixing well. Chill. Roll out a third of the dough at a time on a lightly floured board until ⅛ inch thick. Cut into rounds; lift onto waxed paper that you have heavily covered with granulated sugar, and turn each round with a spatula so both sides are sugar-coated. Place on an ungreased baking sheet and prick each wafer about 4 times with a fork. Bake in a moderately hot oven (375°) for 10 to 12 minutes, or until golden brown. Cool. Makes about 4 dozen wafers.

For the filling cream butter and powdered sugar together thoroughly. Add egg yolk and vanilla, and beat until smooth and creamy. Put 2 wafers together with a thick layer of filling.

Butter Almond Fingers

1 cup slivered almonds
1¾ cups flour
1½ teaspoons baking powder
½ teaspoon salt
⅛ teaspoon nutmeg
1½ cups sugar
½ cup (¼ pound) butter
3 eggs
½ teaspoon grated lemon peel
½ teaspoon almond extract
½ teaspoon vanilla
¾ cup finely ground almonds

Thickly butter a 13 by 9-inch baking pan. Sprinkle almonds over bottom of pan. Set aside. Sift flour, measure, then sift again with baking powder, salt, and nutmeg. In a mixing bowl cream together sugar and butter. Add eggs one at a time, beating thoroughly after each addition. Add lemon peel, almond extract, and vanilla; stir until blended. Fold in flour mixture, then ground almonds. Spoon batter over the slivered almonds and spread gently. Bake in a slow oven (300°) for 45 minutes, or until a light brown. While still warm cut into 1 by 3-inch bars. Makes 2½ dozen.

Kourabiedes

These tender, almost fragile Greek cookies are quite similar to the round and rich Mexican Tea (or Wedding) Cakes.

1½ cups butter
2 tablespoons powdered sugar
1 egg yolk
½ cup coarsely grated or finely chopped almonds
3½ cups flour (approximately)
2 pounds powdered sugar (approximately)

Cream butter until light and fluffy. Mix in the 2 tablespoons sugar and egg yolk, creaming well. Beat in almonds. Sift flour, measure and gradually add just enough to make a soft dough that you can shape with your hands. Pinch off pieces of dough the size of a large walnut and roll between your hands, shaping into half moons or stylized S shapes. Place on an ungreased baking sheet and bake in a slow oven (275°) for 45 minutes, or until very lightly browned. Remove from oven and let cool in pan until lukewarm. Sift powdered sugar over butcher paper, arranged in a shallow pan, and carefully transfer cookies from baking sheet to sugared paper. Sift more powdered sugar over the top, coating them at least ¼ inch thick with sugar. Let stand until cool, then store in a crock. Makes about 30.

Swedish Spritz Cookies

3 cups flour
½ teaspoon baking powder
1 cup (½ pound) butter
1 cup sugar
3 egg yolks
¼ cup light cream
½ teaspoon almond extract

Sift flour and measure; sift with baking powder. Cream butter and sugar together until fluffy. Add the egg yolks and beat well. Stir in flour mixture until well blended. Blend in cream and almond extract. Force through cooky press onto a baking sheet, forming the dough into rings, bars, rosettes, and figure S's. Bake in a moderately hot oven (375°) for 8 to 10 minutes. Cool on a rack. Makes 3 to 5 dozen cookies, depending on size.

Swiss Bonnets

4 egg whites
1 cup sugar
1 cup filberts, finely ground
½ cup almonds, finely ground
¼ teaspoon salt
About 3½ dozen whole filberts or almonds

Whip egg whites until stiff, gradually beating in sugar until smooth and glossy. Measure out 1 cup of the meringue and set aside. Fold ground nut meats and salt into remaining meringue mixture. Drop by spoonfuls on greased baking sheet. Bake in a slow oven (300°) for 10 minutes. Remove pan from oven and dot cookies with the 1 cup meringue. Set a filbert or almond on top of each dot of meringue. Return to oven and bake 10 minutes longer. Cool on wire racks. Makes 3½ dozen.

Beverages

UNDER THE wide-spreading word "beverages," you find coffee and tea, punches and mulled wine, chocolate and milk drinks.

Looking over the field, we are inclined to take the business of coffee very seriously, and place the punches in the department of frivolity. Punches are for parties; and you can be as frivolous as you like in the serving of them.

To make the pastel-pretty fruit punches even more colorful, you can float strawberries, pineapple chunks, orange or lemon wheels, and sprigs of mint on the top, or you can include them on toothpick spears in each serving.

You can also use ice decoratively, by freezing flowers or fruits into the cubes, or into larger molded blocks. (If the party is held on a long, hot summer day, it is a good idea to freeze some of the punch itself into cubes to avoid over-dilution.) To make the glasses frosty and cool-looking, rub a cut lemon or lime around the rim, and dip rims immediately into granulated sugar; chill the glasses until ready to use.

The coffees, of course, are prima donnas, and enjoy unorthodox service. Serve them as the coffee houses do—in water goblets, wine glasses, brandy snifters, pilsner glasses, small tumblers.

The mulled wine is a fireside drink, and will settle for a homely mug. But to enjoy it to its fullest, put some chestnuts into the fire to roast.

Tomato Juice Juleps

Crush a few leaves of mint in the bottom of each glass, fill with finely chipped ice, and then pour in tomato juice to the top. Serve with a big wedge of lemon, and stick a sprig of mint in each glass.

Hot Tomato Juice Cocktail

3 cups tomato juice
2 tablespoons sugar
½ teaspoon salt
1 clove garlic, crushed
1 tablespoon Worcestershire
2 dashes of Tabasco
½ cup or less of juice from dill pickles
½ cup whipping cream
1 tablespoon prepared horse-radish

Combine tomato juice, sugar, salt, garlic, Worcestershire, Tabasco, and dill pickle juice. Bring to a boil and pour into bouillon cups. Garnish each serving with the cream, whipped and mixed with the horse-radish. Serves 6.

Mock Champagne Cocktail

½ cup sugar
½ cup water
½ cup grapefruit juice
¼ cup orange juice
2 cups ginger ale, chilled
3 tablespoons grenadine syrup
Lemon peel

Combine sugar and water in a saucepan; boil slowly for 10 minutes, stirring only until sugar is dissolved; cool. Mix sugar-water syrup, grapefruit juice, and orange juice; chill thoroughly. Just before serving, add ginger ale and grenadine; mix well. Serve in champagne or sherbet glasses and put a twist of lemon peel in each glass. Serves 8 to 10.

Cranberry Juice Punch

4 cups cranberry juice
1 cup pineapple juice
1 cup orange juice
2 cups lemon juice
1½ cups sugar
½ cup water
1 cup ginger ale

Combine cranberry, pineapple, orange, and lemon juices. Sweeten with the sugar and water which have been boiled together a few minutes to make a simple syrup. Just before serving, stir in ginger ale. Makes enough for 25 punch cup servings.

Golden Punch

The full, rich flavor of this punch can stand diluting slightly with decorative ice cubes or an ice block.

2 cans (6 oz. each) frozen orange juice concentrate
2 cans (6 oz. each) frozen concentrate for lemonade
2 cans (12 oz. each) apricot nectar
2 cans (1 pt. 2 oz. each) pineapple juice

Add water to frozen concentrates as directed on the cans. Combine with the apricot nectar and pineapple juice. Chill. Makes 6 quarts or about 50 servings.

Oriental Punch

¾ cup sugar
6 whole cloves
1 cinnamon stick
½ teaspoon ground ginger
1 cup water
½ cup fresh mint leaves
  Juice of 2 large lemons
  Juice of 3 oranges
2 drops peppermint flavoring
2½ cups ice cubes
  Mint sprigs for garnish

Combine sugar, cloves, cinnamon stick, ginger, and water in a saucepan; boil for 3 minutes. Drop mint leaves into syrup, cover, and let stand until cool; strain. Combine the cooled syrup with the lemon and orange juice and peppermint flavoring. Place ice cubes in 8 large frosted glasses, pour over punch, and garnish with mint. Serves 8.

Holiday Punch

3 cans (6 oz. each) frozen pineapple juice concentrate
3 cans (6 oz. each) frozen orange juice concentrate
2 cans (6 oz. each) frozen concentrate for lemonade or limeade
½ cup white corn syrup
1 bottle (one-fifth gallon) muscatel, sherry, or white port wine
3 quarts cold water
2 quarts sparkling water or ginger ale

Combine the 3 fruit juice concentrates, corn syrup, and wine. Mix well and refrigerate for several hours, or overnight, to blend flavors. Pour chilled liquids into the punch bowl over a block of ice (or add ice cubes); add water and sparkling water. Blend. Makes about 3 gallons.

Red Wine Punch

½ cup sugar
⅔ cup water
3 strips lemon peel
6 whole cloves
  3-inch stick of cinnamon
1 cup pineapple juice
½ cup lemon juice
2 cups orange juice
1 bottle (one-fifth gallon) Burgundy

Boil together sugar, water, lemon peel, cloves, and cinnamon for 10 minutes. Strain and cool. Add pineapple, lemon and orange juices, and wine. Makes enough for 16 punch cup servings.

White Wine Punch

Slices of fresh citrus fruits garnish this flavorful punch. Start making it a day before the party to let flavors mingle. Leave the split vanilla bean in the punch when you serve it.

1 medium sized pineapple, peeled and cut into fine chunks
½ cup brown sugar, firmly packed
½ whole nutmeg, grated
1 vanilla bean, slit in half lengthwise
Sections of 2 grapefruit
Sections of 2 oranges
Zest (outer peel) of 1 lime
Juice of 2 limes
1 bottle (one-fifth gallon) chilled dry white table wine
6 cups fruit juice (orange, pineapple, grapefruit, or a combination)

The day before the party, place in a large bowl or pitcher the pineapple, brown sugar, nutmeg, and vanilla bean. Mix and cover. Place in a cool place (not in refrigerator), and allow to stand 12 to 24 hours. Add grapefruit and orange sections. Twist strips of lime zest to extract oil and drop into punch. Add lime juice, wine, and fruit juice. Pour over ice in a large punch bowl. Makes about 2½ quarts.

Hot Pineapple Cider

1 quart cider
2 cups unsweetened pineapple juice
1 cup fresh mint leaves
4 cups ginger ale

Combine cider, pineapple juice, and crushed mint leaves. Bring to a boil. Strain and bring to a boil again. Add unchilled ginger ale and serve immediately. Serves 12.

Double Boiler Mulled Wine

1 cinnamon stick, 2 inches long
1 teaspoon whole cloves
⅛ of a whole nutmeg
3 tablespoons lemon juice
½ cup sugar
1 bottle (one-fifth gallon) dry red table wine (Burgundy, Zinfandel)
1½ cups port
Sliced lemon rounds

Rub the cinnamon stick with a grater, or use a mortar and pestle until it is well broken up. Grind the cloves and nutmeg in a nutmeg grinder. Place the spices in the top of a double boiler with the lemon juice, sugar, red table wine, and port. Place over hot water and heat for 20 minutes, or until sugar is thoroughly dissolved and spice flavor has permeated the mixture. Place a lemon round in each mug or cup and ladle the mulled wine into the cups. Serves 8.

Hot Buttered Cranberry Punch

Serve this bright red punch piping hot in mugs with cinnamon sticks for stirrers.

½ to ¾ cup brown sugar, firmly packed
¼ teaspoon each salt and nutmeg
½ teaspoon each cinnamon and allspice
¾ teaspoon ground cloves
4 cups water
2 cans (1 lb. each) jellied cranberry sauce
1 quart canned pineapple juice
Butter
Whole cinnamon sticks (optional)

Mix the sugar and spices with 1 cup of the water and bring to a boil. In a large pan, crush cranberry sauce with a fork; add remaining 3 cups water, and beat until smooth. Add pineapple juice and the spiced syrup; simmer about 5 minutes. Serve hot, topped with a dot of butter, and add cinnamon sticks for stirrers if you wish. Makes 2½ quarts, 20 servings.

Spiced Tea

1 teaspoon whole cloves
1 cinnamon stick
2½ tablespoons black tea
3 quarts cold water
3 cups orange juice
1½ cups lemon juice
1½ cups sugar

Use a clean piece of linen toweling or a double thickness of cheesecloth to make two spice bags. Tie the whole cloves and cinnamon stick in one bag; tie the tea in the second bag. Pour the cold water in a large kettle; add the tied spices and heat water to boiling. Remove pan from heat. Take out the tied spices and add the tea bag. Cover pan and let steep 5 minutes; remove tea.

In a separate pan, heat orange juice, lemon juice, and sugar until sugar is dissolved. Pour hot fruit mixture into spiced tea. Keep hot until ready to serve, but do not boil. Makes 25 servings.

French Chocolate

When you pour hot milk over the chocolate base, the whipped cream in the base rises in a frothy topping.

2½ squares (1 oz. each) unsweetened chocolate
½ cup water
¾ cup sugar
Pinch of salt
½ cup whipping cream
6 cups milk

To prepare chocolate base, heat chocolate and water together until blended. Add sugar and salt; stirring, boil 4 minutes; cool. When ready to serve, whip cream and fold into the chocolate syrup. Spoon 1 rounded tablespoon chocolate mixture into each cup. Heat milk to scalding point; pour over chocolate in cups. Serves 8. (You can store base in refrigerator in a covered container for several days.)

Viennese Coffee

Viennese coffee may be spiced, served with hot milk, or served plain. For a simple version, brew extra-strength coffee, pour into cups, and top with a drift of sweetened whipped cream. Dust the cream lightly with powdered nutmeg or cinnamon.

Belgian Coffee

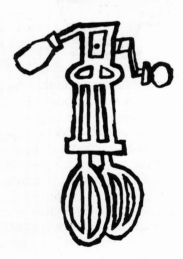

A creamy, sweetened meringue mixture spooned into heated cups, then topped with strong, fragrant coffee makes the brew called Belgian Coffee. Beat 1 egg white until stiff and fold in 1 cup of cream, whipped. Sweeten to taste. Half-fill heated coffee cups with egg white mixture and fill with hot coffee. Serve immediately. Makes about 6 servings.

Dutch Coffee

A Seattle coffee house suggests that a Hollander's choice of coffee goes something like this: Place a cinnamon stick in each serving cup, fill with freshly brewed black coffee, stir in 1 tablespoon heavy cream, and float a pat of yellow butter on top. Serve with sugar.

Syrian Demitasse

The Syrians brew their after-dinner coffee so that it wafts a delicate cardamom aroma. Place 2 or 3 crushed cardamom seeds in each demitasse cup and fill with double strength coffee. (Use 8 level tablespoons coffee with 2 measuring cups water.) Serve with sugar.

Caffé Borgia

The Italians probably named this drink after the aristocratic Borgia family of the 15th and 16th centuries. Pour equal parts hot chocolate (made with milk) and double strength coffee into heated cups. Top with a heaping spoonful of lightly sweetened whipped cream; sprinkle with grated orange peel and shaved bittersweet chocolate.

Irish Coffee

Coffee house proprietors tell us that renowned Irish coffee is one of their most popular menu offerings. Here's how they make it. Into a warmed table wine glass, place 2 teaspoons of sugar; fill glass about ⅔ full of strong, hot coffee. Stir. Add 2 tablespoons of Irish whiskey, and top with softly whipped cream. Makes 1 serving.

Russian Coffee

You top this combination of chocolate and coffee with sweetened whipped cream or not, as you choose. Try it for breakfast.

½ oz. semi-sweet chocolate
¼ cup sugar
⅛ teaspoon salt
¼ cup water
½ cup each milk and whipping cream
   or 1 cup light cream
2 cups freshly brewed strong, hot
   coffee
1 teaspoon vanilla

In the top of a double boiler, melt chocolate over hot water. Add sugar, salt, and water. Place over direct heat and simmer for 5 minutes, stirring. Add milk and cream and heat, but do not allow to boil. Add coffee and vanilla. Beat with a rotary beater until foamy and serve immediately. Serves 4.

Mexican Coffee

½ teaspoon cinnamon
1½ cups strong black coffee
   Sugar to taste
½ cup whipping cream
¼ teaspoon each nutmeg and
   cinnamon

Stir cinnamon into coffee. Pour into 4 demitasse cups. Sweeten to taste and top each cup with a generous dollop of whipped cream which has been spiced with the nutmeg and cinnamon. Serves 4.

Coffee Hawaiian

In this coffee you taste the sweetness of coconut.

2 cups milk
1 cup flaked or shredded coconut
2 tablespoons sugar
2 cups freshly brewed, strong, hot coffee

Heat milk until a film forms on top. Add flaked coconut and sugar. Cover and allow to stand in the refrigerator overnight. Strain milk and reheat slowly. Combine milk with hot coffee. Serve with a topping of toasted coconut, if desired. Makes 6 coffee-cup servings.

This coffee can also be served chilled. Pour into brandy snifters or glass tumblers and serve as an afternoon refreshment.

Wine

ON THE FOLLOWING PAGES we pay homage to the fine wines of California, and to the benefits they offer the good cook in preparing and presenting a memorable repast.

California has been producing quality wines for more than a century. A happy combination of terrain, sun, and soil, and the early arrival of Europeans skilled in wine making, have given California an honored place among the world's great wine-making regions.

The semi-circular area around San Francisco Bay produces fine table wines. California's Central Valley produces excellent dessert and appetizer wines (the Ports, Sherries, Vermouths, and others) and also lower priced table wines. Southern California is particularly noted for appetizer and dessert wines.

Of course, it is quite misleading to compare California and European wines, or to argue their relative merit. They are different wines. As one celebrated wine expert points out, it is as pointless to compare a white Bordeaux with a white Burgundy as to compare a white Bordeaux with a California Semillon.

California table wines sometimes carry *generic* names which simply relate them to similar wines of Europe. Typical generics: White wines—Sauterne, Chablis, Rhine wine; red wines—Burgundy, Claret. But gaining in favor is the practice of *varietal* labeling. A varietal is named for the wine grape variety used to make the wine. Varietal labeling is a new language to many wine buyers, but it also is a more precise language, and easy to learn.

You will find no mention here of the respectable wines made in upstate New York, in Ohio, or elsewhere east of California. Part of this is honest prejudice; the origins of this cook book are in the West. But part also is recognition of fact: *Vitis vinifera,* Europe's classic wine grape family, in America thrives only in California.

Appetizer Wines

Appetizer wines, as their class name indicates, are popular for serving before meals. The two best known appetizer or "aperitif" wines are Sherry and Vermouth.

Sherry, the most popular appetizer wine, has a characteristic "nutty" flavor and pale to dark amber color. For pre-dinner serving, dry (which simply means "not sweet") or extra dry Sherry is the usual choice. The sweeter types of Sherry (which may be marked *Sweet* or *Cream* or *Golden* Sherry) are more likely to be served with cookies or fruit cake or crackers and cheese for afternoon or evening refreshments.

Vermouth is wine that is flavored with herbs and other aromatic substances. There are two types—dry or French Vermouth, which is pale amber in color, and sweet or Italian Vermouth, which is dark amber. French type Vermouth should always be used in making dry Martini cocktails—otherwise they will not be dry. The Italian type is used in making Manhattans and other sweet or slightly sweet mixed drinks. Vermouth, and drinks containing it, should always be served icy cold. Chilled Vermouth, either French or Italian type, may be served straight, in small glasses, with merely a twist of lemon peel added, or as Vermouth-and-soda in tall glasses with plenty of ice, plus a dash of bitters and a twist of lemon peel.

Varietal Table Wines

California's first varietal wines were bottled more than a half century ago. But the varietals weren't subject to uniform standards until 1939. A Federal law now requires that a varietal wine be made at least 51 per cent from that grape variety. This

CHART OF VARIETAL WINES OF CALIFORNIA

		GENERIC NAME	VARIETAL NAME	EXPERTS' RATING	COMMENTARY
W H I T E	CHILL	Chablis	CHARDONNAY (OR PINOT CHARDONNAY)	☆☆☆☆	Chardonnay is the aristocrat, very sparse yielder. It and Pinot Blanc are very dry without being acid. Chenin Blanc is the more accurate varietal name for White Pinot. Both it and Folle Blanche produce wines that are light, dry, fruity. Most available: Chardonnay, White Pinot. Least: Folle Blanche.
			PINOT BLANC	☆☆☆	
			WHITE PINOT (OR CHENIN BLANC)	☆☆☆	
			FOLLE BLANCHE	☆	
	CHILL	Sauterne	SAUVIGNON BLANC	☆☆☆	Sauvignon Blanc is spare yielder. Semillon is chief Sauterne grape, made into either a sweet or dry table wine.
			SEMILLON	☆☆	
	CHILL	Rhine Wine	WHITE RIESLING (OR JOHANNISBERGER RIESLING)	☆☆☆☆	White Riesling is called plain Riesling in Europe. It does best in our coolest climates, produces wine of pronounced fragrance. Some say Gewürztraminer is separate variety; others say just a strain of the Red Traminer. Some Traminers notably spicy. Grey Riesling (so called, though not a true Riesling) makes a mild wine.
			SYLVANER	☆☆	
			TRAMINER (OR GEWURZTRAMINER)	☆☆	
			GREY RIESLING	☆	
	CHILL	Champagne	CHAMPAGNE BRUT, EXTRA DRY, SEC, CALIFORNIA		Brut is driest; others usually sweeter in order listed. Bottle-fermented is most expensive. If made by bulk, or Charmat, process, must be so labeled.
P I N K	CHILL	Vin Rosé	GRENACHE	☆☆	Grenache and Gamay are most available, but there's scattering of other varietals, many non-varietals.
			GAMAY	☆	
			PINK CHAMPAGNE OR ROSE CHAMPAGNE		Made like champagne, from rosé wine (usually bears pink label).
R E D	SERVE AT ROOM TEMPERATURE	Burgundy	PINOT NOIR	☆☆☆☆	Aristocratic Pinot Noir rates top quality among Burgundies. More than a dozen wineries produce it, available in a wide range of quality. Gamay is also made into rosé wine. Some put Barbera, Charbono, Grignolino (below) in separate "Italian type" wine group.
			BARBERA	☆☆	
			GAMAY (OR GAMAY BEAUJOLAIS)	☆	
			CHARBONO	☆	
		Claret	CABERNET SAUVIGNON	☆☆☆☆	Cabernet Sauvignon always one of top red varietals. Cabernet usually means Sauvignon, but might be other Cabernet. Zinfandel's origin a mystery, grown only in California.
			ZINFANDEL	☆☆	
			GRIGNOLINO	☆	
			SPARKLING BURGUNDY OR RED CHAMPAGNE		Made from red wine (usually dark red label), often fairly sweet.

law, however, sets only a minimum. Today a number of producers make varietal wines 100 per cent from named varieties.

Winemakers call the truly distinguished wine grape varieties "shy bearers." These wines yield only 1 to 1.5 tons of grapes per acre, compared to 6 or more tons of table or raisin grapes per acre. Juice of the aristocratic wine grapes also takes more care in handling and longer aging. Consequently the table wines that result are more expensive to buy.

There are exceptions, of course. The winemaker's care and attention to a wine's quality are the all-important factors.

California's common table wines continue to sell in much greater volume than the varietals. And as a group, these everyday California wines rate well in comparison with similar wines made anywhere else in the world. But California's fine varietal wines are another matter. Their quality, at its best, brings them respectful attention from wine experts the world over.

Dessert Wines

Among the rich, sweet, full-bodied dessert wines, there are four prime favorites: ruby-red Port, amber Muscatel and Tokay, and white Port. Other dessert wines such as Angelica, Malaga, and sweet or cream Sherry also are popular.

Although dessert wines are sweet in flavor, no sugar is added in their making. Instead, their fermentation is arrested before all the natural sugar of the grapes has been converted into wine alcohol. This is done by the addition of a small amount of pure grape brandy. The same method is followed in preparing appetizer wines. As a result of the addition of the grape brandy, appetizer and dessert wines may be kept indefinitely after the bottle has been opened, whereas the more perishable table wines should be used within a few days.

Cooking with Wine

Cooking with wine *is* an art. It need not be complicated, but it shouldn't be done haphazardly. Temper wine cookery with the same good taste and finesse you employ with other seasonings. Experience will help you develop skill.

All types of wine have a place in cooking and food preparation. Your choice depends on the use you intend.

For a minimum stock of wine for cooking, choose a medium Sherry (medium refers to the quality of sweetness or dryness). It is the most versatile wine, with an affinity for almost any dish.

An adequate, flexible stock of wines for cooking might include one bottle of each of these: a Burgundy or other red table wine, a Sauterne or other white table wine, a medium Sherry, and a sweet dessert wine such as ruby Port. With this selection you can supply the wine ingredients of almost any recipe, although you might occasionally have to use a Burgundy, for example, in a recipe that designates Claret.

Wines are pretty much interchangeable as long as they are of the same type—red, white, sweet, dry. When a recipe calls for a dry white table wine, it's usually safe to use a dry Sauterne, a Chablis, or a Rhine wine; when dry red wine is indicated, Claret or Burgundy; for a sweet or dessert wine, Port, Muscatel, Tokay, or mellow Sherry.

When wine is to be served as a beverage, one good approach is to use some of the drinking wine in preparing the meal's wine-seasoned food. Obvious exceptions, of course, are foods best seasoned with the sweeter wines, such as Sherry, Madeira, and Port.

When used as a seasoning, wine may serve to blend and balance the inherent flavors of the foods in a dish. It can accentuate and point up natural food flavors in much the way lemon juice does. Or it can be the principal flavoring for a dish, contributing its own fruity taste and aroma.

The acid in wine gives it tenderizing qualities, especially useful with meat cookery. The wine acid softens meat tissues exposed to it through marinating or long simmering.

If wine is to be used to accentuate and blend other flavors or to tenderize, add it in the beginning. If the flavor of the wine itself is to be its contribution, add the wine just before serving, so none of its quality is lost.

Quantity depends, of course, on your use of the wine; if you're simmering meat in a wine sauce, you may use as much as a cup of wine for each pound of meat. But if you're adding just a seasoning note, 1 teaspoon for each serving may give you the fillip you want. Use the wine cookery chart for initial proportions when you experiment with wine cooking.

Try to cook wine-seasoned dishes in a covered container. Even if you're only chilling fruits in wine, cover them to prevent evaporation and to hold in the entire wine essence.

WINE COOKERY CHART

These recommendations are intended as suggestions, not hard-and-fast rules. This qualification applies especially to the column on amounts of wine to use. Many experienced cooks add wine entirely by taste, just as they do salt. Use these amounts as rough estimates, to be made more precise when you flavor each individual dish.

	FOODS	AMOUNT	WINES
Soups	Cream soups	1 or 2 teaspoons per serving	White table wines or Sherry
	Meat and vegetable soups	1 or 2 teaspoons per serving	Red table wines or Sherry
Seafoods	Fish and shellfish	½ cup per pound	White table wines
Poultry and Game	Chicken, broiled (for basting) or sauté	¼ cup per pound	White or red table wines
	Chicken, fricassee	¼ cup per pound	White table wines
	Gravy for roast or fried chicken and turkey	2 tablespoons per cup	White or red table wines or Sherry
	Rabbit, braised	¼ cup per pound	White or red table wines
	Duck (wild or tame), roast (for basting)	¼ cup per pound	Red table wines
	Venison, roast (for basting), pot roast, or stew	¼ cup per pound	Red table wines
	Pheasant, roast (for basting) or sauté	¼ cup per pound	White or red table wines or Sherry
Meats	Beef, pot roast or stew	¼ cup per pound	Red table wines
	Lamb and veal, pot roast or stew	¼ cup per pound	White table wines or Rosé
	Pork, roast (for basting)	¼ cup per pound	Red or white table wines or Rosé
	Gravy for roasts	2 tablespoons per cup	Red or white table wines or Sherry
	Ham (whole), baked (for basting)	2 cups	Port, Muscatel, or Rosé
	Liver, braised	¼ cup per pound	Red or white table wines
	Kidneys, braised	¼ cup per pound	Sherry or red table wines
	Tongue, boiled	½ cup per pound	Red table wines
Cheese Dishes	Soufflés and other lightly flavored dishes	½ to 1 cup per pound of cheese	White table wines
	Robust-flavored cheese dishes	½ to 1 cup per pound of cheese	Red table wines
Egg Dishes	Scrambled, omelets, baked	1 teaspoon to 1 tablespoon per egg	White table wines
Sauces	Cream sauce and variations	1 tablespoon per cup	Sherry or white table wines
	Brown sauce and variations	1 tablespoon per cup	Sherry or red table wines
	Tomato sauce	1 tablespoon per cup	Sherry or red table wines
	Cheese sauce	1 tablespoon per cup	Sherry or red or white table wines
	Dessert sauces	1 tablespoon per cup	Port, Muscatel or sweet Sherry
Casseroles	Meat, poultry, seafood, egg, cheese	1 tablespoon per cup of sauce	Use wine suggested for protein ingredient
Fruits	Compotes and fruit cups	1 tablespoon per serving	Port, Muscatel, Sherry
Desserts	Puddings, refrigerator desserts	1 tablespoon per serving	Any sweet dessert wine, sweet Sauterne, sweet Champagne

When wine is used in cooking, the alcohol content evaporates; only the flavor of the wine remains. (Alcohol vaporizes at 172.4° F.; water boils at 212°.)

You can cook foods flavored with wine in any utensil. But when marinating, use glass or enamelware to prevent possible reaction from long contact of the wine and metal.

Wine-seasoned dishes can appear in almost any course — appetizer, soup, meat, vegetable, dessert, beverage. And you can use wine in almost any cooking method — basting, saucing, baking, marinating, or dressing a salad.

Tips on Wine Storage

Wine perishability varies according to the particular wine and the weather. In general, wines' keeping qualities vary in relation to their alcohol content. Dessert and appetizer wines, with about 20 per cent alcohol, can be expected to keep their original qualities for several months after they are opened.

But table wines containing 10 to 14 per cent alcohol may begin oxidizing as soon as air reaches them. Their perishability is compared to that of fresh milk; it is often suggested that they be used within a few days after opening. It is a good idea to recork them immediately after using, then store them in your refrigerator for further use.

However, there are exceptions to these general rules. Some of today's less expensive table wines, in processing, undergo treatment with sulfur dioxide to arrest further fermentation.

Here's one practical solution to the storage problem: Purchase appetizer and dessert wines in "fifths" (bottles containing ⅘ quart). Buy table wines for everyday cooking in "tenths" (12.8 oz., ⅘ pint, or "half bottles"). Tenths are marketed by many wineries, but they may not be displayed on your dealer's open shelves; you may have to ask for them.

If you do choose to buy wines in large-quantity containers, rebottle the wine as soon as it is opened to reduce the surface exposed to air. Use clean, small bottles that can be tightly capped. Soft drink bottles with flexible plastic caps, or clean small wine bottles with screw-top lids, will do. Fill as full as you can, leaving the smallest possible air space.

Drop a bit of olive oil on the top of an opened bottle of wine destined only for cooking; it will help seal out the air.

Party Food

A VERY PLEASANT CHANGE has recently come over the collection of foods loosely grouped as appetizers, canapés, hors d'oeuvres. Party food has become in the last few years more imaginative and more exciting. Dips and spreads still have their place—and you'll find some good ones in this chapter—but they are accompanied by tantalizing "hot bites" from the oven or broiler, and are served with appealing "scoopers"—chilled shrimp, raw vegetables.

The eye-appealing cheese tray has come into importance, providing enough variety to suit the tastes of every guest. Along with the familiar Swiss, jack, Cheddar, Edam, Gouda, Muenster, and blue cheeses, the cheese tray might include a smokey Italian Provolone, a Greek Feta, a domestic Fontinella, or a Dutch Leyden. And with the cheeses comes an opportunity for more variety—an assortment of breads and crackers in varying colors, textures, and shapes.

Another party food idea that has recently come to the fore is that of miniature kebabs—colorful arrays of meat, fruit, and vegetables, cut in bite-size pieces and arranged on disposable bamboo skewers. Prepared by the hostess ahead of time, and broiled over a *hibachi* or barbecue by the guests themselves, these exceptional appetizers lend themselves nicely to the informality of today's entertaining.

Olive-Filled Cheese Balls

Bake them in the morning, and reheat them at party time.

1 cup shredded sharp Cheddar cheese
2 tablespoons butter
½ cup flour
Dash of cayenne
25 medium olives, well drained (pitted ripe or stuffed green)

Cream together cheese and butter. Blend in flour and cayenne. Drop teaspoonfuls of dough on waxed paper. Wrap each teaspoonful of dough around an olive, covering completely. Bake in a hot oven (400°) for 15 minutes. Makes about 25 balls.

Water Chestnut Appetizers

1 can (5 oz.) water chestnuts
¼ cup soy
¼ cup sugar
4 slices of bacon

Drain water chestnuts and marinate in soy for 30 minutes. Roll each chestnut in sugar, then wrap with a strip of bacon (cut each slice of bacon in half crosswise and lengthwise), and secure with a cocktail pick. Arrange on a cake rack in a shallow pan or on broiler. Bake in a hot oven (400°) for 20 minutes. Drain on paper toweling.

Before serving, return to a moderate oven (350°) for about 5 minutes to reheat and crisp the chestnuts. Makes about 16 appetizers.

Chicken Almond Puffs

All the chicken flavor is baked into these crisp little cream puff appetizers.

1 cup flour
¼ teaspoon salt
½ cup (¼ pound) butter
1 cup chicken stock or broth
4 eggs
½ cup finely diced cooked chicken
2 tablespoons chopped toasted almonds
Few grains paprika

Sift the flour, measure, and sift again with the salt. Combine the butter and chicken stock in a pan; keep over low heat until the butter is melted. Add the flour all at once and stir vigorously over low heat until the mixture forms a ball and leaves the sides of the pan. Remove from the heat. Add the eggs, one at a time, and beat thoroughly after each one is added. Continue beating until a thick dough is formed. Stir in the chicken, almonds, and paprika. Drop by small teaspoonfuls onto a greased baking sheet. Bake in a very hot oven (450°) for 10 minutes. Reduce heat to 350°, and bake 5 to 10 minutes longer or until browned. Makes 4 to 5 dozen.

(You can make these with 1 stick prepared cream puff mix: Use chicken stock in place of the water called for; stir in chicken, almonds, paprika.)

Meal Planner
by Jane Ross
SAFEWAY'S FOOD CONSULTANT

*XMAS COOKIES TO MAIL

```
* * * * * * * * * * * * * * * * * * * * * * * * * * * *
*                                                       *
*    CHEWY COCONUT SQUARES        SPICED ORANGE FLOWERS  *
*                                                       *
*  PEANUT BUTTEROONS   COFFEE NUT MACAROONS   CRESCENTS  *
*                                                       *
*        GLAZED ALMOND COOKIES        NOELS             *
*                                                       *
*                    FABULOUS FUDGE                     *
*                                                       *
* * * * * * * * * * * * * * * * * * * * * * * * * * * *
```

CHEWY COCONUT SQUARES

1/2 cup soft Lucerne butter
1 1/2 cups light brown sugar, packed
1 1/2 cups sifted Kitchen craft flour
1/4 teaspoon salt

1 teaspoon Crown Colony vanilla
2 eggs
1 cup chopped walnuts
1 can (3 1/2) oz. flaked coconut

Cream butter and 1/2 cups sugar until light. Add 1 cup flour and mix well. Pat into greased 13 x 9 x 2 inch pan. Bake in moderate oven 375 F. 10 minutes. Mix 1 cup sugar, 1/4 cup flour and remaining ingredients. Spread evenly over baked mixture.. Bake 20 minutes. While warm cut into about 4 dozen squares. Cool in pan. Wrap separately in transparent plastic wrap. Pack in crumpled tissue paper in firm box so cookies cannot slide around.

SPICED ORANGE FLOWERS

1 cup soft Lucerne butter
1 1/2 cup sugar
1 tablespoon grated orange rind
1 egg
3 tablespoons orange juice

3 cups sifted Kitchen Craft flour
1 teaspoon baking powder
1/2 teaspoon salt
1/2 teaspoon each Crown Colony allspice and nutmeg
Candied red and green cherries

Cream butter and sugar until light. Beat in rind, egg and juice. Add sifted dry ingredients and mix well until smooth. Chill if necessary to make stiff enought to roll. Then roll to 1/8 inch thickness and cut with 2 inch diamond shaped cutter. Put on sheet and bring 2 longest points of each to center, overlaping slightly. Decorate with cherries. Bake in hot oven 400 F. 8 to 10 minutes.
Makes 8 dozens

PEANUT BUTTEROONS

2/3 cup confectioners sugar
1/2 cup peanut butter

2 egg whites

Gradually beat sugar into the peanut butter. Beat egg white until stiff and fold into first mixture. Drop from teaspoon on foil covered sheet and bake in 375 F. oven 10 minutes.

COFFEE NUT MACAROONS

2 egg whites
1 1/3 cups sugar
2 tablespoons instant coffee

2/3 cup salted cashews
1 teaspoon vanilla

Beat egg whites until stiff, but not dry. Mix sugar and coffee, gradually add to egg whites, beating constantly until blended. Fold in nuts and vanilla. Drop by teaspoons onto greased sheets. Bake 325 F. about 15 minutes. Makes 48

CRESCENTS

1 cup butter or margarine
1/2 cup sugar
2 teaspoon vanilla
1 3/4 cups sifted flour

1/3 cup each chopped almond,
  pecans and filberts
1/4 teaspoon salt
Confectioners sugar

Cream butter, gradually beat in 1/2 cup sugar. Add 1 teaspoon vanilla, flour,
nuts and salt. Chill well. Shape in crescents (half moon) using 1/2 tablespoons dough for each, put on sheets. Bake in slow oven (300 F.) 18 to 20
minutes. Roll in 1 cup confectioners sugar and 1 teaspoon vanilla mixed with
sugar.   Makes 6 dozens.

GLAZED ALMOND COOKIES

1 cup butter or margarine
1 cup sugar
1/2 teaspoon each of almond and vanilla
2 eggs, separated
1/2 teaspoon salt

3/4 cup chopped blanched
  almonds
2 2/3 cups flour, cake
  flour
48 unblanched whole almonds

Cream butter and sugar until light. Beat in flavorings and egg yolks. Add
chopped nuts, flour and salt, mix well. Roll in 1 inch balls, dip in unbeaten
egg whites and put 2 inch apart on greased sheets. Put a whole almond in
center of each ball and push down to flatten cookie. Bake in moderate oven
350 F. about 10 minutes. (Good keepers and shippers). Makes 4 dozens.

NOELS

1/3 cup soft butter
1 teaspoon vanilla
3/4 cup light brown sugar
1 egg
1 1/4 cups sifted Kitchen Craft flour
1/2 teaspoon salt

1/4 teaspoon baking powder
1/2 teaspoon soda
1/2 cup sour cream
36 pitted dates
36 walnut halves
Icing

Cream butter and vanilla, gradually beat in sugar. Add egg and beat well. Sift
dry ingredients and add alternately with sour cream. Stuff dates with walnut
halves and roll in dough. When well covered,drop from fork on greased sheet.
Bake in hot oven 400 F. about 10 minutes. When cool, spread with icing.
ICING
Melt 2 tablespoons butter, blend in 1 cup confectioners sugar, 1 teaspoon vanilla
and 1 tablespoon cream. Makes 3 dozens.

FABULOUS FUDGE

2 cups sugar
1/8 teaspoon salt
2 squares unsweetened chocolate
1 small can evaporated milk

2 tablespoons white corn syrup
2 tablespoons butter
1/2 teaspoon vanilla

Combine sugar, salt, chocolate, milk and corn syrup in a heavy pan. Heat,
stirring constantly, just until the sugar dissolves and chocolate melts. Remove
spoon. Cook rapidly without stirring to read 236 F on thermometer, remove from
heat. Add butter and vanilla (no stirring yet) then let cool on a rack to 110 F.
Bottom of pan should feel lukewarm. Beat 2 to 3 minutes or until fudge starts to
thicken and lose its glossiness, pour into buttered pan. Let stand until set
only 2 to 3 minutes, cut at once in squares.   Makes 1 1/4 pounds.

NUTS IN SHELL		NUTS SHELLED
Walnuts, 1 pound	makes	2 cups
Almonds, 1 pound	"	2 cups
Pecans, 1 pound	"	2 1/4 cups

SHELLED NUTS	
Walnuts, 4 ounces	1 cup
Almonds, 5 ounces	1 cup
Pecans, 3 ounces	1 cup
Filberts, 4 ounces	1 cup

Cheese and Filbert Balls

1 cup (¼ pound) shredded sharp
  Cheddar cheese
¼ cup (4 tablespoons) butter
½ cup flour
¼ teaspoon salt
1 cup ground filberts
1 teaspoon paprika

Using your hands, mix together the cheese, butter, flour, salt, ½ cup of the filberts, and paprika. When well blended, roll teaspoonfuls of the dough in little marbles, roll balls in the other ½ cup of filberts, and arrange on cooky sheets. Chill, then bake in a moderate oven (350°) for 10 minutes, or until lightly browned. Makes about 3 dozen.

Oyster-Stuffed Mushrooms

Oysters, of course, are just one of the stuffings for mushroom caps. Others: cheese, seasoned bread crumbs, anchovies.

24 large fresh mushroom caps
¼ cup (4 tablespoons) butter
6 green onions, finely chopped
24 small Olympia oysters
  Melted butter
  Salt

Sauté mushroom crowns gently in the ¼ cup butter for 3 minutes, stirring carefully so caps do not break. Remove from pan and place on a greased cooky sheet, hollow side up. Sauté onions until limp in the remaining butter; put about ¼ teaspoon chopped onion inside each mushroom cap. Dip oysters in melted butter; place 1 inside each mushroom; sprinkle lightly with salt. Heat under the broiler until the edges of the oysters start to curl. Serve at once.

Green Pepper-Cheese Broil

Flecks of green pepper and crumbled bacon flavor this thin cheese spread, which thickens as it broils on bread squares.

1 strip bacon
¼ cup (4 tablespoons) butter
1 package (3 oz.) pimiento cream
  cheese
3 tablespoons finely chopped green
  pepper
1 clove of garlic, mashed or minced
1 egg
8 thin slices bread

Dice bacon and fry until crisp. Cream butter with cream cheese. Stir in bacon and drippings, green pepper, and garlic. Beat egg lightly and stir in, blending thoroughly. Trim crusts off bread and cut each slice in quarters or narrow strips. Toast one side of bread under broiler; remove from oven. Turn bread over and spread cheese mixture on untoasted side. Return to oven and broil until cheese bubbles and browns slightly. Serve hot. Makes about 32 hors d'oeuvres.

Peanut Butter and Bacon Rollups

Remove crusts from the very thin-sliced pumpernickel bread. Roll slices with rolling pin to prevent their cracking. Spread with smooth peanut butter and cut each slice into 4 strips. Cut bacon strips in half crosswise and lengthwise. Roll up peanut butter strips, wrap bacon around them, fasten with toothpick. Refrigerate until ready to broil. Cook bacon on all sides.

Chicken Liver Appetizers

Wrap one anchovy fillet around each well chilled or partially frozen chicken liver; then wrap a 3-inch bacon strip around the anchovy. Secure with toothpicks. Cook in hot deep fat (375°) for 3 minutes or until bacon is crisp. Drain on paper toweling. Serve hot.

Curried Shrimp

Slit cooked, deveined shrimp down back; stuff with slice of blue cheese; reshape. Make a thick waffle batter, substituting sherry for milk and curry powder for the sugar called for in your recipe. (If you use a packaged mix, use 1 teaspoon curry powder with 1 cup mix.) Dip cheese-stuffed shrimp in batter, drain, and fry in deep fat at 375° until golden brown. Drain shrimp on layers of absorbent paper. Serve hot.

Filbert Cocktail Fritters

¼ cup (4 tablespoons) butter
½ cup boiling water or consommé
½ cup sifted flour
  Few grains of salt
 2 eggs
 1 cup blanched filberts, finely shaved
  Salt

Melt butter in the boiling water or consommé; add flour and salt. Stir vigorously over low heat until mixture forms ball and leaves side of pan. Remove from heat; add eggs, one at a time, beating well after each addition. Heat deep fat to 375°. Spread filberts on a pan, and drop the dough in ½ teaspoonfuls. Roll lightly in the nuts and fry in deep fat, a few at a time, until a golden brown. Drain on paper towels and sprinkle with salt. Serve hot. Makes about 5 dozen.

Chicken-Water Chestnut-Mushroom Kebabs

Miniature kebabs, on disposable bamboo skewers, appeal to everyone. Use your favorite spicy barbecue sauce as a marinade for these.

Cut chicken or turkey breasts into small squares. Marinate in a barbecue sauce about 1 hour, then sauté in a little butter to cook partially. Arrange on skewers with canned mushrooms and slices of canned water chestnuts, starting with mushrooms. Dip in sauce before broiling.

Shrimp-Mushroom-Green Pepper Kebabs

Use small shrimp, shelled and deveined; drop into boiling water and simmer 5 minutes. Marinate shrimp about 1 hour in a barbecue sauce. Arrange on bamboo skewers with small pieces of green pepper and canned whole or sliced mushrooms. Dip in sauce before broiling.

Skewered Beef or Turkey Cubes

Sesame seeds and soy contribute unusual flavor to broiled cubes of meat.

Cut raw top quality beef or raw turkey or chicken breasts into tiny cubes. Marinate in Sesame Soy Sauce (below) for ½ to 1 hour, or put cubes on bamboo skewers and dip into sauce just before broiling.

Sesame Soy Sauce

1 cup sesame seeds
1 cup soy
1 cup water
1 clove garlic, crushed
1 tablespoon sugar
½ cup vinegar
½ cup sherry
1 large apple, finely grated

Put the sesame seeds into a dry frying pan; stir continually over medium heat until they are brown. Remove from heat. Using a mortar and pestle, grind about ¼ cup of the seeds at a time until they reach the consistency of peanut butter. (Or combine sesame seeds and soy, and whirl in a blender.) Add all the remaining ingredients. Let stand at least 24 hours to blend flavors. Makes about 1 quart.

Ham-Cheese Cubes

2 tablespoons prepared horse-radish
2 tablespoons mayonnaise
1 teaspoon Worcestershire
½ teaspoon seasoned salt
⅛ teaspoon pepper
1 large package (8 oz.) cream cheese
6 thin slices boiled ham

Beat all ingredients except ham together until creamy and of spreading consistency. Place one ham slice on a piece of waxed paper. With a spatula, spread some of the creamed mixture over it. Place another slice of ham on top of creamed mixture and spread with more of the cheese. Repeat this process, ending with a ham slice on top.

Wrap securely in waxed paper and place in freezer or freezing compartment of refrigerator for 2 hours or more. About an hour before time to serve, remove from refrigerator and cut lengthwise and crosswise into ½-inch cubes. Pierce each cube with a colored toothpick. Place on a dish, garnish, and serve. Makes 80 or more cubes.

Prawns with Soy and Sesame Seeds

Push cocktail picks through small cooked prawns, then dip first in soy and then in toasted sesame seeds. The soy makes the seeds stick to the prawns.

Artichoke Appetizers

Each artichoke leaf is a container for a tasty morsel of cheese and shrimp.

1 large artichoke
Water
1 teaspoon salad oil
1 bay leaf, crushed
½ teaspoon salt
1 package (3 oz.) cream cheese
¼ teaspoon Tabasco
½ teaspoon garlic powder
Salt to taste
About 2 tablespoons light cream
About ¼ pound small shrimp
Paprika

Cook the artichoke in a tightly covered container in water to cover; add the oil, bay leaf, and salt to the cooking water. Simmer about 30 minutes, or until tender; cool, then remove the leaves. Use the leaves that are firm enough to handle and have a good edible portion on the ends. Blend the cream cheese with Tabasco, garlic powder, additional salt to taste, and cream to make a smooth paste. Spread this filling on the base of each leaf. Place a small shrimp on top of the filling and sprinkle with paprika. Arrange on a round plate or tray in the shape of a sunflower so each leaf is easy to pick up. Makes about 18.

Curried Avocado Dip

2 medium sized avocados
4 tablespoons lemon juice
2 slices bacon
¾ teaspoon curry powder
1 clove garlic, minced or mashed
1 tablespoon minced chives
1 tablespoon mayonnaise
1 teaspoon Worcestershire
¼ teaspoon Tabasco
½ teaspoon chili powder
   Salt to taste

Carefully cut the avocados in half lengthwise and remove the seeds. With a spoon remove the pulp, being sure to leave firm shells of two of the halves. Sprinkle these shells with 1 tablespoon of the lemon juice. Cook bacon until crisp, and chop into fine bits. Mash avocado pulp, add bacon and all the remaining ingredients, including the remaining lemon juice; beat until smooth. Heap the mixture into the 2 prepared shells; chill. Serve as a dip for crisp crackers, corn chips, tostadas, or small points of hot buttered rye toast.

Raw Vegetable Dip

In choosing your vegetables, mix the conventional (celery, carrots, onions) with the adventuresome (raw sliced turnips, sweet red onion wedges, zucchini sticks).

¼ pound blue cheese
½ large (8 oz.) package cream cheese
3 tablespoons dry vermouth
1 small clove garlic, mashed or minced
   Commercial sour cream

Combine the blue cheese, cream cheese, vermouth, and garlic. Add enough sour cream to make mixture thin enough for dunking the vegetables.

Lobster Spread or Dip

1 large package (8 oz.) cream cheese
2 tablespoons crumbled Roquefort or blue cheese
½ cup commercial sour cream
½ clove garlic, mashed, or a dash of garlic powder
2 teaspoons instant minced onion or 2 tablespoons finely chopped green onion
1 tablespoon lemon juice
1 tablespoon water
1 can (6½ oz.) lobster or 1 cup fresh or frozen lobster meat
   Chopped parsley

Soften cream cheese. Beat in Roquefort cheese, sour cream, garlic, onion, lemon juice, and water. Stir in lobster meat (and its liquor, if canned meat is used), breaking up the large pieces. (If you use fresh lobster, you may wish to thin the mixture slightly with cream.) Pile into serving dish or lobster shell and sprinkle with chopped parsley. Makes about 2 cups.

Hot Cheese Dip

½ pound sharp Cheddar cheese
2 slices cooked bacon, crumbled
1 medium sized onion, finely chopped

Shred or chop cheese and turn into a small baking dish. Stir in bacon and onion. Bake in a hot oven (400°) for 20 minutes or until cheese bubbles all over. Place baking dish in center of chop plate and surround with crisp crackers, bread sticks, or rye wafers. Serves 6.

Camembert Spread or Dip

An unusual but effective combination of cheeses. Try it with Melba rye toast or buffet-size rye bread.

1 large package (8 oz.) cream cheese
1 package (4 oz.) soft Camembert cheese
2 cups (1 pint) small curd cottage cheese
⅓ cup grated Parmesan cheese
 About 1 teaspoon seasoned salt
 Toasted sesame seeds or dill seeds (optional)

Soften cream cheese; beat in the Camembert (including the skin) until smooth. Combine with cottage cheese, Parmesan cheese, and seasoned salt to taste. Sprinkle sesame or dill seeds on top, if you wish. Makes about 3½ cups.

Crab and Olive Spread

To make it spreadable, flake the crab meat well.

1 cup flaked crab meat (well packed in cup)
1 can (4½ oz.) chopped ripe olives
2 hard cooked eggs, coarsely chopped
4 tablespoons (¼ cup) mayonnaise
1 tablespoon Worcestershire
2 tablespoons lemon juice
2 teaspoons prepared horse-radish
2 teaspoons catsup
1 teaspoon minced chives

Place the crab meat, chopped olives, chopped eggs, mayonnaise, Worcestershire, lemon juice, horse-radish, and catsup in a bowl; mix until well blended. Spoon spread into a serving bowl and sprinkle with minced chives. Provide a butter knife and serve with whole wheat or rye crisp crackers or corn chips. Makes 1½ cups.

Index